No. 2412
$19.95

THE
CESSNA
172

BILL CLARKE

TAB BOOKS Inc.
Blue Ridge Summit, PA 17214

FIRST EDITION

FIRST PRINTING

Copyright © 1987 by TAB BOOKS Inc.

Printed in the United States of America

Reproduction or publication of the content in any manner, without express permission of the publisher, is prohibited. No liability is assumed with respect to the use of the information herein.

Library of Congress Cataloging in Publication Data

Clarke, Bill (Charles W.)
   The Cessna 172.

   Includes index.
   1. Cessna 172 (Private planes) I. Title.
TL686.C4C56   1987   629.133'343   87-1928
ISBN 0-8306-0912-1
ISBN 0-8306-2412-0 (pbk.)
Questions regarding the content of this book
should be addressed to:

   Reader Inquiry Branch
   Editorial Department
   TAB BOOKS Inc.
   P.O. Box 40
   Blue Ridge Summit, PA 17214

Front cover: top two photographs courtesy of Cessna Aircraft Company, P.O. Box 1521, Wichita, Kansas; bottom photograph courtesy of Marion Pyles, Air Pix Aviation Photography.

Contents

Acknowledgments

This book was made possible by the kind assistance and contributions of:

Dean Humphrey, Lorretta Kelly, and Alice Helson of Cessna Aircraft.
Ken Johnson of AVCO Lycoming.
Dennis Jakoboski of Teledyne Continental.
AVEMCO Aviation Insurance.
A.O.P.A.
Cessna Owner Organizations.
Federal Aviation Administration.
Randolph Products Co.
Smithsonian Institute.
Joe Christy.

. . . and all those other wonderful "airplane" people who provided me with photographs, descriptions, advice, hardware, and friendship.

Introduction

The Cessna 172 airplanes are the most popular and the most affordable of all the four-place airplanes produced in recent years.

This guide will assist the pilot, the owner, and the would-be-owner in gaining a complete understanding of these airplanes.

In this book, you will learn all about the various year/models and their differences. Read about the chronic problems—and how to fix them. Learn about modifications that can be made to improve the 172's performance and comfort.

If you're thinking of purchasing a used 172, you will discover where and how to locate a good used one—and, more importantly, how to keep from getting stung in the process. Although the prospective buyer may have a basic idea of what the advertised airplane looks like, he should have a source to review for further information about the airplane, its equipment, and its value. This book is such a source. A price guide, based on the current used airplane market, is provided at the back of the book. A walk-through of all the purchase paperwork will be detailed, with examples of the forms shown.

Read how to care for your plane, and learn what preventive maintenance you may legally perform yourself. See what an annual is all about. There is even a chapter about float flying and the new avenues of adventure to be found on the water. An avionics section is included to aid you in making practical/economical decisions when you decide to upgrade your avionics.

Hangar-fly the 172 series and see what their pilots have to say. Hear from the mechanics who service them, and read what the National Transportation Safety Board has to say about the 172 and other small family airplanes.

In summary, this guide was written to aid the Cessna model 172 owner/pilot by exposing him to as much background material as possible in one handy-sized reference guide.

1929 CESSNA DC-6A -- FIRST AIRCRAFT PRODUCED BY CESSNA PAWNEE DIVISION

1975 CESSNA SKYHAWK -- 100,000TH SINGLE-ENGINE AIRPLANE PRODUCED BY CESSNA PAWNEE DIVISION

The first Cessna production airplane and the most popular production airplane. (courtesy Smithsonian Institution)

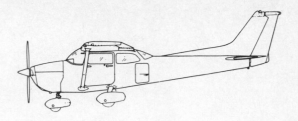

Chapter 1

History of the Cessna 172

On a June day in 1911, a 31-year-old farmer/mechanic from Rago, Kansas, cranked up the Elbridge engine of his homemade wood-and-fabric airplane and made his first short yet successful flight. Thus Clyde Cessna became the first person to build and fly an airplane west of the Mississippi River and east of the Rockies, and laid the cornerstone of today's Cessna Aircraft Company—the world leader in general aviation production and sales (Fig. 1-1).

Thereafter, until America's entry into World War I curtailed civilian flying, Clyde Cessna designed and built one airplane every year—and, with firm faith in his own designs, flew them on exhibitions ranging over wide geographic areas. Each year he improved and refined his basic design. But he built no airplanes for sale. Barnstorming was more profitable than airplane sales—and certainly more fun (Fig. 1-2).

In the winter of 1916-17, Cessna accepted an invitation from the Jones Motor Car Company to build his newest airplane in their plant in Wichita, Kansas. Thus he pioneered the manufacture of powered aircraft in Wichita—starting that city on its road to fame as the air capitol of the world.

On July 5, 1917, he set a notable speed record of 124.62 mph on a cross-country flight from Blackwell, Oklahoma, to Wichita. This record was only the first of many racing and competition triumphs to be scored by Cessna airplanes.

In 1925, with a total of six successful airplane designs to his

1

Fig. 1-1. Clyde Cessna (right) and his nephew Dwane Wallace. Dwane became president of Cessna in 1936. (courtesy Cessna Aircraft Company)

credit, Cessna joined Walter Beech and Lloyd Stearman in establishing the Travel Air Manufacturing Company in Wichita, and became its president. He remained with Travel Air until he sold out to Beech in 1927.

Fig. 1-2. C. V. Cessna and his aeroplane at Burdett, KS, 1914. (courtesy Cessna Aircraft Company)

3

In that same year, Cessna built his first production model airplane. This was the four-place full-cantilever high-winged "Comet" monoplane. On December 31, 1927, the Cessna Aircraft Company came into being.

EARLY CESSNA MILESTONES

1928: Cessna goes into production with the "A" series, the first full cantilever-wing airplane to enter production in this country (Fig. 1-3). Cessna AW wins Class A Transcontinental Air Derby from New York to Los Angeles.

1929: Cessna builds a new factory southwest of Wichita on 80 acres of land.

1930: Cessna builds the CG-2 glider to offset the "depression market" sag.

1931: A Cessna AW wins the *Detroit News* Trophy Race and "World's Most Efficient Airplane" award.

1933: Cessna builds their first retractable landing gear airplane, the CR-2 Racer. Also, the Cessna CR-3 Racer sets a world speed record for airplanes with engines having less than 500 cubicinches of displacement—242.35 mph at the 1933 American Air Races.

1935-36: The Cessna Model C-34 wins the *Detroit News* Trophy Race and "World's Most Efficient Airplane" award in 1935 and 1936, then takes permanent possession of the trophy (Fig. 1-4).

1937: Cessna goes into production of the Airmaster C-37.

1938-40: Cessna manufactures the Models C-145 and C-165 Airmasters.

1940-45: Cessna builds over 5400 Bobcats (Model T-50) for World War II use. This is Cessna's first twin-engine airplane and the first use of a low-wing design by the company (Fig. 1-5).

1942: Cessna builds a new plant in Hutchinson, Kansas. 750 Waco CG-4A Gliders are built.

1946: Cessna returns to commercial production with the Models 120 and 140, introducing spring landing gear with these models, and converts production facilities from welded steel tubing and wood techniques to all-metal methods (Fig. 1-6).

Cessna diversifies aircraft production with industrial hydraulic components.

1947: Cessna builds furniture in the Hutchinson plant. Production begins on the five-place Models 190 and 195, Cessna's first all-metal airplanes.

Fig. 1-3. "A" Series airplane, about 1928. (courtesy Cessna Aircraft Company)

5

Fig. 1-4. C-34. Dwane Wallace used such an airplane to race, often using his winnings to meet the Cessna payroll. (courtesy Cessna Aircraft Company)

Fig. 1-5. Cessna T-50, sometimes called the "Bamboo Bomber." One famous T-50 was called the *Song Bird* in the 1950s TV series *Sky King*. (courtesy Cessna Aircraft Company)

Fig. 1-6. Cessna 120/140 series was the first of the postwar Cessnas. (courtesy Cessna Aircraft Company)

1948: Cessna enters the four-place airplane market with the Model 170.

The 170

The Cessna four-place line of airplanes started in 1948 with the introduction of the Model 170 (Figs. 1-7, 1-8).

The first 170s had metal fuselages, fabric-covered wings, and two wing struts on each side. Of course they had conventional landing gear, as did most airplanes of that era. The 170 was powered with a Continental C-145-2 engine.

In 1949 the 170 was updated to the 170A model. Gone were the dual wing struts and the fabric-covered wings. The wings were now all-metal. There was also a slight change in the tail fin. The same Continental engine was supplied as standard; as an option, there was the Franklin O-300. Additionally, there was an optional 18-gallon auxiliary fuel tank. The A Model was in production for three years.

The last of the 170 series was the 170B, introduced in 1952. The 170B came with the Continental C-145-2 engine or the Franklin 165, and had the large flaps we have all become used to on Cessnas. The B Model was produced through 1957.

By 1957, the year after the 172 was introduced, the demand for the "easy drive-it" airplane saw sales lagging on the conventional-geared 170, and gaining with the 172. Basically, the original 172 was a 170 with a nosewheel and a different rudder. After building 5136 Model 170 airplanes, production was halted. Even though the 170s ended production nearly 30 years ago, they are still popular today.

Specifications
Model: 170 all
Engine

Make	: Continental
Model	: C-145-2 (or Franklin option)
hp	: 145
TBO	: 1800

Seats: 4
Speed

Max	: 140 mph
Cruise	: 120 mph
Stall	: 52 mph

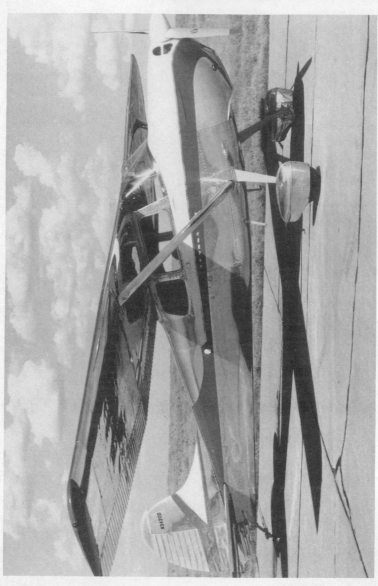

Fig. 1-7. This Cessna 170B was built in the early '50s, and is just as modern as today. (courtesy Cessna Aircraft Company)

Fuel Capacity: 42 gal
Rate of Climb: 690 fpm
Transitions
    Takeoff over 50' obs: 1820 ft
    Ground run: 700 ft
    Landing over 50' obs: 1145 ft
    Ground roll: 500 ft
Weights
    Gross: 2200 lbs
    Empty: 1260 lbs
Dimensions
    Length: 25 ft 0 in
    Height: 6 ft 5 in
    Span: 36 ft 0 in

Support

The International Cessna 170 Club was officially formed in order to keep the 170 flying as inexpensively and as easily as possible. Its purpose is to furnish information about service, parts, and flying techniques to its members. In addition, general aviation gossip, insurance and safety data, as well as other "essential" information is exchanged.

The club issues a quarterly magazine, *The 170 News*. It contains photos, news items, want ads, articles, and letters. They also put out a newsletter 11 times a year which includes additional want ads; these are free to members.

The club has an annual convention in the summer which is advertised as a "week of family fun with a little education thrown in." There are also regional get-togethers.

For further information about the International Cessna 170 Club, contact:

International Cessna 170 Association
P.O. Box 86
Hartville, MO 65667
Phone: (417) 741-6557

CONTINUING HISTORY

1949: Cessna converts to metal-covered wings on Model 120, 140, and 170 airplanes. This ends the fabric-covered airplane era for Cessna. This was the first year of the 170A.

1950: Cessna re-enters military prime contract business with

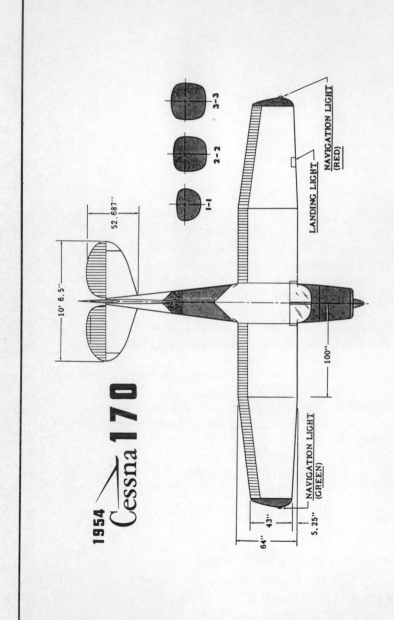

1954 Cessna 170

NAVIGATION LIGHT (RED)

LANDING LIGHT

NAVIGATION LIGHT (GREEN)

52.687"

10' 6.5"

1-1 2-2 3-3

100"

64"

43"

5.25"

12

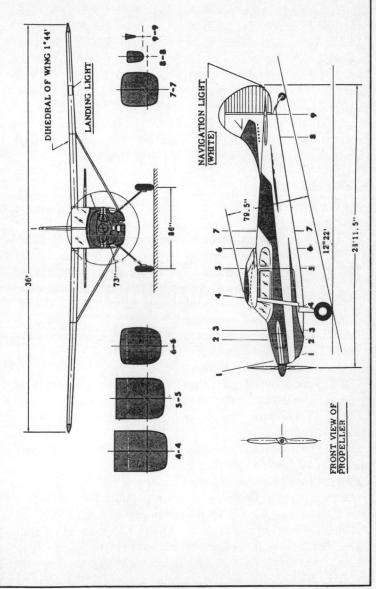

Fig. 1-8. The 1954 Cessna 170. (courtesy Cessna Aircraft Company)

the Bird Dog (L-19). This model incorporates Cessna's first high-lift wing flaps.

1952: Cessna Industrial Hydraulics Division is established at Hutchinson, Kansas. Cessna introduces the "Para-Lift" wing flaps in commercial airplanes (Model 170B).

1953: The Model 180 enters production. (The 180 will later become famous as a bushplane in Alaska and other remote regions of the world.) Cessna flies its first jet airplane, the XT-37A.

1955: Cessna goes into production on the T-37A (Fig. 1-9).

1956: Cessna introduces the tricycle landing gear with Models 172 and 182 (Fig. 1-10). New sales phrases herald the 172, and will be heard for many years: *Land-O-Matic*, referring to the tricycle landing gear, and the system of "driving" the airplane into the air and back onto the ground; and *Para-Lift Flaps*, referring to the exceptionally large flaps that have since become standard on all Cessna high-wing singles.

MODERN HISTORY

1957: Sales lag on the conventional-gear Model 170 and production is halted.

1958: The Cessna Model 175 is introduced. It is essentially a 172 with a geared, 175-hp engine.

1959: Cessna phases out the T-37A and starts production of the T-37B jet trainer. Cessna re-enters the two-place airplane market with the Model 150. Cessna purchases Aircraft Radio Corporation as a wholly-owned subsidiary.

1960: All Cessna production airplanes adopt swept tails except the Models 150 and 180. Cessna purchases 49 percent interest in Reims Aviation, Reims, France.

1961: Production is started on the Skyknight, Cessna's first supercharged twin-engine airplane.

1962: Omni-Vision wraparound windshields are introduced on Models 210 and 182.

1963: Omni-Vision is introduced on Model 172 series. Cessna produces its 50,000th airplane, a Skyhawk (172).

1964: Cessna is presented the President's "E" Award for excellence in exporting. Cessna receives a contract for 170 T-41A (Model 172) aircraft for USAF pilot training (Fig. 1-11).

1965: Delivery of the 10,000th Model 172—to a flying club in Elaine, Arkansas—takes place. Production reaches the milestone of one airplane every 23 minutes during the eight-hour working day (Figs. 1-12, 1-13).

Fig. 1-9. The U.S. Air Force T-37 jet trainer. (courtesy Cessna Aircraft Company)

Fig. 1-10. 1956 Cessna 172, the first of many. (courtesy Cessna Aircraft Company)

Fig. 1-11. The T-41, military primary trainer. (courtesy Cessna Aircraft Company)

Fig. 1-12. Pawnee Division of Cessna, where the 172s were built. (courtesy Cessna Aircraft Company)

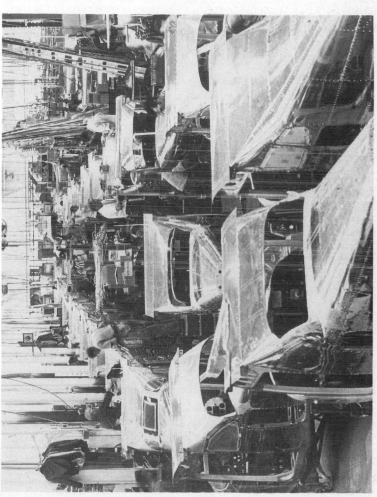

Fig. 1-13. The assembly line that once produced an airplane every 23 minutes. (courtesy Cessna Aircraft Company)

1966: Cessna takes a big step to broaden the base of the private aircraft market by launching a worldwide learn-to-fly campaign, increasing production of the 1966 Model 150 two-place trainer to 3000 units and reducing the price of the aircraft by more than 10 percent to make it more readily available. Cessna delivers its 60,000th airplane to an Oklahoma supermarket manager. Agreement with DINFIA to manufacture aircraft in Argentina receives approval of the Argentine government.

1967: The 75,000th Cessna airplane is delivered. Cessna makes deliveries of three versions of the T-41 to the Air Force, the Air Force Academy, and the Army. The first A-37s are delivered, marking the first time a general aviation manufacturer has built a combat-designated airplane.

1968: Deliveries are made on the 10,000th Model 150 and the 10,000th Model 182/Skylane. The 1000th T-37 jet trainer is delivered to the U.S. Air Force.

1974: The number of delivered Cessna 172 airplanes surpasses that of the Piper Cubs and Super Cubs at 20,000 (Fig. 1-14).

1975: Cessna passes the 110,000-airplane mark in total production.

1978: Cessna has pilot training centers in 33 countries worldwide.

1978: Cessna produced 9197 airplanes for the year.

1980: The "Silver Anniversary" of the Model 172 airplane; more than 31,000 have been delivered.

1983: Cessna posts the first yearly loss in the company's 55-year history.

1984: Cessna enters the "black hole" of zero production of some models; selling prices have become more than the purchasers are willing to pay.

THE 172 FAMILY

The beginning of production of the Model 172 airplanes—and its many improved versions—started a success story unlike any other in modern aviation.

In 1955 Cessna introduced the 172. It has been accepted as has no other lightplane, an acceptance based upon the airplane's simplicity and economy, coupled with its abilities.

The 172s provide a means of air transport that is non-taxing on the pilot, as there are no complex systems or controls to handle, just straightforward flying. By the same token, with simplicity in the pilots' workload comes simplicity in the aircraft itself.

Fig. 1-14. Pawnee Division's 100,000th airplane. (courtesy Cessna Aircraft Company)

There are no complex and expensive propeller or landing gear systems to maintain.

Of course, the 172 is known for being economical in operation also. There is no more thirst for avgas than there is for expensive maintenance. At the time of its introduction, the 172 provided this simplicity and economy to a market then ready for family airplanes.

Perhaps the single most important virtue of the 172—in the eyes of the mid-1950s' buyer—was the tricycle landing gear. Also important was the construction of the airframe; the 172 was all-metal, and in its class there was nothing to compare.

The list of four-place conventional-geared airplanes dropped from production between 1946 and 1956 included the Piper Pacer (replaced with the Tri-Pacer, also a tri-geared airplane), the Aeronca Sedan, the Luscombe 11 Sedan, the Stinson Voyager, and the Taylorcraft Ranchwagon. Most of these airplanes were also partially or completely fabric-covered.

On the other end of the scale of four-place airplanes were the Beechcraft Bonanzas and Navions. Both types of airplanes were considerably more complex, and therefore more expensive and complicated to operate. They were built and used by an entirely different segment of the aviation market.

All told, the 172 was—and still is—a hard-working, honest airplane capable of providing economical and reliable air transportation.

The Model 172 is not completely alone on the Cessna family tree. Over the years, Cessna has tried to capitalize on a good thing—although often unsuccessfully—by adding different models of the basic 172 airframe to their product line.

Model 175

In 1958 the Model 175 was introduced. At the time of its introduction, Cessna said of the 175: "It is an entirely new airplane with new performance figures and a new purpose in life." Other than power, it was really just a 172—a point proven in 1963, when it reverted to being called a 172 (Fig. 1-15).

The 1975 boasted a 175-hp geared Continental GO-300 engine. Although Cessna tried to push these planes, they did not achieve a high level of success, and production was halted after only a few years. One of the reasons for its non-acceptance was the high (3200) rpm engine operation. This high engine speed was reduced to 2400 propeller rpm via a gearbox. The high rpm seemed unnatural, and pilots would not accept it. Additionally, the high speed wore the

Fig. 1-15. A 1961 Cessna 175B. (courtesy Cessna Aircraft Company)

engine out faster, and the gearboxes had a high (expensive) failure rate.

The 175s are all over 20 years old now, and, depending upon the engine situation, can represent good buys. The original geared engine had a low TBO, as you will see in the specifications, and is considerably more expensive to repair/rebuild than the non-geared O-300 engine found in the Model 172. As a result of the engine problems, many owners saw fit to replace the geared engine with a standard powerplant. Properly done, these engines enhance the desirability of the 175. However, no matter what is changed, the airframe is still a Model 175. In 1963 Cessna began calling it the "172 Powermatic," but it was really just a Model 175 with a new name (its specifications were the same as the 1962 Model 175).

Specifications

Year: 1958 to 1962
Model: 175
Range and Speed:

Maximum cruise speed:	139	mph
Range:		
52 Gallons, No Reserve:	595	mi
	4.3	hrs
Maximum Range		
52 Gallons, No Reserve:	720	mi
(39 percent power at 10,000 ft):	102	mph
	7.0	hrs
Rate of Climb at Sea Level:	850	fpm
Service Ceiling:	15,900	ft
Baggage:	120	lbs
Wing Loading: (lbs/sq ft)	13.4	
Power Loading: (lbs/hp)	13.4	
Fuel Capacity		
Standard:	52	gal
Engine: '58	Continental GO-300A	
'59	Continental GO-300A	
'60	Continental GO-300C	
'61	Continental GO-300D	
	GO-300C in Standard	
'62	Continental GO-300E	
TBO:	1200	hrs
Power:	175	hp
Wingspan:	36 ft 0	in
Wing Area: (sq ft)	175	

Length:	25 ft 0	in
Height:	8 ft 06	in
Gross Weight:	2350	lbs
Empty Weight: (Skylark)	1395	lbs
(Standard)	1325	lbs
Useful Load: (Skylark)	955	lbs
(Standard)	1025	lbs

Note: Speed for the Skylark version will be slightly more than the standard 175 by approximately 2 mph. There is a corresponding difference in range. All other performance figures remain the same.

Model 172 XP

Much later in the 172's history, Cessna again introduced a version with greater power. This was the Hawk XP series, first produced in 1977. These sported the Teledyne Continental IO-360 fuel-injected engine of 195 hp. As with the earlier Model 175, production lasted only five years. Many claimed little was gained in performance to justify the added initial purchase expense and continued higher operating expense of the larger engine. The XPs did find acceptance as floatplanes, and their pilots/owners will tell you the extra power is the deciding factor (Fig. 1-16).

Specifications

Year: 1977 to 1981
Model: R 172
      Hawk XP and Hawk XP II

Speed		
Top Speed at Sea Level:	134	kts
Cruise, 80 percent power at 5500 ft:	131	kts
Range (with 45 minute reserve)		
Cruise, 80 percent power at 5500 ft:	485	nm
49 Gallons Usable Fuel:	3.7	hrs
Cruise, 80 percent power at 6000 ft:	635	nm
66 Gallons Usable Fuel:	4.9	hrs
Maximum Range at 10,000 ft:	595	nm
49 Gallons Usable Fuel:	5.6	hrs
Maximum Range at 10,000 ft:	815	nm
66 Gallons Usable Fuel:	8.7	hrs
Rate of Climb at Sea Level:	870	fpm
Service Ceiling:	17,000	ft
Takeoff		
Ground Run:	850	ft

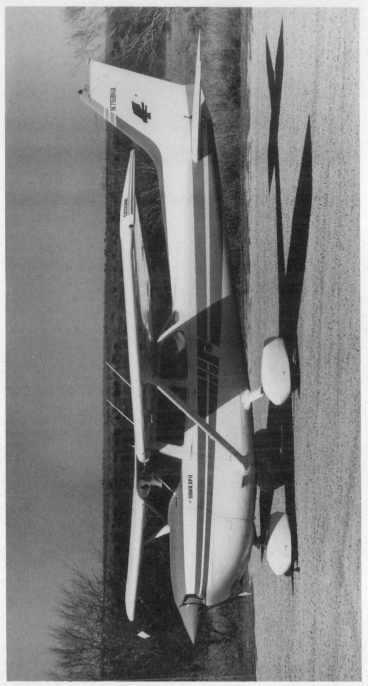

Fig. 1-16. A 1980 Cessna Hawk XP. (courtesy Cessna Aircraft Company)

Over 50 ft Obstacle:	1360	ft
Landing		
Ground Roll:	620	ft
Over 50-ft Obstacle:	1270	ft
Stall Speed		
Flaps Up, Power Off:	53	kts
Flaps Down, Power Off:	46	kts
Baggage:	200	lbs
Wing Loading: (lbs/sq ft)	14.7	
Power Loading: (lbs/hp)	13.1	
Fuel Capacity		
Standard:	52	gal
w/Optional tanks:	68	gal
Oil Capacity:		
Engine: '77	Continental IO-360-K	
'78	Continental IO-360-K	
'79	Continental IO-360-KB	
'80	Continental IO-360-KB	
'81	Continental IO-360-KB	
TBO. (1500 hrs on K model)	2000	hrs
Power: (at 2600 rpm)	195	hp
Propeller: (diameter) C/S	76	in
Wingspan:	35 ft 10	in
Wing Area: (sq ft)	174	
Length:	27 ft 02	in
Height:	8 ft 09	in
Maximum Weight:	2550	lbs
Empty Weight: (Hawk XP)	1549	lbs
(Hawk XP II)	1573	lbs
Useful Load: (Hawk XP)	1001	lbs
(Hawk XP II)	977	lbs

RG Models

In 1980 a retractable gear version of the 172 was introduced. Called the Cutlass RG, it sold for about $19,000 above the basic cost of a Model 172. Although offering better speeds than the standard 172, operating and maintenance costs are predictably higher. The engine used is the AVCO Lycoming 180-hp O-360. As of 1985 the Cutlass RG remained in produced, outlasting the other variants in lifespan (Fig. 1-17).

Specifications
Year: 1980 to 1985

Fig. 1-17. The Cutlass RG. (courtesy Cessna Aircraft Company)

Model: 172 Cutlass RG

Speed
  Top Speed at Sea Level: 145 kts
  Cruise, 75 percent power: 140 kts

Range, 75 percent power at 9000 ft
  62 Gallons, 45 min. Reserve: 720 nm
                                     5.3 hrs

Maximum Range at 10,000 ft:
  62 Gallons   840 nm
                                     7.7 hrs

Rate of Climb at Sea Level: 800 fpm
Service Ceiling: 16,800 ft
Takeoff
  Ground Run: 1060 ft
  Over 50-ft Obstacle: 1775 ft
Landing
  Ground Roll: 625 ft
  Over 50-ft Obstacle: 1340˙ ft
Stall Speed
  Flaps Up, Power Off: 54 kts
  Flaps Down, Power Off: 50 kts
Baggage: 200 lbs
Fuel Capacity
  Standard: 66 gal
Engine: Lycoming O-360-F1A6
TBO: 2000 hrs
Power: (at 2700 rpm)   180 hp
Propeller: Constant Speed
Wingspan: 36 ft 01 in
Wing Area: (sq ft)   174
Length: 26 ft 11 in
Height: 8 ft 09 in
Gross Weight: 2650 lbs
Empty Weight: (Cutlass RG)   1615 lbs
           (Cutlass RG II)   1644 lbs
Useful Load: (Cutlass RG)   1043 lbs
           (Cutlass RG II)   1014 lbs

Cutlass

The latest offering is the non-retractable Cutlass. It was introduced in 1983, and is also powered with a 180-hp engine. At the time of this writing, it is far too soon to determine if this latest variant of the 172 will meet with more success than any of the other "improved" versions. After all, it really is difficult to improve upon anything that has been as successful as the original 172.

Specifications

Year: 1983 to 1985
Model: 172 Q Cutlass
Speed

Top Speed at Sea Level:	124	kts
Cruise, 75 percent power:	122	kts

Range, 75 percent power at 8500 ft

50 Gallons, 45 min. Reserve:	475	nm
	4.0	hrs
62 Gallons, 45 min. Reserve:	620	nm
	5.2	hrs

Maximum Range at 10,000 ft:

50 Gallons	600	nm
	6.4	hrs
62 Gallons	775	nm
	8.2	hrs

Rate of Climb at Sea Level:	680	fpm
Service Ceiling:	17,000	ft

Takeoff

Ground Run:	960	ft
Over 50-ft Obstacle:	1690	ft

Landing

Ground Roll:	575	ft
Over 50-ft Obstacle:	1335	ft

Stall Speed

Flaps Up, Power Off:	53	kts
Flaps Down, Power Off:	48	kts
Baggage:	120	lbs

Fuel Capacity

Standard:	54	gal
Long range tanks:	68	gal
Engine:	Lycoming 0-360-A4N	
TBO:	2000	hrs
Power: (at 2700 rpm)	180	hp
Propeller:	Fixed Pitch	
Wingspan:	36 ft 01	in
Wing Area: (sq ft)	174	

Length:		26 ft 11 in
Height:		8 ft 09 in
Gross Weight:		2550 lbs
Empty Weight:	(Cutlass)	1480 lbs
	(Cutlass II)	1500 lbs
Useful Load:	(Cutlass)	1078 lbs
	(Cutlass II)	1058 lbs

PRODUCTION FIGURES

The following charts depict the production periods and quantities of the Model 172 and 175 airplanes:

Model:	172		175
1955	173	(1956 models)	
1956	1419		
1957	939		
1958	790		702
1959	874		727
1960	1015		501
1961	903		126
1962	809		50
1963	1146		13
1964	1401		
1965	1436		
1966	1597		
1967	839		
1968	1206		
1969	1170		
1970	759		
1971	827		
1972	984		
1973	1550		
1974	1786		
1975	1885		
1976	2085	w/Hawk XP	
1977	2309	w/Hawk XP	
1978	2023	w/Hawk XP	
1979	1875	w/Hawk XP	
1980	1177	w/Cutlass RG and Hawk XP	
1981	979	w/Cutlass RG and Hawk XP	
1982	330	w/Cutlass RG	
1983	251		
1984	195		
1985	n/a		

Note: These are the totals for the U.S.-made versions only. The totals are slightly higher if Reims Aviation (the French version) 172s are included.

In total, there have been over 37,000 Cessna 172 airplanes produced. This is the record for any type/model of airplane ever manufactured in the world—even greater than the German Messerschmitt 109 of World War II fame. (Yet this does not even include the 175 Models or the Reims 172s!) The Cessna 172 airplanes are assuredly the most popular airplanes ever built.

SERIAL NUMBERS

The following list gives the serial number ranges for all years and models of the 172 airplanes:

Year	Beginning	Ending
Model 172		
1956	28000	29174
1957	29175	29999
	36000	36215
1958	36216	36965
1959	36966	36999
	46001	46754
1960	46755	47746
1961	47747[1]	48734
1962	48735	49544
1963	49545	50572
1964	50573	51822
1965	51823	53392
1966	53393	54892
1967	54893	56512
1968	56513	57161
1969	57162	58486
1970	58487	59223
1971	59224	59903
1972	59904	60758
1973	60759	61898
1974	61899	63458
1975	63459	65684
1976	65685	67584
1977	67585	69309
1978	69310	71034
1979	71035	72884
1980	72885	74009

Year	Beginning	Ending
1981	74001	75034
1982	75035	75759
1983	75760	76079
1984	76080	76259
1985	76260	up

Model 175
1958	55001	55703
1959	55704	56238
1960	56239	56777
1961	56778	57002
1962	57003	57119

Powermatic
1963	P17257120	P17257189

Hawk XP
1977	R1722000	R1722724
1978	R1722725	R1722929
1979	R1722930	R1723199
1980	R1723200	R1723399
1981	R1723400	R1723454

Cutlass RG
1980	RG0001	RG0570
1981	RG0571	RG0890
1982	RG0891	RG1099
1983	RG1100	RG1144
1984	RG1145	RG1177
1985	RG1178	up

Cutlass Q
1983	75869[2]	76079
1984	76080	76259
1985	76260	up

1. Starting in 1961, the numbers 172 were added to the front of all Model 172 serial numbers (ie: 17271035)
2. The Cutlass Q Models share the standard 172 serial number sequence.

172 CHANGES

Over the years many changes have been made to the Model 172 airplane. These changes and improvements are detailed in the following list. Not included are the color scheme and interior styling changes, for these are owner-changeable at any time.

1955 (November): The Cessna 172 is introduced at a price of $8995 for the 1956 model.

Among the features that will make it the "most popular airplane" are the "Land-O-Matic" gear and the "Para-Lift" flaps.

1958: The Model 175 is introduced with the more powerful Continental geared GO-300 engine (Figs. 1-18, 1-19).

Also in 1958, a new world's endurance flight record is set by a 172 remaining aloft for a total of 1200 hours, 16 minutes and 10 seconds (this was 50 days in the air).

1959: Electric fuel gauges are offered, along with the die-cast wheels and gear-toothed brakes.

1960: Swept-back vertical tail is added, and 172s are made available on floats (Fig. 1-20).

The cost of a 1960 Model 172 is $9450.

1961: The "Skyhawk" name is added to upgraded models that include certain equipment (avionics and appearance) packages.

1962: Available for the first time is an autopilot, and gone is the pull handle starter; it is replaced with a key starter button.

The wingtips and speed fairings have been redesigned (they will fit all models from 150 through 180).

For pilot comfort, new six-way adjustable seats are introduced.

Fig. 1-18. Cowling of a 172.

Fig. 1-19. Cowling of a 175. Notice the raised area to house the gearbox.

Family seats are introduced to allow the 172 to carry as many as six passengers (Fig. 1-21).

The Model 172 sells for $9,895, while the Skyhawk sells for $11,590.

The 175 is dropped from production.

1963: Omni-Vision is added. Now you can see what is behind you.

Also changed is the two-piece windshield; it is replaced with a single piece unit (Fig. 1-22).

New rudder/brake pedals are installed.

The Model 172 Powermatic is added to the 172 line. It is really an updated Model 175.

The basic 172 sells for $10,245, the 172 Powermatic for $13,275, the Skyhawk for $11,995, and the Skyhawk Powermatic for $14,650.

1964: Gone are the manual flaps; electric flaps are added to the 172s.

Push-to-reset circuit breakers are installed on the electric panel.

1966: The 172 sells for $12,450 and the Skyhawk for $13,300.

1967: Short-stroke nose gear is added, offering less drag and better appearance.

A shock-mounted cowl is installed resulting in lower noise levels in the cabin.

Fig. 1-20. Swept-back tail on a "fastback."

Fig. 1-21. It is possible to carry six in the 172—with a weight limitation. (courtesy Cessna Aircraft Company)

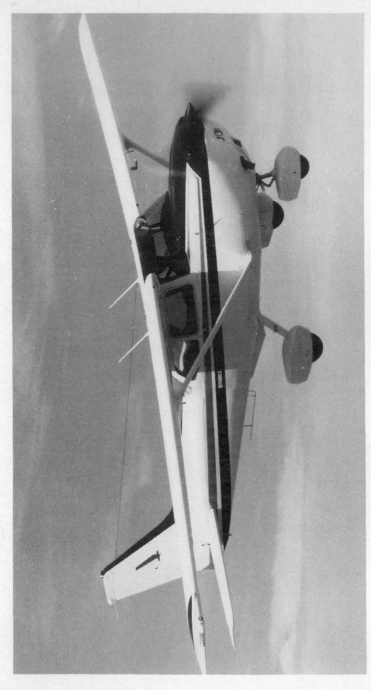

Fig. 1-22. This late model shows both the Omni-Vision and the one-piece windshield. (courtesy Cessna Aircraft Company)

A pneumatic stall warning horn becomes standard on all versions, as are plastic wing tips.

The 172 sells for $10,950 and the Skyhawk for $12,750.

1968: The "Blue Streak" Lycoming O-320-E2D 150-hp engine replaces the Continental (five more hp and 45 pounds less weight).

"T" arrangement of instruments is introduced.

1969: Long-range fuel tanks of 52-gallon capacity are offered as an option.

A dorsal fin is installed, and the rudder restyled.

The rear windows are increased in size by 16 square inches.

The 172 sells for $12,500 and the Skyhawk for $13,995.

1970: Conical-camber wingtips are added for better performance (Figs. 1-23, 1-24), and fully articulating seats are available, as an option, for passenger comfort.

1971: Tubular-strut landing gear replaces the "flat spring" type gear. It has a tread width over one foot wider than the older style (Figs. 1-25, 1-26).

The 172 sells for $13,425 and the Skyhawk for $14,995. 1972: A new, enlarged, dorsal fin is added (Figs. 1-27, 1-28).

The cabin doors and baggage door are made by metal-to-metal bonding (no rivets).

1973: A new "Camber-lift" wing for improved low-speed handling characteristics is introduced.

Fig. 1-23. Original wingtips of the first 172s.

Fig. 1-24. Improved conical tips.

1974: The Skyhawk II package is introduced. This package includes a second NAV/COMM, an ADF, and a XPNDR.

The baggage compartment is increased in size, and optional dual nose-mounted landing lights are available (Figs. 1-29, 1-30).

1975: The 172 sells for $16,055, the Skyhawk for $17,890, and the Skyhawk II for $20,335.

Fig. 1-25. Original flat steel main gear.

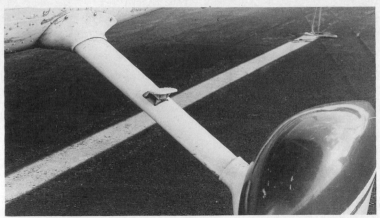

Fig. 1-26. Improved tubular steel main gear.

Fig. 1-27. Pre-1972 fin.

Fig. 1-28. Post-1972 fin.

41

Fig. 1-29. Single landing light.

1976: The instrument panel is changed to hold the ever-increasing amount of avionics available.

1977: The Skyhawk/100 (for 100 octane LL avgas) is introduced.

Fig. 1-30. Double landing lights.

A new engine of 160 hp, the AVCO Lycoming O-320-H2AD, is installed in the 100s.

Rudder trim is available as an option, and a pre-selectable flap control is standard.

The new Hawk XP is introduced with a 195-hp fuel-injected engine using a constant-speed prop. It is really an updated Reims Rocket (built under license in France) and similar to the military T-41.

The Skyhawk/100 sells for $22,300, the Skyhawk/100 II for $24,990, the Hawk XP for $29,950 and the Hawk XP II for $32,650.

1978: A 28 volt electric system is installed, and air conditioning becomes available as an option.

The Hawk XP is certified for floats.

1979: Flap extension speed is increased to 110 KIAS on the Skyhawk and Hawk XP models.

Optional integral fuel cells become available for the Hawk XP, increasing the usable fuel to 66 gallons.

1980: This is the Silver Anniversary year for the 172. Over 31,000 have been built.

A slimmer door post allows for increased visibility.

A rounded leading edge has been added on the elevator.

1981: A new engine, the AVCO Lycoming O-320-D2J, is installed.

Maximum flap extension is reduced from 40 degrees to 30 degrees on all models.

A wet wing optional fuel tank is available, making a total fuel capacity of 62 gallons usable for the Skyhawk.

This is the last year for the Hawk XP.

The Skyhawk sells for $33,950, the Skyhawk II for 31,810, the Skyhawk with the Nav/Pac for $42,460, the Hawk XP for $41,850, the Hawk XP II for $45,935, and the Hawk XP II with Nav/Pac for $50,790.

1982: Landing lights are installed in the leading edge of the wing, and are more than doubled in power (Fig. 1-31).

1983: Sound reduction improvements are made, including a thick plexiglass windshield and side windows. New type cabin door latching pins are introduced.

1984: The Skyhawk sells for $44,000, the Skyhawk II for $48,940, and the Skyhawk II with Nav/Pac for $54,380.

1985: The base price for a Skyhawk is $49,600. That is stripped down, with none of the necessary avionics for today's flying.

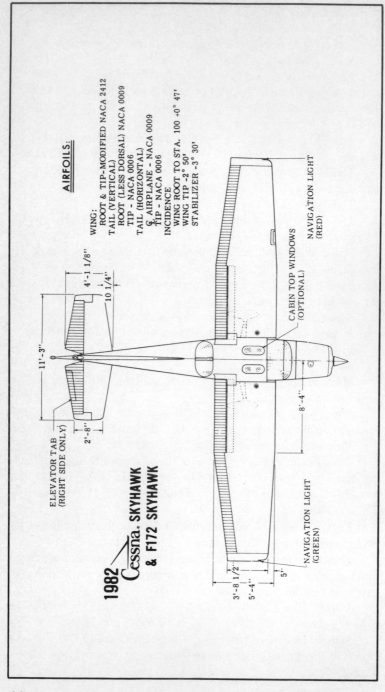

AIRFOILS:

WING:
   ROOT & TIP-MODIFIED NACA 2412
TAIL (VERTICAL)
   ROOT (LESS DORSAL) NACA 0009
   TIP - NACA 0006
TAIL (HORIZONTAL)
   ₵ AIRPLANE - NACA 0009
   TIP - NACA 0006
INCIDENCE
   WING ROOT TO STA. 100 +0° 47'
   WING TIP -2° 50'
   STABILIZER -3° 30'

ELEVATOR TAB
(RIGHT SIDE ONLY)

4'-1 1/8''

10 1/4''

11'-3''

2'-8''

1982 Cessna. SKYHAWK
& F172 SKYHAWK

CABIN TOP WINDOWS
(OPTIONAL)

NAVIGATION LIGHT
(RED)

8'-4''

NAVIGATION LIGHT
(GREEN)

3'-8 1/2''

5'-4''

5''

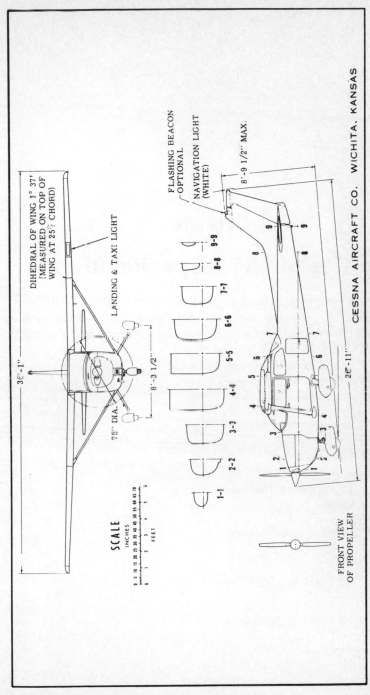

Fig. 1-31. Scale drawing of the 1982 Cessna 172. (courtesy Cessna Aircraft Company)

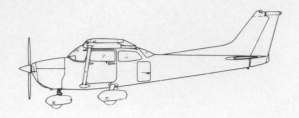

Chapter 2

Cessna 172 Specifications

The photographs on these pages depict many versions of the Cessna Model 172 airplanes. Notice the differences between the various year models, and compare these to the model changes described in Chapter 1 (Figs. 2-1 through 2-6).

The following are the official specifications for each year/model of the Cessna 172 airplanes.

1956
Year: 1956
Model: 172

Speed
    Top Speed at Sea Level: 135 mph
    Cruise   124 mph
Range
    Cruise (recommended):   519 mi
                                    4.2 hrs
                                    124 mph
    Maximum Range at 7500 ft: 620 mi
                                    6.4 hrs
                                    97 mph
Rate of Climb at Sea Level: 660 fpm
Service Ceiling: 13,300 ft
Baggage: 120 lbs
Wing Loading: (lbs/sq ft)   12.6

Fig. 2-1. The early 172s have straight tails and are referred to as "straight tails" or "straight-tailed fastbacks." "Fastback" refers to the lack of rear cabin windows. (courtesy Smithsonian Institution)

47

Fig. 2-2. This 1962 Model 172 is called a "swept-tail fastback." (courtesy Smithsonian Institution)

Fig. 2-3. The 172 pictured here is a typical late model Skyhawk. This particular plane is a 1964. (courtesy Cessna Aircraft Company)

Fig. 2-4. Notice the unfaired landing gear. This is a 172, not a Skyhawk, and is somewhat plainer in appearance. (courtesy Cessna Aircraft Company)

Fig. 2-5. In 1977 the "100 versions" of the Skyhawk appeared. The 100 indicates 100 LL avgas. It also equates to the O-320-H2AD engine. (courtesy Cessna Aircraft Company)

51

Fig. 2-6. The Cessna Skyhawk as it appears today. Notice the one-piece windshield, the lower stance of the landing gear, and the very modern paint scheme. (courtesy Cessna Aircraft Company)

Power Loading: (lbs/hp)	15.2	
Fuel Capacity		
Standard:	42	gal
Engine:	Continental O-300A	
TBO:	1500	hrs
Power:	145	hp
Wingspan:	36 ft 00	in
Wing Area: (sq ft)	175	
Length:	25 ft 00	in
Height:	8 ft 06	in
Gross Weight:	2200	lbs
Empty Weight:	1260	lbs
Useful Load:	940	lbs

1957

Year: 1957
Model: 172

Speed		
Top Speed at Sea Level:	135	mph
Cruise	124	mph
Range		
Cruise (recommended):	519	mi
	4.2	hrs
	124	mph
Maximum Range at 7500 ft:	620	mi
	6.4	hrs
	97	mph
Rate of Climb at Sea Level:	660	fpm
Service Ceiling:	13,300	ft
Baggage:	120	lbs
Wing Loading: (lbs/sq ft)	12.6	
Power Loading: (lbs/hp)	15.2	
Fuel Capacity		
Standard:	42	gal
Engine:	Continental O-300A	
TBO:	1500	hrs
Power:	145	hp
Wingspan:	36 ft 00	in
Wing Area: (sq ft)	175	
Length:	25 ft 00	in
Height:	8 ft 06	in
Gross Weight:	2200	lbs
Empty Weight:	1260	lbs
Useful Load:	940	lbs

1958

Year: 1958
Model: 172

Speed
    Top Speed at Sea Level: 135 mph
    Cruise   124 mph
Range
    Cruise (recommended):   519 mi
                                     4.2 hrs
                                  124 mph
    Maximum Range at 7500 ft: 620 mi
                                   6.4 hrs
                                   97 mph

Rate of Climb at Sea Level: 660 fpm
Service Ceiling: 13,300 ft
Baggage: 120 lbs
Wing Loading: (lbs/sq ft)   12.6
Power Loading: (lbs/hp)   15.2
Fuel Capacity
    Standard: 42 gal
Engine: Continental O-300A
TBO: 1500 hrs
Power: 145 hp
Wingspan: 36 ft   00 in
Wing Area: (sq ft)   175
Length: 25 ft   00 in
Height: 8 ft   06 in
Gross Weight: 2200 lbs
Empty Weight: 1260 lbs
Useful Load: 940 lbs

1959

Year: 1959
Model: 172

Speed
    Top Speed at Sea Level: 135 mph
    Cruise   124 mph
Range
    Cruise (recommended):   519 mi
                                     4.2 hrs
                                  124 mph
    Maximum Range at 7500 ft: 620 mi

		6.4	hrs
		97	mph
Rate of Climb at Sea Level:		660	fpm
Service Ceiling:	13,300	ft	
Baggage:		120	lbs
Wing Loading: (lbs/sq ft)		12.6	
Power Loading: (lbs/hp)		15.2	
Fuel Capacity			
Standard:		42	gal
Engine:	Continental O-300A		
TBO:		1500	hrs
Power:		145	hp
Wingspan:	36 ft 00	in	
Wing Area: (sq ft)		175	
Length:	25 ft 00	in	
Height:	8 ft 06	in	
Gross Weight:		2200	lbs
Empty Weight:		1260	lbs
Useful Load:		940	lbs

1960

Year: 1960
Model: 172 A

Speed		
Top Speed at Sea Level:	140	mph
Cruise, 70 percent power at 8000 ft:	131	mph
Range		
Cruise, 70 percent power at 8000 ft:	545	mi
37 Gallons, No Reserve:	4.2	hrs
	131	mph
Maximum Range at 10,000 ft:	790	mi
37 Gallons, No Reserve:	8.3	hrs
	95	mph
Rate of Climb at Sea Level:	730	fpm
Service Ceiling:	15,100	ft
Takeoff		
Ground Run:	780	ft
Over 50-ft Obstacle:	1370	ft
Landing		
Ground Roll:	680	ft
Over 50-ft Obstacle:	1115	ft
Baggage:	120	lbs
Wing Loading: (lbs/sq ft)	12.6	

Power Loading: (lbs/hp)	15.2	
Fuel Capacity		
Standard:	42	gal
Oil Capacity:	8	qts
Engine:	Continental O-300C	
TBO:	1800	hrs
Power:	145	hp
Propeller:	1C171/EM 7654 McCauley	
Wingspan:	36 ft 00	in
Wing Area: (sq ft)	174	
Length:	26 ft 04	in
Height:	8 ft 11	in
Gross Weight:	2200	lbs
Empty Weight:	1252	lbs
Useful Load:	948	lbs

1961

Year: 1961
Model: 172 B

Speed		
Top Speed at Sea Level:	139	mph
Cruise, 75 percent power at 7000 ft:	131	mph
Range		
Cruise, 75 percent power at 7000 ft:	535	mi
39 Gallons, No Reserve:	4.1	hrs
	131	mph
Optimum Range at 10,000 ft:	780	mi
39 Gallons, No Reserve:	7.8	hrs
	100	mph
Rate of Climb at Sea Level:	700	fpm
Service Ceiling:	14,550	ft
Takeoff		
Ground Run:	825	ft
Over 50-ft Obstacle:	1430	ft
Landing		
Ground Roll:	690	ft
Over 50-ft Obstacle:	1140	ft
Baggage:	120	lbs
Wing Loading: (lbs/sq ft)	12.9	
Power Loading: (lbs/hp)	15.5	
Fuel Capacity		
Standard:	42	gal
Oil Capacity:	8	qts
Engine:	Continental O-300C	

TBO:	1800	hrs
Power:	145	hp
Propeller: (diameter)	76	in
Wingspan:	36 ft 02	in
Wing Area: (sq ft)	175	
Length:	26 ft 06	in
Height:	8 ft 11	in
Gross Weight:	2250	lbs
Empty Weight:	1260	lbs
Useful Load:	990	lbs

Year: 1961
Model: 172 B Skyhawk

Speed		
Top Speed at Sea Level:	140	mph
Cruise, 75 percent power at 7000 ft:	131	mph
Range		
Cruise, 75 percent power at 7000 ft:	540	mi
39 Gallons, No Reserve:	4.1	hrs
	131	mph
Optimum Range at 10,000 ft;	780	mi
39 Gallons, No Reserve:	7.8	hrs
	100	mph h
Rate of Climb at Sea Level:	730	fpm
Service Ceiling:	15,100	ft
Takeoff		
Ground Run:	875	ft
Over 50-ft Obstacle:	1370	ft
Landing		
Ground Roll:	600	ft
Over 50-ft Obstacle:	1115	ft
Baggage:	120	lbs
Wing Loading: (lbs/sq ft)	12.9	
Power Loading: (lbs/hp)	15.5	
Fuel Capacity		
Standard:	42	gal
Oil Capacity:	8	qts
Engine:	Continental O-300D	
TBO:	1800	hrs
Power:	145	hp
Propeller: (diameter)	76	in
Wingspan:	36 ft 02	in
Wing Area: (sq ft)	175	
Length:	26 ft 06	in

Height:	8 ft 11	in
Gross Weight:	2200	lbs
Empty Weight:	1325	lbs
Useful Load:	875	lbs

1962

Year: 1962
Model: 172 C

Speed
Top Speed at Sea Level:	139	mph
Cruise, 75 percent power at 7000 ft:	131	mph

Range
Cruise, 75 percent power at 7000 ft:	535	mi
39 Gallons, No Reserve:	4.1	hrs
	131	mph
Optimum Range at 10,000 ft:	780	mi
39 Gallons, No Reserve:	7.8	hrs
	100	mph

Rate of Climb at Sea Level:	700	fpm
Service Ceiling:	14,550	ft

Takeoff
Ground Run:	825	ft
Over 50-ft Obstacle:	1430	ft

Landing
Ground Roll:	690	ft
Over 50-ft Obstacle:	1140	ft
Baggage:	120	lbs
Wing Loading: (lbs/sq ft)	12.9	
Power Loading: (lbs/hp)	15.5	

Fuel Capacity
Standard:	42	gal
Oil Capacity:	8	qts
Engine:	Continental O-300C	
TBO:	1800	hrs
Power:	145	hp
Propeller: (diameter)	76	in
Wingspan:	36 ft 02	in
Wing Area: (sq ft)	175	
Length:	26 ft 06	in
Height:	8 ft 11	in
Gross Weight:	2250	lbs
Empty Weight:	1260	lbs
Useful Load:	990	lbs

Year: 1962
Model: 172 C Skyhawk

Speed
    Top Speed at Sea Level: 140 mph
    Cruise, 75 percent power at 7000 ft: 132 mph
Range
    Cruise, 75 percent power at 7000 ft: 540 mi
    39 Gallons, No Reserve: 4.1 hrs
                                   132 mph
    Optimum Range at 10,000 ft: 780 mi
    39 Gallons, No Reserve: 7.8 hrs
                                   100 mph
Rate of Climb at Sea Level: 700 fpm
Service Ceiling: 14,550 ft
Takeoff
    Ground Run: 825 ft
    Over 50-ft Obstacle: 1430 ft
Landing
    Ground Roll: 690 ft
    Over 50-ft Obstacle: 1140 ft
Baggage: 120 lbs
Wing Loading: (lbs/sq ft)   12.9
Power Loading: (lbs/hp)   15.5
Fuel Capacity
    Standard: 42 gal
Oil Capacity: 8 qts
Engine: Continental O-300D
TBO: 1800 hrs
Power: 145 hp
Propeller: (diameter)   76 in
Wingspan: 36 ft 02 in
Wing Area: (sq ft)   175
Length: 26 ft 06 in
Height: 8 ft 11 in
Gross Weight: 2250 lbs
Empty Weight: 1330 lbs
Useful Load: 990 lbs

1963
Year: 1963
Model: 172 D

Speed
    Top Speed at Sea Level: 138 mph

Cruise, 75 percent power at 7000 ft:	130	mph
Range		
Cruise, 75 percent power at 7000 ft:	595	mi
39 Gallons, No Reserve:	4.6	hrs
	130	mph
Optimum Range at 10,000 ft:	720	mi
39 Gallons, No Reserve:	7.1	hrs
	102	mph
Rate of Climb at Sea Level:	645	fpm
Service Ceiling:	13,100	ft
Takeoff		
Ground Run:	865	ft
Over 50-ft Obstacle:	1525	ft
Landing		
Ground Roll:	520	ft
Over 50-ft Obstacle:	1250	ft
Baggage:	120	lbs
Wing Loading: (lbs/sq ft)	13.2	
Power Loading: (lbs/hp)	15.9	
Fuel Capacity		
Standard:	42	gal
Oil Capacity:	8	qts
Engine:	Continental O-300C	
TBO:	1800	hrs
Power:	145	hp
Propeller: (diameter)	76	in
Wingspan:	36 ft 02	in
Wing Area: (sq ft)	174	
Length:	26 ft 06	in
Height:	8 ft 11	in
Gross Weight:	2300	lbs
Empty Weight:	1260	lbs
Useful Load:	1040	lbs

Year: 1963
Model: 172 D Skyhawk

Speed		
Top Speed at Sea Level:	139	mph
Cruise, 75 percent power at 7000 ft:	131	mph
Range		
Cruise, 75 percent power at 7000 ft:	600	mi
39 Gallons, No Reserve:	4.6	hrs
	131	mph
Optimum Range at 10,000 ft:	720	mi

39 Gallons, No Reserve:	7.1	hrs
	102	mph
Rate of Climb at Sea Level:	645	fpm
Service Ceiling:	13,100	ft
Takeoff		
Ground Run:	865	ft
Over 50-ft Obstacle:	1525	ft
Landing		
Ground Roll:	520	ft
Over 50-ft Obstacle:	1250	ft
Baggage:	120	lbs
Wing Loading: (lbs/sq ft)	13.2	
Power Loading: (lbs/hp)	15.9	
Fuel Capacity		
Standard:	42	gal
Oil Capacity:	8	qts
Engine:	Continental O-300D	
TBO:	1800	hrs
Power:	145	hp
Propeller: (diameter)	76	in
Wingspan:	36 ft 02	in
Wing Area: (sq ft)	174	
Length:	26 ft 06	in
Height:	8 ft 11	in
Gross Weight:	2300	lbs
Empty Weight:	1330	lbs
Useful Load:	970	lbs

Year: 1963
Model: 172 Powermatic

Speed		
Top Speed at Sea Level:	150	mph
Cruise, 75 percent power at 7000 ft:	142	mph
Range		
Cruise, 75 percent power at 7000 ft:	550	mi
41.5 Gallons, No Reserve:	3.9	hrs
	142	mph
Optimum Range at 10,000 ft:	720	mi
41.5 Gallons, No Reserve:	6.9	hrs
	104	mph
Rate of Climb at Sea Level:	950	fpm
Service Ceiling:	17,800	ft
Takeoff		
Ground Run:	600	ft
Over 50-ft Obstacle:	1205	ft

Landing

Ground Roll:	610	ft
Over 50-ft Obstacle:	1200	ft
Baggage:	120	lbs
Wing Loading: (lbs/sq ft)	14.1	
Power Loading: (lbs/hp)	14.0	

Fuel Capacity

Standard:	52	gal
Oil Capacity:	10	qts
Engine:	Continental GO-300E	
TBO:	1200	hrs
Power:	175	hp
Propeller: (diameter) C/S	84	in
Wingspan:	36 ft 02	in
Wing Area: (sq ft)	175	
Length:	26 ft 06	in
Height:	8 ft 11	in
Gross Weight:	2450	lbs
Empty Weight:	1410	lbs
Useful Load:	1040	lbs

1964

Year: 1964
Model: 172 E

Speed

Top Speed at Sea Level:	138	mph
Cruise, 75 percent power at 7000 ft:	130	mph

Range

Cruise, 75 percent power at 7000 ft:	595	mi
39 Gallons, No Reserve:	4.6	hrs
	130	mph
Optimum Range at 10,000 ft:	720	mi
39 Gallons, No Reserve:	7.1	hrs
	102	mph
Rate of Climb at Sea Level:	645	fpm
Service Ceiling:	13,100	ft

Takeoff

Ground Run:	865	ft
Over 50-ft Obstacle:	1525	ft

Landing

Ground Roll:	520	ft
Over 50-ft Obstacle:	1250	ft
Baggage:	120	lbs
Wing Loading: (lbs/sq ft)	13.2	

Power Loading: (lbs/hp)			15.9	
Fuel Capacity				
Standard:			42	gal
Oil Capacity:			8	qts
Engine:		Continental O-300C		
TBO:			1800	hrs
Power:			145	hp
Propeller: (diameter)			76	in
Wingspan:	36 ft		02	in
Wing Area: (sq ft)			174	
Length:	26 ft		06	in
Height:	8 ft		11	in
Gross Weight:			2300	lbs
Empty Weight:			1255	lbs
Useful Load:			1045	lbs

Year: 1964
Model: 172 E Skyhawk

Speed		
Top Speed at Sea Level:	139	mph
Cruise, 75 percent power at 7000 ft:	131	mph
Range		
Cruise, 75 percent power at 7000 ft:	600	mi
39 Gallons, No Reserve:	4.6	hrs
	131	mph
Optimum Range at 10,000 ft:	720	mi
39 Gallons, No Reserve:	7.1	hrs
	102	mph
Rate of Climb at Sea Level:	645	fpm
Service Ceiling:	13,100	ft
Takeoff		
Ground Run:	865	ft
Over 50-ft Obstacle:	1525	ft
Landing		
Ground Roll:	520	ft
Over 50-ft Obstacle:	1250	ft
Baggage:	120	lbs
Wing Loading: (lbs/sq ft)	13.2	
Power Loading: (lbs/hp)	15.9	
Fuel Capacity		
Standard:	42	gal
Oil Capacity:	8	qts
Engine:	Continental O-300D	
TBO:	1800	hrs

Power:	145	hp
Propeller: (diameter)	76	in
Wingspan:	36 ft 02	in
Wing Area: (sq ft)	174	
Length:	26 ft 06	in
Height:	8 ft 11	in
Gross Weight:	2300	lbs
Empty Weight:	1320	lbs
Useful Load:	980	lbs

1965

Year: 1965
Model: 172 F

Speed

Top Speed at Sea Level:	138	mph
Cruise, 75 percent power at 7000 ft:	130	mph

Range

Cruise, 75 percent power at 7000 ft:	595	mi
39 Gallons, No Reserve:	4.6	hrs
	130	mph
Optimum Range at 10,000 ft:	720	mi
39 Gallons, No Reserve:	7.1	hrs
	102	mph
Rate of Climb at Sea Level:	645	fpm
Service Ceiling:	13,100	ft

Takeoff

Ground Run:	865	ft
Over 50-ft Obstacle:	1525	ft

Landing

Ground Roll:	520	ft
Over 50-ft Obstacle:	1250	ft
Baggage:	120	lbs
Wing Loading: (lbs/sq ft)	13.2	
Power Loading: (lbs/hp)	15.9	

Fuel Capacity

Standard:	42	gal
Oil Capacity:	8	qts
Engine:	Continental O-300C	
TBO:	1800	hrs
Power:	145	hp
Propeller: (diameter)	76	in
Wingspan:	36 ft 02	in
Wing Area: (sq ft)	174	

Length:	26 ft 06 in
Height:	8 ft 11 in
Gross Weight:	2300 lbs
Empty Weight:	1260 lbs
Useful Load:	1040 lbs

Year: 1965
Model: 172 F Skyhawk

Speed
| Top Speed at Sea Level: | 139 mph |
| Cruise, 75 percent power at 7000 ft: | 131 mph |

Range
Cruise, 75 percent power at 7000 ft:	600 mi
39 Gallons, No Reserve:	4.6 hrs
	131 mph
Optimum Range at 10,000 ft:	720 mi
39 Gallons, No Reserve:	7.1 hrs
	102 mph

| Rate of Climb at Sea Level: | 645 fpm |
| Service Ceiling: | 13,100 ft |

Takeoff
| Ground Run: | 865 ft |
| Over 50-ft Obstacle: | 1525 ft |

Landing
Ground Roll:	520 ft
Over 50-ft Obstacle:	1250 ft
Baggage:	120 lbs
Wing Loading: (lbs/sq ft)	13.2
Power Loading: (lbs/hp)	15.9

Fuel Capacity
Standard:	42 gal
Oil Capacity:	8 qts
Engine:	Continental O-300D
TBO:	1800 hrs
Power:	145 hp
Propeller: (diameter)	76 in
Wingspan:	36 ft 02 in
Wing Area: (sq ft)	174
Length:	26 ft 06 in
Height:	8 ft 11 in
Gross Weight:	2300 lbs
Empty Weight:	1320 lbs
Useful Load:	980 lbs

1966

Year: 1966
Model: 172 G

Speed
    Top Speed at Sea Level: 138 mph
    Cruise, 75 percent power at 7000 ft: 130 mph
Range
    Cruise, 75 percent power at 7000 ft: 595 mi
    39 Gallons, No Reserve: 4.6 hrs
                                      130 mph

    Optimum Range at 10,000 ft: 720 mi
    39 Gallons, No Reserve: 7.1 hrs
                                      102 mph

Rate of Climb at Sea Level: 645 fpm
Service Ceiling: 13,100 ft
Takeoff
    Ground Run: 865 ft
    Over 50-ft Obstacle: 1525 ft
Landing
    Ground Roll: 520 ft
    Over 50-ft Obstacle: 1250 ft
Baggage: 120 lbs
Wing Loading: (lbs/sq ft)   13.2
Power Loading: (lbs/hp)   15.9
Fuel Capacity
    Standard: 42 gal
Oil Capacity: 8 qts
Engine: Continental O-300C
TBO: 1800 hrs
Power: 145 hp
Propeller: (diameter)   76 in
Wingspan: 36 ft 02 in
Wing Area: (sq ft)   174
Length: 26 ft 06 in
Height: 8 ft 11 in
Gross Weight: 2300 lbs
Empty Weight: 1260 lbs
Useful Load: 1040 lbs

Year: 1966
Model: 172 G Skyhawk

Speed
    Top Speed at Sea Level: 139 mph

Cruise, 75 percent power at 7000 ft:	131	mph
Range		
Cruise, 75 percent power at 7000 ft:	600	mi
39 Gallons, No Reserve:	4.6	hrs
	131	mph
Optimum Range at 10,000 ft:	720	mi
39 Gallons, No Reserve:	7.1	hrs
	102	mph
Rate of Climb at Sea Level:	645	fpm
Service Ceiling:	13,100	ft
Takeoff		
Ground Run:	865	ft
Over 50-ft Obstacle:	1525	ft
Landing		
Ground Roll:	520	ft
Over 50-ft Obstacle:	1250	ft
Baggage:	120	lbs
Wing Loading: (lbs/sq ft)	13.2	
Power Loading: (lbs/hp)	15.9	
Fuel Capacity		
Standard:	42	gal
Oil Capacity:	8	qts
Engine:	Continental O-300D	
TBO:	1800	hrs
Power:	145	hp
Propeller: (diameter)	76	in
Wingspan:	36 ft 02	in
Wing Area: (sq ft)	174	
Length:	26 ft 06	in
Height:	8 ft 11	in
Gross Weight:	2300	lbs
Empty Weight:	1320	lbs
Useful Load:	980	lbs

1967

Year: 1967
Model: 172 H

Speed		
Top Speed at Sea Level:	138	mph
Cruise, 75 percent power at 7000 ft:	130	mph
Range		
Cruise, 75 percent power at 7000 ft:	595	mi
39 Gallons, No Reserve:	4.6	hrs
	130	mph

Optimum Range at 10,000 ft:	720	mi
39 Gallons, No Reserve:	7.1	hrs
	102	mph
Rate of Climb at Sea Level:	645	fpm
Service Ceiling:	13,100	ft
Takeoff		
Ground Run:	865	ft
Over 50-ft Obstacle:	1525	ft
Landing		
Ground Roll:	520	ft
Over 50-ft Obstacle:	1250	ft
Baggage:	120	lbs
Wing Loading: (lbs/sq ft)	13.2	
Power Loading: (lbs/hp)	15.87	
Fuel Capacity		
Standard:	42	gal
Oil Capacity:	8	qts
Engine:	Continental O-300D	
TBO:	1800	hrs
Power:	145	hp
Propeller: (diameter)	76	in
Wingspan:	36 ft 02	in
Wing Area: (sq ft)	174	
Length:	26 ft 11	in
Height:	8 ft 09	in
Gross Weight:	2300	lbs
Empty Weight:	1275	lbs
Useful Load:	1025	lbs

Year: 1967
Model: 172 H Skyhawk

Speed		
Top Speed at Sea Level:	139	mph
Cruise, 75 percent power at 7000 ft:	131	mph
Range		
Cruise, 75 percent power at 7000 ft:	600	mi
39 Gallons, No Reserve:	4.6	hrs
	131	mph
Optimum Range at 10,000 ft:	720	mi
39 Gallons, No Reserve:	7.1	hrs
	102	mph
Rate of Climb at Sea Level:	645	fpm
Service Ceiling:	13,100	ft
Takeoff		
Ground Run:	865	ft

Over 50-ft Obstacle:	1525	ft
Landing		
Ground Roll:	520	ft
Over 50-ft Obstacle:	1250	ft
Baggage:	120	lbs
Wing Loading: (lbs/sq ft)	13.2	
Power Loading: (lbs/hp)	15.87	
Fuel Capacity		
Standard:	42	gal
Oil Capacity:	8	qts
Engine:	Continental O-300D	
TBO:	1800	hrs
Power:	145	hp
Propeller: (diameter)	76	in
Wingspan:	36 ft 02	in
Wing Area: (sq ft)	174	
Length:	26 ft 11	in
Height:	8 ft 09	in
Gross Weight:	2300	lbs
Empty Weight:	1340	lbs
Useful Load:	960	lbs

1968

Year: 1968
Model: 172 I

Speed		
Top Speed at Sea Level:	139	mph
Cruise, 75 percent power at 9000 ft:	131	mph
Range		
Cruise, 75 percent power at 9000 ft:	615	mi
38 Gallons, No Reserve:	4.7	hrs
	131	mph
Optimum Range at 10,000 ft:	640	mi
	5.5	hrs
	117	mph
Rate of Climb at Sea Level:	645	fpm
Service Ceiling:	13,100	ft
Takeoff		
Ground Run:	865	ft
Over 50-ft Obstacle:	1525	ft
Landing		
Ground Roll:	520	ft
Over 50-ft Obstacle:	1250	ft
Baggage:	120	lbs

Wing Loading: (lbs/sq ft)	13.2
Power Loading: (lbs/hp)	15.33
Fuel Capacity	
Standard:	42 gal
Oil Capacity:	8 qts
Engine:	Lycoming O-320 E2D
TBO:	2000 hrs
Power:	150 hp
Gross Weight:	2300 lbs
Empty Weight:	1230 lbs
Useful Load:	1070 lbs

Year: 1968
Model: 172 I Skyhawk

Speed	
Top Speed at Sea Level:	140 mph
Cruise, 75 percent power at 9000 ft:	132 mph
Range	
Cruise, 75 percent power at 9000 ft:	620 mi
38 Gallons, No Reserve:	4.7 hrs
	132 mph
Optimum Range at 10,000 ft:	655 mi
	5.5 hrs
	118 mph
Rate of Climb at Sea Level:	645 fpm
Service Ceiling:	13,100 ft
Takeoff	
Ground Run:	865 ft
Over 50-ft Obstacle:	1525 ft
Landing	
Ground Roll:	520 ft
Over 50-ft Obstacle:	1250 ft
Baggage:	120 lbs
Wing Loading: (lbs/sq ft)	13.2
Power Loading: (lbs/hp)	15.33
Fuel Capacity	
Standard:	42 gal
Oil Capacity:	8 qts
Engine:	Lycoming O-320 E2D
TBO:	2000 hrs
Power:	150 hp
Gross Weight:	2300 lbs
Empty Weight:	1300 lbs
Useful Load:	1000 lbs

1969

Year: 1969
Model: 172 K

Speed
Top Speed at Sea Level:	139	mph
Cruise, 75 percent power at 9000 ft:	131	mph

Range
Cruise, 75 percent power at 9000 ft:	615	mi
38 Gallons, No Reserve:	4.7	hrs
	131	mph
Optimum Range at 10,000 ft:	640	mi
	5.5	hrs
	117	mph

Rate of Climb at Sea Level:	645	fpm
Service Ceiling:	13,100	ft

Takeoff
Ground Run:	865	ft
Over 50-ft Obstacle:	1525	ft

Landing
Ground Roll:	520	ft
Over 50 ft Obstacle:	1250	ft
Baggage:	120	lbs
Wing Loading: (lbs/sq ft)	13.2	
Power Loading: (lbs/hp)	15.33	

Fuel Capacity
Standard:	42	gal
Oil Capacity:	8	qts
Engine:	Lycoming O-320 E2D	
TBO:	2000	hrs
Power:	150	hp
Gross Weight:	2300	lbs
Empty Weight:	1230	lbs
Useful Load:	1070	lbs

Year: 1969
Model: 172 K Skyhawk

Speed
Top Speed at Sea Level:	140	mph
Cruise, 75 percent power at 9000 ft:	132	mph

Range
Cruise, 75 percent power at 9000 ft:	620	mi
38 Gallons, No Reserve:	4.7	hrs
	132	mph

Optimum Range at 10,000 ft:	655	mi
	5.5	hrs
	118	mph
Rate of Climb at Sea Level:	645	fpm
Service Ceiling:	13,100	ft
Takeoff		
Ground Run:	865	ft
Over 50-ft Obstacle:	1525	ft
Landing		
Ground Roll:	520	ft
Over 50-ft Obstacle:	1250	ft
Baggage:	120	lbs
Wing Loading: (lbs/sq ft)	13.2	
Power Loading: (lbs/hp)	15.33	
Fuel Capacity		
Standard:	42	gal
Oil Capacity:	8	qts
Engine:	Lycoming O-320 E2D	
TBO:	2000	hrs
Power:	150	hp
Gross Weight:	2300	lbs
Empty Weight:	1300	lbs
Useful Load:	1000	lbs
	9000	ft:

1970

Year: 1970
Model: 172 K

Speed
| Top Speed at Sea Level: | 139 | mph |
| Cruise, 75 percent power at 9000 ft: | 131 | mph |

Range
Cruise, 75 percent power at 9000 ft:	615	mi
38 Gallons, No Reserve:	4.7	hrs
	131	mph
Cruise, 75 percent at 9000 ft:	775	mi
48 Gallons, No Reserve:	5.9	hrs
	131	mph
Optimum Range at 10,000 ft:	640	mi
38 Gallons, No Reserve:	5.5	hrs
	117	mph
Optimum Range at 10000 ft:	820	mi
48 Gallons, No Reserve:	7.0	hrs
	117	mph

Rate of Climb at Sea Level:	645	fpm
Service Ceiling:	13,100	ft
Takeoff		
Ground Run:	865	ft
Over 50-ft Obstacle:	1525	ft
Landing		
Ground Roll:	520	ft
Over 50-ft Obstacle:	1250	ft
Stall Speed		
Flaps Up, Power Off:	57	mph
Flaps Down, Power Off:	49	mph
Baggage:	120	lbs
Wing Loading: (lbs/sq ft)	13.2	
Power Loading: (lbs/hp)	15.3	
Fuel Capacity		
Standard:	42	gal
w/optional tanks:	52	gal
Oil Capacity:	8	qts
Engine:	Lycoming O-320 E2D	
TBO:	2000	hrs
Power: (at 2700 rpm)	150	hp
Propeller: (diameter)	76	in
Wingspan:	35 ft 09	in
Wing Area: (sq ft)	174	
Length:	26 ft 11	in
Height:	8 ft 09	in
Gross Weight:	2300	lbs
Empty Weight:	1245	lbs
Useful Load:	1055	lbs

Year: 1970
Model: 172 K Skyhawk

Speed		
Top Speed at Sea Level:	140	mph
Cruise, 75 percent power at 9000 ft:	132	mph
Range		
Cruise, 75 percent power at 9000 ft:	620	mi
38 Gallons, No Reserve:	4.7	hrs
	132	mph
Cruise, 75 percent power at 9000 ft:	780	mi
48 Gallons, No Reserve:	5.9	hrs
	132	mph
Optimum Range at 10,000 ft:	655	mi
38 Gallons, No Reserve:	5.5	hrs

	118	mph
Optimum Range at 10000 ft:	830	mi
48 Gallons, No Reserve:	7.0	hrs
	118	mph
Rate of Climb at Sea Level:	645	fpm
Service Ceiling:	13,100	ft
Takeoff		
Ground Run:	865	ft
Over 50-ft Obstacle:	1525	ft
Landing		
Ground Roll:	520	ft
Over 50-ft Obstacle:	1250	ft
Stall Speed		
Flaps Up, Power Off:	57	mph
Flaps Down, Power Off:	49	mph
Baggage:	120	lbs
Wing Loading: (lbs/sq ft)	13.2	
Power Loading: (lbs/hp)	15.3	
Fuel Capacity		
Standard:	42	gal
w/optional tanks:	52	gal
Oil Capacity:	8	qts
Engine:	Lycoming O-320 E2D	
TBO:	2000	hrs
Power:	150	hp
Propeller: (diameter)	76	in
Wingspan:	35 ft 09	in
Wing Area: (sq ft)	174	
Length:	26 ft 11	in
Height:	8 ft 09	in
Gross Weight:	2300	lbs
Empty Weight:	1315	lbs
Useful Load:	985	lbs

1971

Year: 1971
Model: 172 L

Speed		
Top Speed at Sea Level:	139	mph
Cruise, 75 percent power at 9000 ft:	131	mph
Range		
Cruise, 75 percent power at 9000 ft:	615	mi
38 Gallons, No Reserve:	4.7	hrs
	131	mph

Cruise, 75 percent at 9000 ft:	775	mi
48 Gallons, No Reserve:	5.9	hrs
	131	mph
Optimum Range at 10000 ft:	640	mi
38 Gallons, No Reserve:	5.5	hrs
	117	mph
Optimum Range at 10000 ft:	820	mi
48 Gallons, No Reserve:	7.0	hrs
	117	mph
Rate of Climb at Sea Level:	645	fpm
Service Ceiling:	13,100	ft
Takeoff		
Ground Run:	865	ft
Over 50-ft Obstacle:	1525	ft
Landing		
Ground Roll:	520	ft
Over 50-ft Obstacle:	1250	ft
Stall Speed		
Flaps Up, Power Off:	57	mph
Flaps Down, Power Off:	49	mph
Baggage:	120	lbs
Wing Loading: (lbs/sq ft)	13.2	
Power Loading: (lbs/hp)	15.3	
Fuel Capacity		
Standard:	42	gal
w/optional tanks:	52	gal
Oil Capacity:	8	qts
Engine:	Lycoming O-320 E2D	
TBO:	2000	hrs
Power: (at 2700 rpm)	150	hp
Propeller: (diameter)	76	in
Wingspan:	35 ft 09	in
Wing Area: (sq ft)	174	
Length:	26 ft 11	in
Height:	8 ft 09	in
Gross Weight:	2300	lbs
Empty Weight:	1250	lbs
Useful Load:	1050	lbs

Year: 1971
Model: 172 L Skyhawk

Speed		
Top Speed at Sea Level:	140	mph
Cruise, 75 percent power at 9000 ft:	132	mph

Range

Cruise, 75 percent power at 9000 ft:	620	mi
38 Gallons, No Reserve:	4.7	hrs
	132	mph
Cruise, 75 percent power at 9000 ft:	780	mi
48 Gallons, No Reserve:	5.9	hrs
	132	mph
Optimum Range at 10,000 ft:	655	mi
38 Gallons, No Reserve:	5.5	hrs
	118	mph
Optimum Range at 10,000 ft:	830	mi
48 Gallons, No Reserve:	7.0	hrs
	118	mph

Rate of Climb at Sea Level:	645	fpm
Service Ceiling:	13,100	ft

Takeoff

Ground Run:	865	ft
Over 50-ft Obstacle:	1525	ft

Landing

Ground Roll:	520	ft
Over 50-ft Obstacle:	1250	ft

Stall Speed

Flaps Up, Power Off:	57	mph
Flaps Down, Power Off:	49	mph
Baggage:	120	lbs
Wing Loading: (lbs/sq ft)	13.2	
Power Loading: (lbs/hp)	15.3	

Fuel Capacity

Standard:	42	gal
w/optional tanks:	52	gal
Oil Capacity:	8	qts
Engine:	Lycoming O-320 E2D	
TBO:	2000	hrs
Power: (at 2700 rpm)	150	hp
Propeller: (diameter)	76	in
Wingspan:	35 ft 09	in
Wing Area: (sq ft)	174	
Length:	26 ft 11	in
Height:	8 ft 09	in
Gross Weight:	2300	lbs
Empty Weight:	1300	lbs
Useful Load:	1000	lbs

1972

Year: 1972
Model: 172 L

Speed
    Top Speed at Sea Level: 139 mph
    Cruise, 75 percent power at 9000 ft: 131 mph

Range
    Cruise, 75 percent power at 9000 ft: 615 mi
    38 Gallons, No Reserve: 4.7 hrs
       131 mph

    Cruise, 75 percent at 9000 ft: 775 mi
    48 Gallons, No Reserve: 5.9 hrs
       131 mph

    Optimum Range at 10,000 ft: 640 mi
    38 Gallons, No Reserve: 5.5 hrs
       117 mph

    Optimum Range at 10,000 ft: 820 mi
    48 Gallons, No Reserve: 7.0 hrs
       117 mph

Rate of Climb at Sea Level: 645 fpm
Service Ceiling: 13,100 ft
Takeoff
    Ground Run: 865 ft
    Over 50-ft Obstacle: 1525 ft
Landing
    Ground Roll: 520 ft
    Over 50-ft Obstacle: 1250 ft
Stall Speed
    Flaps Up, Power Off: 57 mph
    Flaps Down, Power Off: 49 mph
Baggage: 120 lbs
Wing Loading: (lbs/sq ft) 13.2
Power Loading: (lbs/hp) 15.3
Fuel Capacity
    Standard: 42 gal
    w/optional tanks: 52 gal
Oil Capacity: 8 qts
Engine: Lycoming O-320 E2D
TBO: 2000 hrs
Power: (at 2700 rpm) 150 hp
Propeller: (diameter) 75 in
Wingspan: 35 ft 09 in
Wing Area: (sq ft) 174
Length: 26 ft 11 in
Height: 8 ft 09 in
Gross Weight: 2300 lbs
Empty Weight: 1265 lbs
Useful Load: 1035 lbs

Year: 1972
Model: 172 L Skyhawk

Speed
    Top Speed at Sea Level: 140 mph
    Cruise, 75 percent power at 9000 ft: 132 mph
Range
    Cruise, 75 percent power at 9000 ft: 620 mi
    38 Gallons, No Reserve: 4.7 hrs
                                         132 mph

    Cruise, 75 percent power at 9000 ft: 780 mi
    48 Gallons, No Reserve: 5.9 hrs
                                         132 mph

    Optimum Range at 10,000 ft: 655 mi
    38 Gallons, No Reserve: 5.5 hrs
                                         118 mph

    Optimum Range at 10,000 ft: 830 mi
    48 Gallons, No Reserve: 7.0 hrs
                                         118 mph

Rate of Climb at Sea Level: 645 fpm
Service Ceiling: 13,100 ft
Takeoff
    Ground Run: 865 ft
    Over 50-ft Obstacle: 1525 ft
Landing
    Ground Roll: 520 ft
    Over 50-ft Obstacle: 1250 ft
Stall Speed
    Flaps Up, Power Off: 57 mph
    Flaps Down, Power Off: 49 mph
Baggage: 120 lbs
Wing Loading: (lbs/sq ft)   13.2
Power Loading: (lbs/hp)   15.3
Fuel Capacity
    Standard: 42 gal
    w/optional tanks: 52 gal
Oil Capacity: 8 qts
Engine: Lycoming O-320 E2D
TBO: 2000 hrs
Power: (at 2700 rpm)   150 hp
Propeller: (diameter)   75 in
Wingspan: 35 ft 09 in
Wing Area: (sq ft)   174
Length: 26 ft 11 in
Height: 8 ft 09 in
Gross Weight: 2300 lbs

Empty Weight:	1305	lbs
Useful Load:	995	lbs

1973
Year: 1973
Model: 172 M

Speed		
Top Speed at Sea Level:	139	mph
Cruise, 75 percent power at 9000 ft:	131	mph
Range		
Cruise, 75 percent power at 9000 ft:	615	mi
38 Gallons, No Reserve:	4.7	hrs
	131	mph
Cruise, 75 percent at 9000 ft:	775	mi
48 Gallons, No Reserve:	5.9	hrs
	131	mph
Optimum Range at 10,000 ft:	640	mi
38 Gallons, No Reserve:	5.5	hrs
	117	mph
Optimum Range at 10,000 ft:	820	mi
48 Gallons, No Reserve:	7.0	hrs
	117	mph
Rate of Climb at Sea Level:	645	fpm
Service Ceiling:	13,100	ft
Takeoff		
Ground Run:	865	ft
Over 50-ft Obstacle:	1525	ft
Landing		
Ground Roll:	520	ft
Over 50-ft Obstacle:	1250	ft
Stall Speed		
Flaps Up, Power Off:	57	mph
Flaps Down, Power Off:	51	mph
Baggage:	120	lbs
Wing Loading: (lbs/sq ft)	13.2	
Power Loading: (lbs/hp)	15.3	
Fuel Capacity		
Standard:	42	gal
w/optional tanks:	52	gal
Oil Capacity:	8	qts
Engine:	Lycoming O-320 E2D	
TBO:	2000	hrs
Power: (at 2700 rpm)	150	hp
Propeller: (diameter)	75	in
Wingspan:	35 ft 10	in

Wing Area: (sq ft)	175.5
Length:	26 ft 11 in
Height:	8 ft 09 in
Gross Weight:	2300 lbs
Empty Weight:	1285 lbs
Useful Load:	1015 lbs

Year: 1973
Model: 172 M Skyhawk

Speed
Top Speed at Sea Level:	140	mph
Cruise, 75 percent power at 9000 ft:	132	mph

Range
Cruise, 75 percent power at 9000 ft:	620	mi
38 Gallons, No Reserve:	4.7	hrs
	132	mph
Cruise, 75 percent power at 9000 ft:	780	mi
48 Gallons, No Reserve:	5.9	hrs
	132	mph
Optimum Range at 10,000 ft:	655	mi
38 Gallons, No Reserve:	5.5	hrs
	118	mph
Optimum Range at 10,000 ft:	830	mi
48 Gallons, No Reserve:	7.0	hrs
	118	mph

Rate of Climb at Sea Level:	645	fpm
Service Ceiling:	13,100	ft

Takeoff
Ground Run:	865	ft
Over 50-ft Obstacle:	1525	ft

Landing
Ground Roll:	520	ft
Over 50-ft Obstacle:	1250	ft

Stall Speed
Flaps Up, Power Off:	57	mph
Flaps Down, Power Off:	51	mph

Baggage:	120	lbs
Wing Loading: (lbs/sq ft)	13.2	
Power Loading: (lbs/hp)	15.3	

Fuel Capacity
Standard:	42	gal
w/optional tanks:	52	gal
Oil Capacity:	8	qts

Engine:	Lycoming O-320 E2D	
TBO:	2000	hrs
Power: (at 2700 rpm)	150	hp
Propeller: (diameter)	75	in
Wingspan:	35 ft 10	in
Wing Area: (sq ft)	175.5	
Length:	26 ft 11	in
Height:	8 ft 09	in
Gross Weight:	2300	lbs
Empty Weight:	1335	lbs
Useful Load:	965	lbs

1974

Year: 1974
Model: 172 M

Speed		
Top Speed at Sea Level:	140	mph
Cruise, 75 percent power at 8000 ft:	135	mph
Range		
Cruise, 75 percent power at 8000 ft:	635	mi
38 Gallons, No Reserve:	4.7	hrs
	135	mph
Cruise, 75 percent at 8000 ft:	795	mi
48 Gallons, No Reserve:	5.9	hrs
	135	mph
Maximum Range at 10,000 ft:	695	mi
38 Gallons, No Reserve:	6.0	hrs
	116	mph
Maximum Range at 10,000 ft:	870	mi
48 Gallons, No Reserve:	7.5	hrs
	116	mph
Rate of Climb at Sea Level:	645	fpm
Service Ceiling:	13,100	ft
Takeoff		
Ground Run:	865	ft
Over 50-ft Obstacle:	1525	ft
Landing		
Ground Roll:	520	ft
Over 50-ft Obstacle:	1250	ft
Stall Speed		
Flaps Up, Power Off:	57	mph
Flaps Down, Power Off:	49	mph
Baggage:	120	lbs

Wing Loading: (lbs/sq ft)	13.2	
Power Loading: (lbs/hp)	15.3	
Fuel Capacity		
Standard:	42	gal
w/optional tanks:	52	gal
Oil Capacity:	8	qts
Engine:	Lycoming O-320 E2D	
TBO:	2000	hrs
Power: (at 2700 rpm)	150	hp
Propeller: (diameter)	75	in
Wingspan:	35 ft 10	in
Wing Area: (sq ft)	174	
Length:	26 ft 11	in
Height:	8 ft 09	in
Gross Weight:	2300	lbs
Empty Weight:	1300	lbs
Useful Load:	1000	lbs

Year: 1974
Model: 172 M Skyhawk and Skyhawk II

Speed		
Top Speed at Sea Level:	144	mph
Cruise, 75 percent power at 8000 ft:	138	mph
Range		
Cruise, 75 percent power at 8000 ft:	650	mi
38 Gallons, No Reserve:	4.7	hrs
	138	mph
Cruise, 75 percent power at 8000 ft:	815	mi
48 Gallons, No Reserve:	5.9	hrs
	138	mph
Maximum Range at 10,000 ft:	700	mi
38 Gallons, No Reserve:	6.0	hrs
	117	mph
Maximum Range at 10,000 ft:	875	mi
48 Gallons, No Reserve:	7.5	hrs
	117	mph
Rate of Climb at Sea Level:	645	fpm
Service Ceiling:	13,100	ft
Takeoff		
Ground Run:	865	ft
Over 50-ft Obstacle:	1525	ft
Landing		
Ground Roll:	520	ft
Over 50-ft Obstacle:	1250	ft
Stall Speed		

Flaps Up, Power Off:	57	mph
Flaps Down, Power Off:	49	mph
Baggage:	120	lbs
Wing Loading: (lbs/sq ft)	13.2	
Power Loading: (lbs/hp)	15.3	
Fuel Capacity		
Standard:	42	gal
w/optional tanks:	52	gal
Oil Capacity:	8	qts
Engine:	Lycoming O-320 E2D	
TBO:	2000	hrs
Power: (at 2700 rpm)	150	hp
Propeller: (diameter)	75	in
Wingspan:	35 ft 10	in
Wing Area: (sq ft)	174	
Length:	26 ft 11	in
Height:	8 ft 09	in
Gross Weight:	2300	lbs
Empty Weight: (Skyhawk)	1345	lbs
(Skyhawk II)	1370	lbs
Useful Load: (Skyhawk)	955	lbs
(Skyhawk II)	930	lbs

1975
Year: 1975
Model: 172 M

Speed		
Top Speed at Sea Level:	140	mph
Cruise, 75 percent power at 8000 ft:	135	mph
Range		
Cruise, 75 percent power at 8000 ft:	635	mi
38 Gallons, No Reserve:	4.7	hrs
	135	mph
Cruise, 75 percent at 8000 ft:	795	mi
48 Gallons, No Reserve:	5.9	hrs
	135	mph
Maximum Range at 10,000 ft:	695	mi
38 Gallons, No Reserve:	6.0	hrs
	116	mph
Maximum Range at 10,000 ft:	870	mi
48 Gallons, No Reserve:	7.5	hrs
	116	mph
Rate of Climb at Sea Level:	645	fpm
Service Ceiling:	13,100	ft

Takeoff
  Ground Run: 865 ft
  Over 50-ft Obstacle: 1525 ft
Landing
  Ground Roll: 520 ft
  Over 50-ft Obstacle: 1250 ft
Stall Speed
  Flaps Up, Power Off: 57 mph
  Flaps Down, Power Off: 49 mph
Baggage: 120 lbs
Wing Loading: (lbs/sq ft) 13.2
Power Loading: (lbs/hp) 15.3
Fuel Capacity
  Standard: 42 gal
  w/optional tanks: 52 gal
Oil Capacity: 8 qts
Engine: Lycoming O-320 E2D
TBO: 2000 hrs
Power: (at 2700 rpm) 150 hp
Propeller: (diameter) 75 in
Wingspan: 35 ft 10 in
Wing Area: (sq ft) 174
Length: 26 ft 11 in
Height: 8 ft 09 in
Gross Weight: 2300 lbs
Empty Weight: 1300 lbs
Useful Load: 1000 lbs

Year: 1975
Model: 172 M Skyhawk and Skyhawk II

Speed
  Top Speed at Sea Level: 144 mph
  Cruise, 75 percent power at 8000 ft: 138 mph
Range
  Cruise, 75 percent power at 8000 ft: 650 mi
  38 Gallons, No Reserve: 4.7 hrs
  138 mph

  Cruise, 75 percent power at 8000 ft: 815 mi
  48 Gallons, No Reserve: 5.9 hrs
  138 mph

  Maximum Range at 10,000 ft: 700 mi
  38 Gallons, No Reserve: 6.0 hrs
  117 mph
  Maximum Range at 10,000 ft: 875 mi

48 Gallons, No Reserve:	7.5	hrs
	117	mph
Rate of Climb at Sea Level:	645	fpm
Service Ceiling:	13,100	ft
Takeoff		
Ground Run:	865	ft
Over 50-ft Obstacle:	1525	ft
Landing		
Ground Roll:	520	ft
Over 50-ft Obstacle:	1250	ft
Stall Speed		
Flaps Up, Power Off:	57	mph
Flaps Down, Power Off:	49	mph
Baggage:	120	lbs
Wing Loading: (lbs/sq ft)	13.2	
Power Loading: (lbs/hp)	15.3	
Fuel Capacity		
Standard:	42	gal
w/optional tanks:	52	gal
Oil Capacity:	8	qts
Engine:	Lycoming O-320 E2D	
TBO:	2000	hrs
Power: (at 2700 rpm)	150	hp
Propeller: (diameter)	75	in
Wingspan:	35 ft 10	in
Wing Area: (sq ft)	174	
Length:	26 ft 11	in
Height:	8 ft 09	in
Gross Weight:	2300	lbs
Empty Weight: (Standard)	1305	lbs
(Skyhawk)	1345	lbs
(Skyhawk II)	1370	lbs
Useful Load: (Standard)	995	lbs
(Skyhawk)	955	lbs
(Skyhawk II)	930	lbs

1976

Year: 1976
Model: 172 M Skyhawk and Skyhawk II

Speed		
Top Speed at Sea Level:	125	kts
Cruise, 75 percent power at 8000 ft:	120	kts
Range (with 45 minute reserve)		
Cruise, 75 percent power at 8000 ft:	450	nm

38 Gallons Usable Fuel:	3.9	hrs
Cruise, 75 percent at 8000 ft:	595	nm
48 Gallons Usable Fuel:	5.1	hrs
Maximum Range at 10,000 ft:	480	nm
38 Gallons Usable Fuel:	4.8	hrs
Maximum Range at 10,000 ft:	640	nm
48 Gallons Usable Fuel:	6.3	hrs
Rate of Climb at Sea Level:	645	fpm
Service Ceiling:	13,100	ft
Takeoff		
Ground Run:	865	ft
Over 50-ft Obstacle:	1525	ft
Landing		
Ground Roll:	520	ft
Over 50-ft Obstacle:	1250	ft
Stall Speed		
Flaps Up, Power Off:	42	kts
Flaps Down, Power Off:	36	kts
Baggage:	120	lbs
Wing Loading: (lbs/sq ft)	13.2	
Power Loading: (lbs/hp)	15.3	
Fuel Capacity		
Standard:	42	gal
w/optional tanks:	52	gal
Oil Capacity:	8	qts
Engine:	Lycoming O-320 E2D	
TBO:	2000	hrs
Power: (at 2700 rpm)	150	hp
Propeller: (diameter)	75	in
Wingspan:	35 ft 10	in
Wing Area: (sq ft)	174	
Length:	26 ft 11	in
Height:	8 ft 09	in
Maximum Weight:	2300	lbs
Empty Weight: (Skyhawk)	1387	lbs
(Skyhawk II)	1412	lbs
Useful Load: (Skyhawk)	913	lbs
(Skyhawk II)	888	lbs

1977

Year: 1977

Model: 172 N Skyhawk/100 and Skyhawk II/100

Speed
   Top Speed at Sea Level: 125 kts

Cruise, 75 percent power at 8000 ft:	122	kts
Range (with 45 minute reserve)		
Cruise, 75 percent power at 8000 ft:	485	nm
40 Gallons Usable Fuel:	4.1	hrs
Cruise, 75 percent at 8000 ft:	630	nm
50 Gallons Usable Fuel:	5.3	hrs
Maximum Range at 10,000 ft:	575	nm
40 Gallons Usable Fuel:	5.7	hrs
Maximum Range at 10,000 ft:	750	nm
50 Gallons Usable Fuel:	7.4	hrs
Rate of Climb at Sea Level:	770	fpm
Service Ceiling:	14,200	ft
Takeoff		
Ground Run:	820	ft
Over 50-ft Obstacle:	1440	ft
Landing		
Ground Roll:	520	ft
Over 50-ft Obstacle:	1250	ft
Stall Speed		
Flaps Up, Power Off:	50	kts
Flaps Down, Power Off:	44	kts
Baggage:	120	lbs
Wing Loading: (lbs/sq ft)	13.2	
Power Loading: (lbs/hp)	14.4	
Fuel Capacity		
Standard:	43	gal
w/optional tanks:	54	gal
Oil Capacity:	6	qts
Engine:	Lycoming O-320-H2AD	
TBO:	2000	hrs
Power: (at 2700 rpm)	160	hp
Propeller: (diameter)	75	in
Wingspan:	35 ft 10	in
Wing Area: (sq ft)	174	
Length:	26 ft 11	in
Height:	8 ft 09	in
Maximum Weight:	2300	lbs
Empty Weight: (Skyhawk)	1379	lbs
(Skyhawk II)	1403	lbs
Useful Load: (Skyhawk)	921	lbs
(Skyhawk II)	897	lbs

1978
Year: 1978

Model: 172 N Skyhawk/100 and Skyhawk II/100

Speed
 Top Speed at Sea Level: 125 kts
 Cruise, 75 percent power at 8000 ft: 122 kts
Range (with 45 minute reserve)
 Cruise, 75 percent power at 8000 ft: 485 nm
 40 Gallons Usable Fuel: 4.1 hrs
 Cruise, 75 percent at 8000 ft: 630 nm
 50 Gallons Usable Fuel: 5.3 hrs
 Maximum Range at 10,000 ft: 575 nm
 40 Gallons Usable Fuel: 5.7 hrs
 Maximum Range at 10,000 ft: 750 nm
 50 Gallons Usable Fuel: 7.4 hrs
Rate of Climb at Sea Level: 770 fpm
Service Ceiling: 14,200 ft
Takeoff
 Ground Run: 805 ft
 Over 50-ft Obstacle: 1440 ft
Landing
 Ground Roll: 520 ft
 Over 50-ft Obstacle: 1250 ft
Stall Speed
 Flaps Up, Power Off: 50 kts
 Flaps Down, Power Off: 44 kts
Baggage: 120 lbs
Wing Loading: (lbs/sq ft) 13.2
Power Loading: (lbs/hp) 14.4
Fuel Capacity
 Standard: 43 gal
 w/optional tanks: 54 gal
Oil Capacity: 6 qts
Engine: Lycoming O-320-H2AD
TBO: 2000 hrs
Power: (at 2700 rpm) 160 hp
Propeller: (diameter) 75 in
Wingspan: 35 ft 10 in
Wing Area: (sq ft) 174
Length: 26 ft 11 in
Height: 8 ft 09 in
Gross Weight: 2300 lbs
Empty Weight: (Skyhawk) 1393 lbs
    (Skyhawk II) 1419 lbs
Useful Load: (Skyhawk) 907 lbs
   (Skyhawk II) 881 lbs

1979

Year: 1979
Model: 172 N Skyhawk/100 and Skyhawk II/100

Speed		
Top Speed at Sea Level:	125	kts
Cruise, 75 percent power at 8000 ft:	122	kts
Range (with 45 minute reserve)		
Cruise, 75 percent power at 8000 ft:	485	nm
40 Gallons Usable Fuel:	4.1	hrs
Cruise, 75 percent at 8000 ft:	630	nm
50 Gallons Usable Fuel:	5.3	hrs
Maximum Range at 10,000 ft:	575	nm
40 Gallons Usable Fuel:	5.7	hrs
Maximum Range at 10,000 ft:	750	nm
50 Gallons Usable Fuel:	7.4	hrs
Rate of Climb at Sea Level:	770	fpm
Service Ceiling:	14,200	ft
Takeoff		
Ground Run:	805	ft
Over 50-ft Obstacle:	1440	ft
Landing		
Ground Roll:	520	ft
Over 50-ft Obstacle:	1250	ft
Stall Speed		
Flaps Up, Power Off:	50	kts
Flaps Down, Power Off:	44	kts
Baggage:	120	lbs
Wing Loading: (lbs/sq ft)	13.2	
Power Loading: (lbs/hp)	14.4	
Fuel Capacity		
Standard:	43	gal
w/optional tanks:	54	gal
Oil Capacity:	6	qts
Engine:	Lycoming O-320-H2AD	
TBO:	2000	hrs
Power: (at 2700 rpm)	160	hp
Propeller: (diameter)	75	in
Wingspan:	35 ft 10	in
Wing Area: (sq ft)	174	
Length:	26 ft 11	in
Height:	8 ft 09	in
Maximum Weight:	2300	lbs
Empty Weight: (Skyhawk)	1379	lbs
(Skyhawk II)	1424	lbs

| Useful Load: (Skyhawk) | 910 lbs |
| (Skyhawk II) | 983 lbs |

1980

Year: 1980
Model: 172 N Skyhawk/100 and Skyhawk II/100

Speed
| Top Speed at Sea Level: | 125 kts |
| Cruise, 75 percent power at 8000 ft: | 122 kts |

Range (with 45 minute reserve)
Cruise, 75 percent power at 8000 ft:	455 nm
40 Gallons Usable Fuel:	3.8 hrs
Cruise, 75 percent at 8000 ft:	600 nm
50 Gallons Usable Fuel:	5.0 hrs
Maximum Range at 10,000 ft:	575 nm
40 Gallons Usable Fuel:	6.1 hrs
Maximum Range at 10,000 ft:	750 nm
50 Gallons Usable Fuel:	7.9 hrs
Rate of Climb at Sea Level:	770 fpm
Service Ceiling:	14,200 ft

Takeoff
| Ground Run: | 775 ft |
| Over 50-ft Obstacle: | 1390 ft |

Landing
| Ground Roll: | 520 ft |
| Over 50-ft Obstacle: | 1250 ft |

Stall Speed
Flaps Up, Power Off:	50 kts
Flaps Down, Power Off:	44 kts
Baggage:	120 lbs
Wing Loading: (lbs/sq ft)	13.2
Power Loading: (lbs/hp)	14.4

Fuel Capacity
Standard:	43 gal
w/optional tanks:	54 gal
Oil Capacity:	6 qts
Engine:	Lycoming O-320-H2AD
TBO:	2000 hrs
Power: (at 2700 rpm)	160 hp
Propeller: (diameter)	75 in
Wingspan:	35 ft 10 in
Wing Area: (sq ft)	174
Length:	26 ft 11 in
Height:	8 ft 09 in

Maximum Weight:	2300	lbs
Empty Weight: (Skyhawk)	1403	lbs
(Skyhawk II)	1430	lbs
Useful Load: (Skyhawk)	904	lbs
(Skyhawk II)	877	lbs

1981

Year: 1981
Model: 172 P Skyhawk and Skyhawk II

Speed		
Top Speed at Sea Level:	123	kts
Cruise, 75 percent power at 8000 ft:	120	kts
Range (with 45 minute reserve)		
Cruise, 75 percent power at 8000 ft:	440	nm
40 Gallons Usable Fuel:	3.8	hrs
Cruise, 75 percent at 8000 ft:	585	nm
50 Gallons Usable Fuel:	5.0	hrs
Cruise, 75 percent at 8000 ft:	755	nm
60 Gallons Usable Fuel:	6.4	hrs
Maximum Range at 10,000 ft:	520	nm
40 Gallons Usable Fuel:	5.6	hrs
Maximum Range at 10,000 ft:	680	nm
50 Gallons Usable Fuel:	7.4	hrs
Maximum Range at 10,000 ft:	875	nm
60 Gallons Usable Fuel:	9.4	hrs
Rate of Climb at Sea Level:	700	fpm
Service Ceiling:	13,000	ft
Takeoff		
Ground Run:	890	ft
Over 50-ft Obstacle:	1825	ft
Landing		
Ground Roll:	540	ft
Over 50-ft Obstacle:	1280	ft
Stall Speed		
Flaps Up, Power Off:	51	kts
Flaps Down, Power Off:	46	kts
Baggage:	120	lbs
Wing Loading: (lbs/sq ft)	13.8	
Power Loading: (lbs/hp)	15.0	
Fuel Capacity		
Standard:	43	gal
w/long range tanks:	54	gal
w/integral long range tanks:	68	gal
Oil Capacity:	8	qts

```
Engine:                              Lycoming O-320-D2J
TBO:                                           2000  hrs
Power:  (at 2700 rpm)                           160  hp
Propeller:  (diameter)                           75  in
Wingspan:                                35 ft  10  in
Wing Area:  (sq ft)                             174
Length:                                  26 ft  11  in
Height:                                   8 ft  09  in
Maximum Weight:                               2400  lbs
Empty Weight:  (Skyhawk)                      1411  lbs
              (Skyhawk II)                    1439  lbs
Useful Load:  (Skyhawk)                        996  lbs
              (Skyhawk II)                      968  lbs
```

1982

Year: 1982
Model: 172 P Skyhawk and Skyhawk II

Speed
    Top Speed at Sea Level: 123 kts
    Cruise, 75 percent power at 8000 ft: 120 kts
Range (with 45 minute reserve)
    Cruise, 75 percent power at 8000 ft: 440 nm
    40 Gallons Usable Fuel: 3.8 hrs
    Cruise, 75 percent at 8000 ft: 585 nm
    50 Gallons Usable Fuel: 5.0 hrs
    Cruise, 75 percent at 8000 ft: 755 nm
    60 Gallons Usable Fuel: 6.4 hrs
    Maximum Range at 10,000 ft: 520 nm
    40 Gallons Usable Fuel: 5.6 hrs
    Maximum Range at 10,000 ft: 680 nm
    50 Gallons Usable Fuel: 7.4 hrs
    Maximum Range at 10,000 ft: 875 nm
    60 Gallons Usable Fuel: 9.4 hrs
Rate of Climb at Sea Level: 700 fpm
Service Ceiling: 13,000 ft
Takeoff
    Ground Run: 890 ft
    Over 50-ft Obstacle: 1625 ft
Landing
    Ground Roll: 540 ft
    Over 50-ft Obstacle: 1280 ft
Stall Speed
    Flaps Up, Power Off: 51 kts

Flaps Down, Power Off:	46	kts
Baggage:	120	lbs
Wing Loading: (lbs/sq ft)	13.8	
Power Loading: (lbs/hp)	15.0	
Fuel Capacity		
Standard:	43	gal
w/long range tanks:	54	gal
w/integral long range tanks:	68	gal
Oil Capacity:	8	qts
Engine:	Lycoming O-320-D2J	
TBO:	2000	hrs
Power: (at 2700 rpm)	160	hp
Propeller: (diameter)	75	in
Wingspan:	35 ft 10	in
Wing Area: (sq ft)	174	
Length:	26 ft 11	in
Height:	8 ft 09	in
Maximum Weight:	2400	lbs
Empty Weight: (Skyhawk)	1430	lbs
(Skyhawk II)	1448	lbs
Useful Load: (Skyhawk)	977	lbs
(Skyhawk II)	959	lbs

1983

Year: 1983

Model: 172 Skyhawk and Skyhawk II

Speed

Top Speed at Sea Level:	123	kts
Cruise, 75 percent power at 8000 ft:	120	kts

Range (with 45 minute reserve)

Cruise, 75 percent power at 8000 ft:	440	nm
40 Gallons Usable Fuel:	3.8	hrs
Cruise, 75 percent at 8000 ft:	585	nm
50 Gallons Usable Fuel:	5.0	hrs
Cruise, 75 percent at 8000 ft:	755	nm
62 Gallons Usable Fuel:	6.4	hrs
Maximum Range at 10,000 ft:	520	nm
40 Gallons Usable Fuel:	5.6	hrs
Maximum Range at 10,000 ft:	680	nm
50 Gallons Usable Fuel:	7.4	hrs
Maximum Range at 10,000 ft:	875	nm
62 Gallons Usable Fuel:	9.4	hrs
Rate of Climb at Sea Level:	700	fpm

Service Ceiling:	13,000	ft
Takeoff		
Ground Run:	890	ft
Over 50-ft Obstacle:	1625	ft
Landing		
Ground Roll:	540	ft
Over 50-ft Obstacle:	1280	ft
Stall Speed		
Flaps Up, Power Off:	51	kts
Flaps Down, Power Off:	46	kts
Baggage:	120	lbs
Wing Loading: (lbs/sq ft)	13.8	
Power Loading: (lbs/hp)	15.0	
Fuel Capacity		
Standard:	43	gal
w/long range tanks:	54	gal
w/integral long range tanks:	68	gal
Oil Capacity:	8	qts
Engine:	Lycoming O-320-D2J	
TBO:	2000	hrs
Power: (at 2700 rpm)	160	hp
Propeller: (diameter)	75	in
Wingspan:	35 ft 10	in
Wing Area: (sq ft)	174	
Length:	26 ft 11	in
Height:	8 ft 09	in
Maximum Weight:	2400	lbs
Empty Weight: (Skyhawk)	1439	lbs
(Skyhawk II)	1466	lbs
Useful Load: (Skyhawk)	968	lbs
(Skyhawk II)	941	lbs

1984

Year: 1984
Model: 172 Skyhawk and Skyhawk II

Speed		
Top Speed at Sea Level:	123	kts
Cruise, 75 percent power:	120	kts
Range 75 percent at 8000 ft		
40 Gallons, 43 min. Reserve:	440	nm
	3.8	hrs
50 Gallons, 45 min. Reserve:	585	nm
	5.0	hrs

62 Gallons, 45 min. Reserve:	775	nm
	6.4	hrs
Maximum Range at 10,000 ft:		
40 Gallons	520	nm
	5.6	hrs
50 Gallons	680	nm
	7.4	hrs
62 Gallons	875	nm
	9.4	hrs
Rate of Climb at Sea Level:	700	fpm
Service Ceiling:	13,000	ft
Takeoff		
Ground Run:	890	ft
Over 50-ft Obstacle:	1625	ft
Landing		
Ground Roll:	540	ft
Over 50-ft Obstacle:	1280	ft
Stall Speed		
Flaps Up, Power Off:	51	kts
Flaps Down, Power Off:	46	kts
Baggage:	120	lbs
Fuel Capacity		
Standard:	43	gal
Long range tanks:	54	gal
Integral long range tanks:	68	gal
Engine:	Lycoming O-320-D2J	
TBO:	2000	hrs
Power: (at 2700 rpm)	160	hp
Propeller:	Fixed Pitch	
Wingspan:	36 ft 01	in
Wing Area: (sq ft)	174	
Length:	26 ft 11	in
Height:	8 ft 09	in
Gross Weight:	2400	lbs
Empty Weight: (Skyhawk)	1438	lbs
(Skyhawk II)	1457	lbs
Useful Load: (Skyhawk)	969	lbs
(Skyhawk II)	950	lbs

1985

Year: 1985
Model: 172 Skyhawk and Skyhawk II

Speed

Top Speed at Sea Level:	123	kts
Cruise, 75 percent power:	120	kts
Range 75 percent at 8000 ft		
40 Gallons, 43 min. Reserve:	440	nm
	3.8	hrs
50 Gallons, 45 min. Reserve:	585	nm
	5.0	hrs
62 Gallons, 45 min. Reserve:	775	nm
	6.4	hrs
Maximum Range at 10,000 ft:		
40 Gallons	520	nm
	5.6	hrs
50 Gallons	680	nm
	7.4	hrs
62 Gallons	875	nm
	9.4	hrs
Rate of Climb at Sea Level:	700	fpm
Service Ceiling:	13,000	ft
Takeoff		
Ground Run:	890	ft
Over 50-ft Obstacle:	1625	ft
Landing		
Ground Roll:	540	ft
Over 50-ft Obstacle:	1280	ft
Stall Speed		
Flaps Up, Power Off:	51	kts
Flaps Down, Power Off:	46	kts
Baggage:	120	lbs
Fuel Capacity		
Standard:	43	gal
Long range tanks:	54	gal
Integral long range tanks:	68	gal
Engine:	Lycoming O-320-D2J	
TBO:	2000	hrs
Power: (at 2700 rpm)	160	hp
Propeller:	Fixed Pitch	
Wingspan:	36 ft 01	in
Wing Area: (sq ft)	•174	
Length:	26 ft 11	in
Height:	8 ft 09	in
Gross Weight:	2407	lbs
Empty Weight: (Skyhawk)	1433	lbs
(Skyhawk II)	1452	lbs
Useful Load: (Skyhawk)	974	lbs
(Skyhawk II)	955	lbs

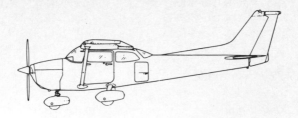

Chapter 3

Cessna 172 Engines

In the basic 172s, there have been only two powerplants installed. These are the Continental O-300 and the Lycoming O-320 engines.

Although only two engines have been used, there have been variations among them. Here is a short list of the original factory-installed engines:

Year	Engine	hp	TBO
1956-59	Cont O-300-A	145	1800
1960	Cont O-300-C	145	1800
1961-67	Cont O-300-D	145	1800
1968-76	Lyco O-320-E2D	150	2000
1977-80	Lyco O-320-H2AD	160	2000
1981-84	Lyco O-320-D2J	160	2000

172 VARIANT ENGINES

Of course, there are other engines found in the 172 variants. These variant airplanes are the Cessna 175, Hawk XP, Cutlass, and Cutlass RG. Following is a list of the factory-installed engines for these models:

Model 175

Year	Engine	hp	TBO
1958-59	Cont GO-300-A	175	1200

Year	Engine	hp	TBO
1960	Cont GO-300-C	175	1200
1961	Cont GO-300-D	175	1200
1962	Cont GO-300-E	175	1200

Model 172 Powermatic

Year	Engine	hp	TBO
1963	Cont GO-300-E	175	1200

Model 172 Hawk XP

Year	Engine	hp	TBO
1977-78	Cont IO-360-K	195	1500
1979-81	Cont IO-360-KB	195	2000

Model 172 Cutlass RG

Year	Engine	hp	TBO
1980-84	Lyco O-360-F1A6	180	2000

Model 172 Cutlass

Year	Engine	hp	TBO
1983-84	Lyco O-360-A4N	180	2000

CONTINENTAL ENGINES

The Continental engines used in the early 172s are long out of production. This does not mean they are not good engines, just that they are no longer made. However, this should be a consideration when making a purchase, as "no longer in production" will mean dwindling parts supplies and higher costs for repairs.

All the Continental engines listed for the 172 series airplanes are of six-cylinder design (Fig. 3-1). In reality, the O-300 engines and the O-200s, as found in the Cessna Model 150, are very close cousins. Many small parts are interchangeable between the O-200-O-300 engines.

The GO-300 engines found on the Model 175s have gear reduc-

Fig. 3-1. The Continental O-300 engine as found in early Cessna 172s. (courtesy Teledyne Continental)

tion units to reduce the rpm of the propeller as compared to the crankshaft. These engines turn at 3200 rpm to develop their rated 175 hp. A propeller of the size used on this plane cannot turn at that speed without the tips going supersonic, hence the gear reduction unit.

The later IO-360 engines found in the Hawk XP are fuel-injected, and are in current production. These are more complex engines than their predecessors, and therefore more expensive to maintain—and, when the time comes, to rebuild.

The O-300 engines all operate on 80/87 octane avgas. The IO-360 requires 100/130 octane.

LYCOMING ENGINES

The three basic engines found in the 172s are all O-320 models. The first is the O-320-E2D, which was first introduced in 1968 and remained through 1976 (Fig. 3-2). This engine is among the most reliable workhorse aircraft powerplants ever produced. It operates on 80/87 avgas.

In 1977, the O-320-H2AD became the standard engine for the 172s. It boasted an extra 10 hp and was designed to utilize 100LL avgas, the latter being considered necessary due to the scarcity of 80-octane fuel. This engine proved to be a complete disaster. Many self-destructed long before the recommended 2000-hour TBO. Catastrophic failure equates to total engine failure, sometimes leaving a trail of oil and parts, and resulting in an unplanned landing.

There have been several ADs (Airworthiness Directives) involving this engine, and many "fixes" to keep these engines running. For more information about the O-320-H2AD engine, see Chapters 4 (ADs and Other Bad News) and 12 (Hangar Flying).

To right the wrong inflicted by the H2AD engine, Cessna introduced the O-320-D2J engine in 1981. It, too, uses 100LL fuel and produces 160 hp.

ENGINE SPECIFICATIONS
Continental O-300

Horsepower:	145 at 2700 rpm
Number of Cylinders:	6 Horizontally Opposed
Displacement:	301.37 cu. in.
Bore:	4.0625 in.
Stroke:	3.875in.

Fig. 3-2. The Lycoming O-320 engine as found in the later Cessna 172s. (courtesy AVCO Lycoming)

Compression Ratio: 7.0:1

Magnetos:	Slick 664
Right:	Fires 26 degrees BTC upper
Left:	Fires 28 degrees BTC lower
Firing Order:	1-6-3-2-5-4
Spark Plugs:	SH20A
Gap:	.018 to .022 in.
Torque:	330 lbs-in.
Carburetor:	Marvel-Schebler MA-3-SPA
Alternator:	14 volts at 60 amps
Starter:	Automatic engagement
Tachometer:	Mechanical
Oil Capacity:	8 qts.
Oil Pressure	
Minimum at idle:	5 psi.
Normal:	30-60 psi.
Maximum (start-up):	100 psi.
Propeller Rotation:	Clockwise (viewed from rear)
Dry Weight:	298 lbs.

Lycoming O-320

Horsepower:

(E2D)	150 at	2700 rpm
(H2AD)	160 at	2700 rpm
(D2J)	160 at	2700 rpm

Number of Cylinders: 4 Horizontally Opposed

Displacement:	319.8 cu. in.
Bore:	5.125 in.
Stroke:	3.875 in.

Compression Ratio

(E2D)	7.0:1
(H2AD)	9.0:1
(D2J)	8.5:1

Magnetos:	Slick 4051 (left) 4050 (right)
Right:	Fires 25 degrees BTC 1-3 upper and 2-4 lower.
Left:	Fires 25 degrees BTC 2-4 upper and 1-3 lower.

(H2AD has D2RN-2021 impulse coupling dual magneto)
(D2J has two Slick magnetos)

Firing Order:	1-3-2-4
Spark Plugs	SH15
Gap:	.015 to .018 in.
Torque:	390 lbs-in.
Carburetor:	Marvel-Schebler MA-4SPA
Alternator:14 volts at	60 amps
	(28volts after 1977)
Starter:	Automatic engagement
Tachometer:	Mechanical
Oil Capacity:	8 qts.

Oil Pressure
Minimum at idle:	25 psi.
Normal:	60-90 psi.
Maximum (start-up):	100 psi.

Propeller Rotation:	Clockwise (viewed from rear)
Dry Weight:	269 lbs.

ENGINE BUZZWORDS

The more you know about engines, the better. Here are a few definitions to help you understand them better:

TBO (Time Between Overhaul): The manufacturer's recommended maximum engine life. It has no legal bearing on airplanes not used in commercial service; it's only an indicator. Many well-cared-for engines last hundreds of hours beyond TBO—but not all.

Remanufacture: The disassembly, repair, alteration, and inspection of an engine. This includes bringing all specifications back to factory new limits. A factory remanufactured engine comes with new logs and zero time.

New limits: The dimensions/specifications used when constructing a new engine. These parts will normally reach TBO with no further attention, save for routine maintenance.

Overhaul: The disassembly, inspection, cleaning, repair, and reassembly of the engine. The work may be done to new limits or to service limits.

Service limits: The dimensions/specifications below which use is forbidden. Many used parts will fit into this category; however, they are unlikely to last the full TBO as they are already partially worn.

Top overhaul: The rebuilding of the head assemblies, but not of the entire engine. In other words, the case of the engine is not split, only the cylinders are pulled. Top overhaul is utilized to bring oil burning and/or low compression engines within specifications. It is a method of stretching the life of an otherwise sound engine. The parts normally repaired/replaced include valves, valve guides, valve springs, lifters, pistons, rings, heads, or complete cyclinders (jugs). A top overhaul is not necessarily an indicator of a poor engine. Its need may have been brought on by such things as pilot abuse, lack of care, lack of use of the engine, or plain abuse (i.e., hard climbs and fast let-downs). An interesting note: The term top overhaul does not indicate the extent of the rebuild job (i.e., number of cylinders rebuilt or the completeness of the job).

Nitriding: A method of hardening cylinder barrels and crankshafts. The purpose is to reduce wear, thereby extending the useful life of the part.

Chrome plating: Used to bring the internal dimensions of the cylinders back to specifications. It produces a hard, machinable, and long-lasting surface. There is one major drawback of chrome plating: longer break-in times. However, an advantage of chrome plating is its resistance to destructive oxidation (rust) within combustion chambers.

Magnaflux/Magnaglow: Terms associated with methods of detecting invisible defects in ferrous metals (i.e., cracks). Parts normally Magnafluxed/Magnaglowed are crankshafts, camshafts, piston pins, rocker arms, etc.

CYLINDER COLOR CODES

Often, when looking at the engine of an airplane, you will notice that the cylinders are marked with paint or banded. The color of the paint or band tells you about the physical properties of the cylinder.

Orange indicates a chrome-plated cylinder barrel.
Blue indicates a nitrided cylinder barrel.
Green means that the cylinder barrel is .010 oversize.
Yellow is used for .020 oversize.

USED ENGINES

Unless you're purchasing an airplane with a brand-new engine on it, you'll need to concern yourself with still more engine facts.

Many airplane ads proudly state the hours on the engine, i.e., 876 SMOH. Basically, this means that there have been 876 hours of use since the engine was overhauled. Not stated is *how* it was used or how *completely* it was overhauled. There are few standards.

TIME vs VALUE

The time (hours) since new or overhaul is an important factor when placing a value on an airplane. The recommended TBO, less the hours currently on the engine, is the time remaining. This is the span you will have to live in.

Three basic terms are usually used when referring to time on an airplane engine:

☐ **Low time**—First 1/3 of TBO.
☐ **Mid time**—Second 1/3 of TBO.
☐ **High time**—Last 1/3 of TBO.

Naturally, other variables come into play when referring to TBO: Are the hours on the engine since new, remanufacture, or overhaul? What type of flying has the engine seen? Was it flown on a regular basis? Lastly, what kind of maintenance did the engine get? The logbook should be of some help in determining any questions about maintenance.

Airplanes that have not been flown on a regular basis—and maintained in a like fashion—will never reach full TBO. Manufacturers refer to regular usage as 20 to 40 hours monthly. However, there are few privately owned airplanes meeting the upper limits of this requirement. Let's face it, most of us don't have the time or money required for such constant use. This 20-to-40 hours monthly equates to 240 to 480 hours yearly. That's a lot of flying.

When an engine isn't run, acids and moisture in the oil will oxidize (rust) engine components. In addition, the lack of lubrication movement will cause the seals to dry out. Left long enough, the engine will seize and no longer be operable.

Just as hard on engines as no use is abuse. Hard climbing and fast descents, causing abnormal heating and cooling conditions, are extremely destructive to air-cooled engines. Training aircraft often exhibit this trait due to their type of usage (i.e., takeoff and landing practice).

Naturally, preventive maintenance should have been accomplished and logged throughout the engine's life (i.e., oil changes, plug changes, etc.). All maintenance must be logged, so say the FARs (Federal Aviation Regulations).

Beware of the engine that has just a few hours on it since an overhaul. Perhaps something is not right with the overhaul, or it was a very cheap job, just to make the plane more salable.

When it comes to overhauls, I recommend the large shops that specialize in aircraft engine rebuilding. I'm not saying that the local FBO can't do a good job; I just feel that the large organizations specializing in this work have more experience and equipment to work with. In addition, they have reputations to live up to, and most will back you in the event of difficulties.

Engines are expensive to rebuild/overhaul. Here are some typical costs for a complete overhaul (based on current average rebuilders pricing):

Engine	Cost
O-300	$6175
GO-300	6925
O-320-E2D	5100
O-320-H2AD	5875
O-320-D2J	5100
O-360	5775
IO-360	7075

These prices include installation.

AVIATION FUELS

The following information is reprinted by permission of AVCO Lycoming, as found in their "Key Reprints" (Key Reprints are available by writing to AVCO Lycoming):

We have received many inquiries from the field expressing concern over the limited availability of 80/87 grade fuel, and the associated questions about the use of higher leaded fuel in engines rated for grade 80/87 fuel. The leading fuel suppliers indicate that in some areas 80/87 grade aviation fuel is not available. It is further indicated that the trend is toward phase-out of 80/87 aviation grade fuel. The low lead 100

LL avgas, blue color, which is limited to 2ml tetraethyl lead per gallon, will gradually become the only fuel available for piston engines. Whenever 80/87 is not available, you should use the lowest lead 100 grade fuel available. Automotive fuels should never be used as a substitute for aviation fuel in aircraft engines.

The continuous use, more than 25 percent of the operating time, with the higher leaded fuels in engines certified for 80 octane fuel can result in increased engine deposits both in the combustion chamber and in the engine oil. It may require increased spark plug maintenance and more frequent oil changes. The frequency of spark plug maintenance and oil drain periods will be governed by the amount of lead per gallon and the type of operation. Operation at full rich mixture requires more frequent maintenance periods; therefore it is important to use properly approved mixture leaning procedures.

To reduce or keep engine deposits at a minimum when using the higher leaded fuels, 100 LL avgas blue or 100 green, it is essential that the following four conditions of operation and maintenance are applied:

A. Fuel management required in all modes of flight operation. (See A, General Rules.)

B. Prior to engine shutdown, run up to 1200 rpm for one minute to clean out any unburned fuel after taxiing in. (See B, Engine Shutdown.)

C. Replace lubricating oil and filters each 50 hours of operation, under normal environmental conditions. (See C, Lubrication Recommendations.)

D. Proper selection of spark plug types and good maintenance are necessary. (See D, Spark Plugs.)

The use of economy cruise engine leaning whenever possible will keep deposits to a minimum. Pertinent portions of the manual leaning procedures as recommended in AVCO Lycoming Service Instruction No. 1094 are reprinted here for reference.

A. General Rules

1. Never lean the mixture from full rich during takeoff, climb, or high-performance cruise operation unless the airplane owner's manual advises otherwise. However, during takeoff from high elevation airports or during climb at

higher altitudes, roughness or reduction of power may occur at full rich mixtures. In such a case the mixture may be adjusted only enough to obtain smooth engine operation. Careful observation of temperature instruments should be practiced.

2. Operate the engine at maximum power mixture for performance cruise powers and at best economy mixture for economy cruise power, unless otherwise specified in the airplane owner's manual.

3. Always return the mixture to full rich before increasing power settings.

4. During let-down and reduced power flight operations it may be necessary to manually lean or leave the mixture setting at cruise position prior to landing. During the landing sequence, the mixture control should then be placed in the full rich position, unless landing at high elevation fields where leaning may be necessary.

5. Methods for manually setting maximum power or best economy mixture.

a. Engine Tachometer—Airspeed Indicator Method: The tachometer and/or the airspeed indicator may be used to locate, approximately, maximum power and best economy mixture ranges. When a fixed-pitch propeller is used, either or both instruments are useful indicators. If the airplane uses a constant-speed propeller, the airspeed indicator is useful. Regardless of the propeller type, set the controls for the desired cruise power as shown in the owner's manual. Gradually lean the mixture from full rich until either the tachometer or the airspeed indicator are reading peaks. At peak indication, the engine is operating in the maximum power range.

b. For Cruise Power: Where best economy operation is allowed by the manufacturer, the mixture is first leaned from full rich to maximum power, then leaning slowly continued until engine operation becomes rough or until engine power is rapidly diminishing as noted by an undesirable decrease in airspeed. When either condition occurs, enrich the mixture sufficiently to obtain an evenly firing engine or the regain of most of the lost airspeed or engine rpm. Some slight engine power and airspeed must be sacrificed to gain best economy mixture setting.

c. Exhaust Gas Temperature Method (EGT): Refer to Service Instruction No. 1094 for procedure.

Recommended fuel management—Manual leaning will not only result in less engine deposits and reduced maintenance cost, but will provide more economical operation and fuel saving.

B. Engine Shutdown

The deposit formation rate can be greatly retarded by controlling ground operation to minimize separation of the non-volatile components of the higher leaded aviation fuels. This rate can be accelerated by (1) Low mixture temperatures and (2) Excessively rich fuel/air mixtures associated with the idling and taxiing operations. Therefore, it is important that engine idling speeds should be set at their proper 600 to 650 rpm range with the idle mixture adjusted properly to provide smooth idling operation. Shutdown procedure recommends setting rpm at 1200 for one minute prior to shutdown.

C. Lubrication Recommendations

Many of the engine deposits formed by the use of the higher leaded fuel are in suspension within the engine oil and are not removed by a full flow filter. When sufficient amounts of these contaminants in the oil reach a high temperature area of the engine they can be baked out, resulting in possible malfunctions such as in exhaust valve guides, causing sticking valves. When using the higher leaded fuels, the recommended oil drain period of 50 hours should not be extended, and if occurrences of valve sticking is noted, all guides should be reamed and a reduction in the oil drain periods and oil filter replacement used.

D. Spark Plugs

Spark plugs should be rotated from the top to bottom on a 50-hour basis, and should be serviced on a 100-hour basis. If excessive spark plug lead fouling occurs, the selection of a hotter plug may be necessary. However, depending on the type of lead deposit formed, a colder plug may better resolve the problem. Depending on the lead content of the fuel and the type of operation, more frequent cleaning of the spark plugs may be necessary. Where the majority of operation is at low power, such as patrol, a hotter plug would be advantageous. If the majority of operation is at high cruise power, a colder plug is recommended.

Color Coding of Avgas

Red: 80 Octane containing .50ml lead/gal.
Blue: 100 Octane containing 2ml lead/gal.
Green: 100 Octane containing 3ml lead/gal.

A Word from the FAA

In April 1977, the use of Tricresyl Phosphate (TCP) was approved for use in Lycoming and Continental engines that do not incorporate turbosuperchargers. TCP is a fuel additive that is available from:

Alcor, Inc.
10130 Jones-Maltsberger Rd.
Box 32516
San Antonio, TX 73284
and from most FBOs.

AUTO FUELS

Recently, there has been considerable controversy and discussion about the use of "auto" fuels (sometimes referred to as *mogas*) in certified aircraft engines. There are pros and cons for both sides; however, I feel that it is up to the individual pilot to make his own choice about the use of non-aviation fuels in his airplane. Consider the following:

One will always hear about economy. Unleaded auto fuel is certainly less expensive than 100LL.

Auto fuel does appear to operate well in the older engines that require 80 octane fuel.

If you have a private gas tank/pump, it might be advantageous to utilize auto fuel. It'll be far easier to locate a jobber willing to keep an auto fuel tank filled than it will be to find an avgas supplier willing to make small deliveries. This is particularly true at private/ranch airstrips.

There may be a lack of consistency among the various gasolines and their additives. In particular, many low-lead auto fuels have alcohol in them. Alcohol is destructive to some parts of the typical aircraft fuel system.

The engine manufacturers claim the use of auto fuel will void warranty service.

Many FBOs are reluctant to make auto fuels available for reasons such as product liability and less profit.

However, just to fuel the fire even further, here is a partial reprint of Advisory Circulry #AC 150/5190-"A, dated 4 Apr 72:

d. Restrictions on self-service.

Any unreasonable restriction imposed on the owners and operators of aircraft regarding the servicing of their own aircraft and equipment may be considered as a violation of agency policy. The owner of an aircraft should be permitted to fuel, wash, repair, paint, and otherwise take care of his own aircraft, provided there is no attempt to perform such services for others. Restrictions which have the effect of diverting activity of this type to a commercial enterprise amount to an exclusive right contrary to law.

If you desire further information about the legal use of auto fuels in your airplane, contact the EAA (Experimental Aircraft Association), which has an ongoing program of testing airplanes and obtaining STCs (Supplemental Type Certificates) for the use of auto fuel.

EAA—STC
Wittman Airfield
Oshkosh, WI 54903

These STCs are available from the EAA for a minimal fee, based upon engine horsepower. The EAA is constantly expanding the list of airplanes and engines for which auto fuel are available.

Here is a list indicating the Cessna models with STCs available:

Model	Engine
172	Continental O-300
	Lycoming O-320-E2D
	Continental GO-300-D
175	Continental GO-300 all

The STCs are for the use of unleaded regular automobile gasoline manufactured to the ASTM Specification D-439 (American Society for Testing Materials, 1916 Race St., Phila, PA 19103). Here is a list of states requiring compliance with this standard for automobile gasolines:

Arizona	Maryland
Arkansas	Montana
Alabama	Nebraska
California	Nevada
Colorado	New Mexico
Connecticut	New York
Florida	N. Carolina
Georgia	S. Carolina
Hawaii	N. Dakota
Idaho	S. Dakota
Iowa	Oklahoma
Indiana	Rhode Island
Kansas	Texas
Louisiana	Tennessee
Maine	Utah
Massachusetts	Virginia
Minnesota	Wisconsin
Mississippi	Wyoming

Auto fuel STCs are also available from:

Petersen Aviation, Inc.
Rt 1 Box 18
Minden, NE 68959
Phone: (308) 832-2200

The Petersen STCs, unlike those from the EAA, allow the use of leaded auto fuels, the latter being considerably cheaper than the no-lead fuels required by the EAA STC.

WARNING

A note of advice: Prior to purchasing the auto fuel STC from the EAA, check with your insurance carrier and get their approval . . . *in writing. Never* use fuel containing alcohol!

ENGINE MONITORING

There are various gauges and instruments available for monitoring what is going on inside the engine.

The tachometer, oil temperature, and oil pressure gauges are all familiar and found on the typical instrument panel. However, there are others that will aid you in closely monitoring your engine:

Exhaust Gas Temperature—the EGT gauge measures the temperature of the exhaust gases as they enter the exhaust manifold. This instrument is extremely valuable for monitoring leaning procedures.

Cylinder Head Temperature—the CHT gauge indicates the temperature of the cylinder heads. Problems such as lack of adequate cooling can be detected by its use.

Carburetor Ice Detector—the Carburetor Ice Detector is designed to actually detect ice, not just low temperature. As ice is a product of both temperature and humidity, mere temperature indication is not satisfactory. The detector utilizes an optical probe in the carburetor throat and is so sensitive that it can detect "frost" up to five minutes before ice begins to form, giving the pilot plenty of time to take corrective action (Fig. 3-3)

All of these gauges are panel-mounted for easy monitoring of engine operating conditions.

EXTENDED WARRANTY

A recent entry into the aviation field is a commercially available extended warranty plan for engines, new, used, or overhauled.

The theory is not new, as automobile dealers have been selling similar coverage for many years. Only recently has this repair insurance been made available to airplane owners.

The warranty—actually called a *service agreement*—covers the major parts of the aircraft engine and protects you from spending large sums of money in repairs. Compared to repair costs, the fee paid for this service agreement is nominal.

The following parts are covered by the service agreement:

☐ Pistons
☐ Piston Rings

□ Connecting Rods
□ Rod Bolts
□ Rod Bearings
□ Crankshaft
□ Bearings
□ Camshaft
□ Timing Gear
□ Valves
□ Valve Guides
□ Valve Springs
□ Valve Spring Keepers
□ Valve Spring Retainers

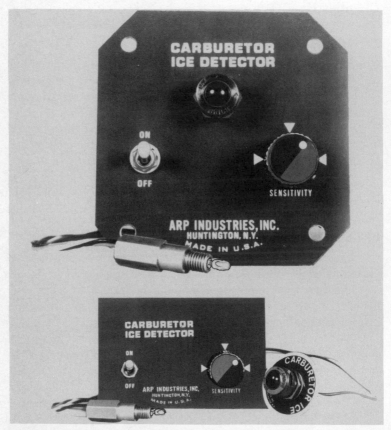

Fig. 3-3. If allowed only one optional engine monitoring device, this would be the author's choice. (courtesy ARP Industries, Inc., 36 Bay Drive East, Huntington, NY 11743)

- [ ] Rocker Arms
- [ ] Rocker Arm Shafts
- [ ] Push Rods
- [ ] Lifters
- [ ] Oil Pump
- [ ] Counter Weight Assemblies
- [ ] Gear Case

The engine case and cylinders are also covered if the mechanical failure was caused by any of the above listed internal engine parts.

For further information, contact:

First Continental Engine Warranty, Inc.
P.O. Box 16098
Jackson, MS 39236
Phone: (800) 233-1099
MS: (601) 352-4207

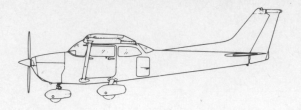

Chapter 4

ADs and Other Bad News

Unfortunately, airplanes are not perfect in design or manufacture; they will, from time to time, require inspection/repairs/service as a result of unforeseen problems. These problems generally affect a large group/number of a particular make/model.

The required procedures are set forth in ADs (Airworthiness Directives). ADs are described in FAR Part 39, and must be complied with. The AD may be a simple one-time inspection, a periodic inspection (i.e., every 50 hours of operation), or a major modification to the airframe/engine.

Some ADs are relatively inexpensive to comply with, as they are basically inspections; others can be very expensive, involving extensive engine or airframe modifications/repairs. ADs are not normally handled like automobile "recalls" with the manufacturer being responsible for the costs involved. Sometimes the manufacturers will offer the parts/labor free of charge, but don't count on it. Even though ADs correct deficient design or poor quality control of parts or workmanship, AD compliance is usually paid for by the owner! There is no large consumer voice involving aircraft manufacturer responsibility.

Notice of an AD will be placed in the Federal Register and sent by mail to registered owners of the aircraft concerned. In an emergency, the information will be sent by telegram to registered owners. Either way, its purpose is to assure the integrity of your flying machine, and your safety.

The records of AD compliance become a part of the aircraft's logbooks. When looking at an airplane with purchase in mind, check for AD compliance.

AD LIST

Basically, the 172 airplanes are relatively AD-free; however, there are some. The following AD list should not be considered the last word; it is only an abbreviated guide to assist the owner/would-be owner/pilot in checking for AD compliance. Not all ADs listed affect all 172 airplanes.

For a complete check of ADs on an airplane, see your mechanic, or contact the AOPA (Aircraft Owners and Pilots Association). The latter will provide a list of ADs for a particular aircraft (by serial number) for a small fee. This type of search is highly accurate, and well worth the money spent.

Model 172

58-8-2: Inspect the exhaust heater on all 172s from SN 36216 and up (1958 only) to prevent carbon monoxide from entering the cabin.

59-10-3: Replace/relocate the flasher switch from SN 28000 through 36003.

68-17-4: Test/rework the stall warning system on all models.

68-19-5: Aircraft is removed from the utility category—those 172s with the Franklin GA-335B engine only.

70-10-6: Replace the solid metal oil pressure line with a flexible hose assembly on 172I and K models.

71-18-1: Provide correct fuel tank capacity information on 172s SN 17248735 through 17256512.

71-22-2: Inspect/replace the nose gear fork after 1000 hours of operation.

72-3-3: Inspect the flap actuator jack screw each 100 hours of operation.

72-7-2: Install a new fuel selector valve, SN 28000 through 17258855.

73-17-1: Placard the auxiliary fuel pump if so equipped.

73-23-7: Replace the wing attachment fittings, SN 17261664 through 172261808.

73-23-01: Replace piston pins, Lycoming O-320 engines.

74-4-1: Inspect the aft bulkhead for cracks, SN17260759 through 17261495.

74-6-2: Inspect/replace muffler if Avcon STCed.

74-8-1: Inspect the autopilot actuators on all 300/400/800 series units.

74-26-9: Inspect Bendix magnetos for solid steel drive shaft bushing and replace as necessary.

75-8-9: Replace the oil pump shaft and impeller on Lycoming O-320 engines.

76-4-3: Modify the ARC PA-500A actuator gear train on all 300/400/800 series autopilots.

76-21-6: Replace the engine oil cooler on certain early models to prevent oil loss, 172M and N.

77-2-9: Replace the flap actuator ball nut assembly on some models, SN17267789 through 17268239.

77-7-7: Modify the oil dipstick tube to allow accurate monitoring of oil levels on O-320-H2AD Lycoming engines.

77-12-8: Test/modify the ground power and electrical system to prevent undesired turning of the propeller.

77-16-1: Check certain McCauley props (see AD for propeller serial numbers).

77-20-7: Replace the valve tappets and rocker arm studs on O-320-H2AD Lycoming engine.

78-12-8: Replace the oil pump gear on O-320-H2AD Lycoming engine.

78-12-9: Replace the crankshaft on O-320-H2AD Lycoming engine.

79-8-3: Remove/modify the cigarette lighter wiring to prevent possible fire, SN 28000 through 29999, 46001 through 47746: 17247747 through 17250572, and 17259224 through 17267584.

79-10-3: Check the engine mounting bolts on 172N models.

79-10-14: Install a vented fuel cap and placard same.

79-13-8: Replace the Airborne dry airpump, if installed after 5-15-79.

79-18-5: Replace LiS02 ELT batteries.

79-18-6: Inspect/modify Bendix magnetos as required per their service bulletin.

80-4-3: Replace the exhaust valve spring seats and hydraulic lifters on O-320-H2AD Lycoming engines to prevent bent push rods.

80-4-8: Install a cover over the map light switch to prevent possible chafing against the fuel lines and a possible fire.

80-6-3: Install a new flap cable clamp 172N models.

80-6-4: Test Slick magneto couplings on all engines.

80-14-7: Inspect the exhaust valve springs and seats on O-320-H2AD Lycoming engines and replace as needed.

80-17-14: Comply with Bendix magneto service bulletins.

80-25-7: Inspect the Stewart Warner oil cooler; replace as listed in AD.

81-5-1: Inspect the fuel quantity gauges and markings for accuracy.

81-15-3: Replace the Brackett engine air filter on all 172s through M model.

81-16-5: Inspect/replace the Slick magneto coil for cracks.

81-16-9: Rework the elevator control system on 172 N models SN 71035 through 74523.

81-18-4: Replace the oil pump impeller and shaft on Lycoming O-320 engines.

82-7-2: Inspect the crankcase breather and seal on 172 through 172 P models.

82-11-5: Comply with Bendix Service Bulletin 617 on magnetos.

82-13-1: Periodic inspection/replace of the gripper bushing block and check pistons/valves on engines with S-1200 series Bendix magnetos.

82-20-1: Inspect the Bendix impulse couplers prior to 300 hours usage on the magnetos.

83-10-3: Modify the control wheel, SN 66940 172 M through 172 P models.

83-17-83: Rebalance the ailerons on some Robertson STOL conversions.

83-22-6: Inspection of the aileron hinges.

84-26-2: Replace the paper air filter elements each 500 hours.

Cutlass RG

80-1-6: Modify the flap actuator assembly.

80-6-4: Test the Slick magneto coupling on all engines.

80-19-8: Rework the fuel mixture control assembly on SN 001 through 573.

80-25-7: Inspect the oil cooler and replace as listed in the AD.

81-5-1: Inspect the fuel quantity gauges and markings for accuracy.

81-5-5: Modify the muffler heater shroud, SN 001 through 789.

81-14-6: Replace the rudder trim to nose gear bungee, SN 001 through 769.

81-16-5: Inspect/replace the Slick magneto coil for cracks.

81-16-9: Rework the elevator control system on 172RG models,

SN 1 through 789.

81-18-4: Replace the oil pump impeller and shaft on Lycoming O-360 engines.

82-20-1: Inspect the Bendix impulse couplers prior to 300 hours usage on the magnetos.

82-27-2: Dye check the propeller blade shank on certain McCauley propellers.

83-14-4: Modify the cabin heater shroud.

83-22-6: Inspection of the aileron hinges.

84-26-2: Replace the paper air filter elements each 500 hours.

Hawk XP

79-13-8: Replace the Airborne dry airpump if installed after 5-15-79.

79-18-5: Replace LiS02 ELT batteries.

80-6-3: Install a new flap cable clamp.

80-6-4: Test Slick the magneto coupling on all engines.

81-5-1: Inspect the fuel quantity gauges and markings for accuracy.

81-13-10: Rework the oil pump drive on certain IO-360 engines.

81-16-5: Inspect/replace the Slick magneto coil for cracks.

81-16-9: Rework the elevator control system on R172 K models, SN R1722930 through R1723425.

82-27-2: Dye check the propeller blade shank on certain McCauley propellers.

83-10-3: Modify the control wheel, R172 K models.

83-22-6: Inspection of the aileron hinges.

84-26-2: Replace the paper air filter elements each 500 hours.

Model 175

62-22-1: Reinstall the vacuum pump on Continental O-300 A engines.

63-22-3: Rework the carburetor on all models.

71-22-2: Inspect/replace the nose gear fork after 1000 hours of operation.

73-17-1: Placard the auxiliary fuel pump if so equipped.

74-26-9: Inspect Bendix magneto for solid steel drive shank bushing. Replace as necessary.

77-16-1: Check certain McCauley props (see AD for propeller serial numbers).

79-8-3: Remove/modify the cigarette lighter wiring.

79-10-14: Install a vented fuel cap and placard same.

79-18-5: Replace LiS02 ELT batteries.

82-7-2: Inspect the crankcase breather and seal on 175 models.

82-20-1: Inspect the Bendix impulse couplers prior to 300 hours usage on the magnetos.

83-22-6: Inspection of the aileron hinges.

DANGEROUS SEATS

"WARNING," says the 1968 Cessna service manual for 172 series airplanes, "It is extremely important that the pilot's seat stops are installed, since acceleration and deceleration could possibly permit the seat to become disengaged from the seat rails and create a hazardous situation, especially during takeoff and landing."

This is *very* serious. How would you feel if you had just started your climbout and suddenly were pitched over backwards, seat and all? From this new position it would be impossible to regain control of the aircraft.

For several years, letters to editors and articles have been appearing in the various general aviation magazines pointing out the seat problem found in the Cessna single-engine airplanes. Basically, the pilot's seat is mounted to two aluminum tracks (rails), sliding back and forth for adjustment. A pin holds the seat position on the track. The following is quoted from *Airworthiness Alerts*, a monthly publication of the FAA Aviation Standards National Field Office, Oklahoma City, OK:

Cessna Single Engine Models

Numerous reports indicate that difficulties continue to be encountered with seat attachments, structures, locking mechanisms, tracks, and stops. When required inspections are made, it is suggested the following items be examined:

1. Check the seat assembly for structural integrity.

2. Inspect the roller brackets for separation and wear.

3. Examine the locking mechanism (actuating arm, linkage, locking pin) for wear and evidence of impending failure.

4. Inspect the floor-mounted seat rails for condition and security, locking pin holes for wear, and rail stops for security.

5. Determine that the floor structure in the vicinity of the rails is not cracked or distorted.

Defective or worn parts are a potential hazard which should be given prompt attention. Accomplish repair and/or replacement of damaged components in accordance with the manufacturer's service publications.

NOTE: This article was previously published in Alerts No. 32, dated March 1981. The same type problems are still being reported.

The NTSB (National Transportation Safety Board) has identified these problems as the probable cause in several fatal accidents.

I *strongly* recommend that you keep this seat problem in mind at preflight time, and *always* check the seat after locking it in place.

H2AD ENGINE

In 1977, Cessna introduced the AVCO Lycoming O-320-H2AD engine. It made for an increase in horsepower from 150 to 160, and was designed to utilize 100 LL avgas. The latter was, at that time, about the only available fuel for piston-powered airplanes. The engine was built at Cessna's request for use in the Model 172s.

The H2AD was less complicated internally than its predecessors. It was designed to require only a minimum amount of machining after casting. The H2AD engine was supposed to be cheaper to build than other aircraft engines. The H proved to be anything *but* economical!

During the time from 1977 until 1981, when the "H" engine was replaced with the D2J engine, Cessna 172 owners were plagued with expensive problems from their engines. Interestingly, other builders of similar-sized aircraft never were affected by H2AD problems, as this engine was never mounted on any production aircraft other than the Cessna 172.

The major problem with the engine was the disintegration (spalling) of the valve tappet and cam surfaces where they make required mechanical contact. The small metal particles then were scattered in the engine lubrication system, causing a ruined engine very quickly.

Lycoming first made a design change in the tappets, camshaft, and rocker arm studs. It did not help. "H" engines were still dropping dead.

In 1978, Cessna introduced the "Blue Streak" program. It was to completely answer all the past problems of the H2AD engine. It didn't work, and the engines kept on breaking apart. Even mandatory oil additives were tried, along with special operating procedures. The spalling continued in the H2AD engines.

122

It's interesting to note that Cessna has attempted to alleviate the problem through various changes and modifications. They even offered a 2000-hour engine warranty, on a prorated basis, to no avail. The engine could neither be fixed nor scared into working for an extended period of time.

The latest (and perhaps final) fix for the H2AD was made from serial number 7976 and up. This involved using a heavier crankcase, redesigned to allow the use of a larger hydraulic tappet.

The end result of all the problems with the H2AD engine was a lot of lost flying time, loads of owner money spent on repairs, and plenty of frustration for all parties concerned.

The Aviation Consumer, printed voice or perhaps the only consumer group in the aviation field, reported in November 1983 that a California court had ordered Cessna to pay damages of $25,000 to a hapless purchaser of a 172 with an "H" engine.

This particular owner's successful suit was based upon a fraud statute: fraud by misrepresentation. The plaintiff felt the aircraft was misrepresented to him due to the many problems he encountered with the O-320-H2AD engine. It was misrepresented in that the plane was not safe, reliable, or of use as advertised. The court agreed.

I have noticed lately that some of the leading engine rebuilders charge different prices for work on the O-320-H2AD than for the earlier E model, or the later D version. The H2AD prices are always higher.

On the brighter side, some 172 owners like their planes so much that they have replaced the H engine with an STCed 180-hp engine. For further information on STCs, see Chapter 10, Modifications and STCs for the 172.

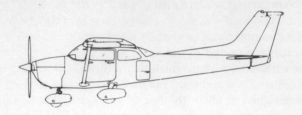

Chapter 5
Selecting a Used 172

The search for a good used Cessna 172 does not usually have to
be wide and exhaustive, because so many have been built. This
is good for the buyer, as it assures an adequate selection from which
to choose.

THE SEARCH

As there are many models and price ranges available, the purchaser is encouraged to set a range of his expectations. This could
be based upon features desired, options available, or—most likely—
the cash available for such a purchase.

Usually, one starts looking at his home field. If you know the
FBO, and feel comfortable with him, then perhaps this is a good
way to do your searching. Tell him what you are looking for. Often an FBO will know of airplanes for sale—or *nearly* for sale, ones
that have yet to be advertised. After all, he is an insider to the
business.

If there is nothing of interest at your field, then broaden the
search. Check the bulletin boards at the local airport(s). Ask around
while you're there, then walk around and look for airplanes with
"For Sale" signs in the windows. You could even put an "Airplane
Wanted" ad on the bulletin boards.

The local newspaper will sometimes have airplanes listed in
the classified ads. However, in this day of specialization, several

publications have become leaders in airplane advertising. Among them are:

Trade-A-Plane
Crossville
Tenn 38555

Air Show Journal
45 West Broadway
Suite 205
Eugene, OR 97401
Phone: (800)-247-9005
or: (503)-344-7813

Aircraft Owners MLS, Inc.
200 N. Adrews Ave.
Fort Lauderdale, FL 33301
        or
1430 Arroyo Way
Walnut Creek, CA 94596
Phone: (800) 327-9630
FL: (305) 402-2524

Other listings of used airplanes can be found in the various flight-oriented magazines *AOPA Pilot, FLYING, Plane & Pilot, Private Pilot*, etc.

Most ads of airplanes for sale that you will see make use of various more or less standard, abbreviations. These abbreviations describe the individual airplane, and tell how it is equipped. Also in the ads will be a telephone number, but seldom a location of where the airplane is located. The clue here is the area code.

Here's a sample ad:

62 C172,3103TT,435 SMOH,May ANN,FGP,
Dual NAV/COM,GS,MB,ELT,NDH. $8750 firm.
800-555-1234

Translated, this ad reads: For sale, a 1962 Cessna 172 airplane with 3103 total hours on the airframe and an engine with 435 hours since a major overhaul. The next annual inspection is due in May.

It is equipped with a full gyro instrument panel, has two navigation and communication radios, a glideslope receiver and indicator, a marker beacon receiver, an Emergency Locator Transmitter, and, best of all, the airplane has no damage history. The price is $8750, and the seller claims he will not bargain. (Most do, however.) Lastly is the telephone number.

As you can see, there sure was a lot of information inside those three little lines.

To assist you in reading these ads, see Appendix A for a complete listing of the popular advertising abbreviations, and Appendix B for a listing of Area Codes and their locations.

THE PRE-PURCHASE INSPECTION

The object of the pre-purchase inspection of a used airplane is to preclude the purchase of a "dog." No one wants to buy someone else's troubles. The pre-purchase inspection must be completed in an orderly, well-planned manner. Take your time during this inspection; a few minutes could well save you thousands of dollars later.

The very first item of inspection is the most-asked question of anyone selling anything: "Why are you selling it?" Of course, if the seller has something to hide, you can't believe his answer. Fortunately, most people will answer honestly. Often the owner is moving up to a larger airplane, and if so he will start to tell you all about his new prospective purchase. Let him talk; you can learn a lot about the owner by listening to him. You can gain insight into his flying habits and how he treated the plane you are considering purchasing. Perhaps he has other commitments (i.e., spouse says sell, or perhaps he can no longer afford the plane). These can be to your advantage, as he is probably anxious to sell. However, there is a warning here also: If the seller is having financial difficulties, consider the quality of maintenance that was performed on the airplane.

Ask the seller if he knows of any problems or defects with the airplane. Again, he will probably be honest; however, there could be things he doesn't know about.

Remember: *Buyer beware;* it is *your* money and *your* safety.

DEFINITIONS

Airworthy: The airplane must conform to the original type certificate, or those STCs (Supplemental Type Certificates) issued for this particular airplane (by serial number). In addition, the airplane must be in safe operating condition relative to wear and deterioration.

Annual Inspection: All small airplanes must be inspected annually by an FAA-certified Airframe and Powerplant mechanic who holds an IA (Inspection Authorization), by an FAA certified repair station, or by the airplane's manufacturer. This is a complete inspection of the airframe, powerplant, and all subassemblies.

100-Hour Inspection: Is of the same scope as the annual, and is required on all commercially operated small airplanes (i.e., rental, training, etc.), and must be accomplished after every 100 hours of operation. This inspection may be performed by an FAA-certified Airframe and Powerplant mechanic without an IA rating. An annual inspection will fulfill the 100-hour requirement, but the reverse is not true.

Preflight Inspection: A thorough inspection, by the pilot, of an aircraft prior to flight. The purpose is to spot obvious discrepancies by inspection of the exterior, interior, and engine of the airplane.

Preventive Maintenance: FAR Part 43 lists a number of maintenance operations that are considered preventive in nature and may be performed by a certificated pilot on an airplane he/she owns, provided the airplane is now flown in commercial service. (These operations are described in Chapter 7 of this book.)

Repairs and Alterations: There are two classes of repairs and/or alterations: *Major* and *Minor*.

Major repairs and alterations must be approved for a return to service by an FAA-certified Airframe and Powerplant mechanic holding an IA authorization, a repair station, or by the FAA.

Minor repairs and alterations may be returned to service by an FAA-certified Airframe and Powerplant mechanic.

Airworthiness Directives: Often called ADs, are defined in FAR Part 39, and must be complied with. As described in Chapter 4, they are a required maintenance/repair step.

Files of ADs and their requirements are kept by mechanics and the FAA offices. A compliance check of ADs is a part of the annual inspection.

Service Difficulty Reports: Referred to as SDRs, are prepared by the FAA from Malfunction or Defect Reports (MDRs) that are initiated by owners, pilots, and mechanics. SDRs are not the word of law that ADs are; however, they should be adhered to for your own safety.

PERFORMING AN INSPECTION

The actual pre-purchase inspection consists of three parts:

1. Walk-around inspection.
2. Test flight.
3. Mechanic's inspection.

The Walk-Around

The walk-around is really a very thorough preflight. It's divided into four simple yet logical steps.

1. The cabin: The first part of the walk-around is to check that all required paperwork is with the airplane. This includes the Airworthiness Certificate, Aircraft Registration Certificate, FCC station license, flight manual or operating limitations, and logbooks (airframe, engine, and propeller), with a current equipment list and weight and balance chart. These are required by the FARs.

While you're inside the airplane looking for the paperwork, notice the general condition of the interior. Does it appear clean, or has it just been scrubbed after a long period of inattention? Look in the corners, just as you would if you were buying a used car. The care given the interior can be a good indication of what care was given to the remainder of the airplane. If you have purchased used cars in the past, and have been successful, you are qualified for this phase of the inspection.

Look at the instrument panel. Does it have what you want/need? Are the instruments in good condition, or are there knobs missing and glass faces broken? Is the equipment all original, or have there been updates made? If updates have been made, are they neat in appearance and workable? (Often updating, particularly in avionics, is done haphazardly—with results that are neither pleasing to the eye or workable to the pilot.)

Look out the windows. Are they clear, unyellowed, and uncrazed? Side windows are not expensive to replace, and you can do it yourself. Windshields are another story, and another—much higher—price.

Check the operation of the doors. They should close and lock with little effort. No outside light should be seen around edges of the doors.

Check the seats for freedom of movement and adjustability. *Check the seat tracks and the adjustment locks for damage. This has been a sore point on 172s for years.*

2. Airframe: While continuing with the walk-around, look for the following:

Is the paint in good condition, or is some of it laying on the ground under the airplane? Paint jobs are expensive, yet necessary for the protection of the metal surfaces from corrosive elements, as well as to please the eye of the beholder. A good paint job can cost in excess of $2500.

Dents, wrinkles, or tears of the metal skin may indicate prior damage—or just careless handling. Each discrepancy must be examined very carefully. Total consideration of all the dings and dents should tell if the airplane has had an easy or a rough life.

Corrosion or rust on surfaces or control systems should be cause for alarm. Corrosion is to aluminum what rust is to iron. It's destructive. Any corrosion or rust should be brought to the attention of a mechanic for his judgment.

The landing gear should be checked for evidence of being sprung. Check the tires for signs of unusual wear that might indicate other structural damage. Also look at the nosewheel oleo strut for signs of fluid leakage and proper extension.

Move all the control surfaces, and check each for damage. They should be free and smooth in movement. When the controls are centered, the surfaces should also be centered. If they are not centered, a problem in the rigging of the airplane may exist.

3. Engine: When checking the engine, search for signs of oil leakage. Do this by looking at the engine, inside the cowl, and on the firewall. If the leaks are bad enough, there will be oil dripping to the ground or onto the nosewheel. Naturally, the seller has probably cleaned all the old oil drips away; however, oil leaves stains. Look for these stains.

Check all the hoses and lines for signs of deterioration or chafing. Also check all the connections for tightness and signs of leakage.

Check control linkages and cables for obvious damage and ease of movement.

Check the battery box and battery for corrosion.

Check the propeller for damage such as nicks, cracks, or gouges. These often small defects cause stress areas on the prop. Any visible damage to a propeller must be checked by a mechanic. Also check it for movement that would indicate looseness of the propeller at the hub.

Check the exhaust pipes for rigidity, then reach inside them and rub your finger along the inside wall. If your finger comes back perfectly clean, you can be assured that someone has washed the inside of the pipe(s)—possibly to remove the oily deposits that form there when an engine is burning a lot of oil. Black oily goo indicates problems for your mechanic to look at. This could be caused by a carburetor in need of adjustment, or a large amount of oil blow-by, the latter indicating an engine in need of large expenditures for overhaul. A light grey dusty coating indicates proper operation. Also check for exhaust stains on the belly of the plane to the rear of the stacks. This area has probably been washed, but look anyway. If you find black oily goo, then, as above, see your mechanic.

4. Logbooks: If you are satisfied with what you've seen up to this point, then go back to the cabin and have a seat. Pull out the logbooks and start reading them. Sitting there will also allow you to look once again around the cockpit.

Be sure you're looking at the proper logs for this particular aircraft, and that they are the original logs. Sometimes logbooks get "lost" and are replaced with new ones. This can happen because of carelessness or theft. The latter is the reason that many owners keep photocopies of their logs in the aircraft and the originals in a safe place. The new logs may be lacking very important information, or could be outright frauds. Fraud is a distinct possibility— and not unheard of. Be really on your guard if the original logs are not available. A complete check of the aircraft's FAA records will give most of the missing information.

Start with the airframe log by looking in the back for the AD compliance section (see Chapter 4 for a list of the ADs). Check that it's up-to-date, and that any required periodic inspections have been made. Now go back to the most recent entry; it probably will be an annual or 100-hour inspection. The annual inspection will be a statement that reads:

March 21, 1985   Total Time: 3126 hrs.
I certify that this aircraft has been inspected in accordance with an annual inspection and was determined to be in air-

worthy condition.

signed here

IA # 0000000

From this point back to the first entry in the logbook you'll be looking for similar entries, always keeping track of the total time, for continuity purposes and to indicate the regularity of usage (i.e., number of hours flown between inspections). Also, you will be looking for indications of major repairs and modifications. This will be signaled by the phrase, "Form 337 filed." A copy of this form should be with the logs, and will tell what work was done. The work may be described in the logbook. Form 337 is filed with the FAA, and copies are a part of the official record of each airplane. They are retrievable from the FAA, for a fee. Be sure there is a current weight and balance sheet with the logbook.

The engine log will be quite similar in nature to the airframe log, and will contain information from the annual/100-hour inspections. Total time will be given, and possibly an indication of time since any overhaul work, although you may have to do some math here. It's quite possible that this log—and engine—will not be the original for the aircraft. As long as the facts are well-documented in the logs, there is no cause for alarm. After all, this would be the case if the original engine was replaced with a remanufactured one.

Pay particular attention to the numbers that indicate the results of a differential compression check. These numbers will give a good indication as to the overall health of the engine. Each is given as a fraction, with the bottom number always being 80. The 80 indicates the air pressure that was utilized for the check. 80 psi (pounds per square inch) is the industry standard. The top number is the air pressure that the combustion chamber was able to maintain while being tested. 80 would be perfect, but it isn't attainable. The figure will always be less. The reason for the lower number is the air pressure loss that results from loose, worn, or broken rings; scored or cracked cylinder walls; or burned, stuck, or poorly seated valves. There are methods mechanics use to determine which of these is the cause and, of course, repair the damage.

Normal readings would be no less than 70/80, and should be uniform (within 2 or 3 lbs) for all cylinders. A discrepancy between cylinders could indicate the need for a top overhaul of one or more cylinders. The FAA says that a loss in excess of 25 percent is cause for further investigation. That would be a reading of 60/80. (Such a low reading as this indicates a very tired engine in need of much work and much money.)

Read the information from the last oil change; it may contain a statement about debris found on the oil screen or in the oil filter. However, oil changes are often performed by owners, and may or may not be recorded in the log. If they are recorded, how regular were they? I prefer every 25 hours, but 50 is acceptable. Is there a record of oil analysis? If so, ask for it. Oil is cheap insurance for long engine life.

If the engine has been top overhauled or majored, there will be a description of the work performed, a date, and the total time on the engine when the work was accomplished.

Check to see if the ADs have been complied with, and the appropriate entries made in the log (see Chapter 4 for a listing of the ADs).

If an AVCO Lycoming O-320-H2AD is installed on the airplane, be very particular about AD compliance—and listen to your mechanic's advice before purchase (see Chapters 3, 4, and 12).

The Test Flight

The test flight is a short flight to determine if the airplane "feels" right to you. It is not meant to be a rip-snort'n, slam-bang, shakeout ride.

I suggest that either the owner or a competent flight instructor accompany you. This will eliminate problems of currency, ratings, etc., with the FAA and the owner's insurance company. It will also foster better relations with the owner.

After starting the engine, pay particular attention to the gauges. Do they jump to life, or are they sluggish? Watch the oil pressure gauge in particular. Did the pressure rise within a few seconds of start? Check the other gauges. Are they indicating as should be expected? Check them during your ground run-up, then again during the takeoff and climbout. Do the numbers match those called for in the operational manual?

After you're airborne, check the radios for proper operation (NAV/COMM, ADF, etc.). This could require you to fly to an airport that is equipped for IFR operations. A short cross-country jaunt will give you a chance to get familiar with the plane.

While you are flying along, pay attention to the gyro instruments. Be sure they are stable.

Check the ventilation and heating system for proper operation.

Do a few turns, some stalls, and some level flight. Does the airplane perform as expected? Can it be trimmed for hands-off flight?

Return to the airport for a couple of landings. Check for proper brake operation and for nosewheel shimmy.

After returning to the parking ramp, open the engine compartment and look again for oil leaks. Also check along the belly for indications of oil leakage and blow-by. A short flight should be enough to "dirty" things up again if they had been dirty to begin with.

Mechanic's Inspection

If you are still satisfied with the airplane and desire to pursue the matter further, then have it inspected by an A&P or AI. This inspection will cost you a few dollars; however, it could save you thousands. The average for a pre-purchase inspection is three to four hours labor at shop rates.

The mechanic will accomplish a search of ADs, a complete check of the logs, and an overall check of the plane. A compression check and a borescope examination must be made. The latter can determine the real condition of the engine by looking into a cylinder and viewing the top of the piston, the valves, and the cylinder walls. This is done by use of a device called a borescope.

POINTS OF ADVICE

Always use your own mechanic for the pre-purchase inspection. By this I mean someone *you* are paying to watch out for *your* interests, not someone who may have an interest in the sale of the plane (i.e., employee of the seller).

Have the plane checked even if an annual was just done, unless you know and trust the AI who did the inspection.

You may be able to make a deal with the owner over the cost of the mechanic's inspection, particularly if an annual is due. It is not uncommon to see airplanes listed for sale with the phrase "annual at date of sale." I am always leery of this, as who is to say just how complete this annual will be? It is coming with the airplane, done by the seller, as part of the sale. Who is looking out for *your* interests? I know that the FARs are very explicit in their requirements, but I am not sure that all mechanics do equal work.

If an airplane seller refuses you anything that has been mentioned in this chapter, then thank him for his time, walk away, and look elsewhere. Do not let a seller control the situation. Your money, your safety, and possibly your very life are at stake. Airplanes are not hot sellers, and there is rarely a line forming to make a purchase. You are the buyer; *you* have the final word.

THE NEW ALTERNATIVE

Searching for a good used airplane can be expensive and very time-consuming. You read ads, make telephone calls (always long distance) and even have to travel great distances to see the airplanes that are advertised.

Often I have seen something that really looked interesting in an ad, called the number, and even thought about going to look at the airplane—that is, except I live in Virginia, and the airplane is in Colorado.

In the past, I have traveled to see what was supposed to be a "10" airplane, and was greated by a gasping "2" or "3." On the one hand I am glad I made the trip; it saved me money, as had I taken the owner at his word, I would have owned a basket of problems. On the other hand, the trip was a complete waste of money, as I came home empty-handed.

The question is: How do you look at an airplane long-distance?

The answer is: Through the use of state-of-the-art electronics and home video systems, it is now possible to inspect an airplane long-distance!

Air Show, an aircraft marketing firm, has recently introduced a complete sales system designed to aid the long-distance buyer. Air Show lists aircrafts for sale and advertises them in national coverage "airplane" papers and magazines. This in itself is not very earthshaking, nor is their use of an "800" toll-free telephone number. However, above just advertising, they offer a unique means of complete visual inspection from all the way across the country.

The folks at Air Show videotape a 15-minute VHS formatted documentary about each airplane they list for sale. For a small fee, the prospective purchaser may have a copy of this sales tape sent to him; then, in the privacy and convenience of his/her own home, may inspect the prospective purchase.

These video recordings follow the same general walk-around that I have recommended earlier in this chapter as the proper way to inspect a used airplane. They are, for the most part, filmed outside, and not under "studio" conditions. The net result is a very informative video representation of the aircraft being "inspected."

For more information about this new service, contact:

Air Show Journal
45 West Broadway
Suite 205
Eugene, OR 97401
Phone: (800) 247-9005
OR: (503) 344-7813

PAPERWORK OF OWNERSHIP

Assuming that you have completely inspected your prospective purchase, and found it acceptable at an agreeable price, you're ready to sit down and complete the paperwork that will lead to ownership.

Title Search

The first step in the paperwork of purchasing an airplane is to assure the craft has a clear title. This is done by a title search.

A title search is accomplished by checking the aircraft's individual records at the Mike Monroney Aeronautical Center in Oklahoma City, Oklahoma. These records include title information, chain of ownership, Major Repair/Alteration (Form 337) information, and other data pertinent to a particular airplane. The FAA files this information by N-number.

The object of a title search is to ascertain that there are no liens or other hidden encumbrances against the ownership of the airplane. This search may be done by you, your attorney, or other representative selected by you.

Since most prospective purchasers would find it inconvenient to travel to Oklahoma City to do the search themselves, it is advisable to contract with a third party specializing in this service to do the searching.

One such organization is the AOPA (Airplane Owners and Pilots Association), 421 Aviation Way, Frederick, MD 21701, Phone: (301) 695-2000. The AOPA has an Oklahoma City office just for this purpose (Phone: (800) 654-4700). There are others that provide similar services.

In addition to title searches, the AOPA offers inexpensive title insurance that will protect you against unrecorded liens, FAA recording mistakes, or other clouds on the title.

Documents

The following documents must be given to you with your airplane:

1. Bill of Sale
2. Airworthiness Certificate
3. Logbooks
    a. Airframe
    b. Engine/propeller
4. Equipment List (including weight and balance data)
5. Flight Manual

Forms to be Completed

AC Form 8050-2, Bill of Sale, is the standard means of recording transfer of ownership (Figs. 5-1, 5-2).

AC Form 8050-1, Aircraft Registration, is filed with the Bill of Sale, or its equivalent (Fig. 5-3). If you are purchasing the airplane under a Contract of Conditional Sale, then that contract must accompany the registration application in lieu of the AC Form 8050-2. The pink copy of the registration is retained by you, and will remain in the airplane until the new registration is issued by the FAA.

AC 8050-41, Release of Lien, must be filed by the seller if he still owes money on the airplane (Fig. 5-4).

AC 8050-64, Assignment of Special Registration Number, will be issued upon written request. All N-numbers consist of the prefix N, followed by:

☐ One to five numbers,
☐ One to four numbers and a letter suffix, or
☐ One to three numbers and a two-letter suffix.

This is similar to obtaining personalized license plates for your automobile, sometimes referred to as "vanity" plates.

FCC (Federal Communications Commission) Form 404, Application for Aircraft Radio Station License, must be completed if you have any radio equipment on board. The tear-off section will remain in your airplane as temporary authorization until the new license is sent to you (Figs. 5-5, 5-6).

Most forms you send to the FAA or FCC will result in the issuance of a document to you. Be patient; it all takes time.

UNITED STATES OF AMERICA

DEPARTMENT OF TRANSPORTATION — FEDERAL AVIATION ADMINISTRATION

AIRCRAFT BILL OF SALE INFORMATION

PRIVACY ACT OF 1974 (PL 93-579) requires that users of this form be informed of the authority which allows the solicitation of the information and whether disclosure of such information is mandatory or voluntary; the principal purpose for which the information is intended to be used; the routine uses which may be made of the information gathered; and the effects, if any, of not providing all or any part of the requested information.

The Federal Aviation Act of 1958 requires the registration of each United States civil aircraft as a prerequisite to its operation. The applicant for registration must submit proof of ownership that meets the requirements prescribed in Part 47 of the Federal Aviation Regulations.

This form identifies the aircraft being purchased, and provides space for purchaser and seller identification and signature. This is intended only to be a suggested bill of sale form which meets the recording requirements of the Federal Aviation Act, and the regulations issued thereunder. In addition to these requirements, the form of bill of sale should be drafted in accordance with the pertinent provisions of local statutes and other applicable federal statutes.

The following routine uses are made of the information gathered:

(1) To support investigative efforts of investigation and law enforcement agencies of Federal, state, and foreign governments.

(2) To serve as a repository of legal documents used by individuals and title search companies to determine the legal ownership of an aircraft.

(3) To provide aircraft owners and operators information about potential mechanical defects or unsafe conditions of their aircraft in the form of airworthiness directives.

(4) To provide supporting information in court cases concerning liability of individual in law suits.

(5) To serve as a data source for management information for production of summary descriptive statistics and analytical studies in support of agency functions for which the records are collected and maintained.

(6) To respond to general requests from the aviation community or the public for statistical information under the Freedom of Information Act or to locate specific individuals or specific aircraft for accident investigation, violation, or other safety related requirements.

(7) To provide data for the automated aircraft registration master file.

(8) To provide documents for microfiche backup record.

(9) To provide data for development of the aircraft registration statistical system.

(10) To prepare an aircraft register in magnetic tape and publication form required by ICAO agreement containing information on aircraft owners by name, address, N-Number, and type aircraft, used for internal FAA safety program purposes and also available to the public (individuals, aviation organizations, direct mail advertisers, state and local governments, etc.) upon payment of user charges reimbursing the Federal Government for its costs.

AC Form 8050-2 (9-82) (0052-00-629-0002)

Fig. 5-1. Privacy Act statement found on FAA forms.

Assistance

There are many forms to complete, and although they are not complicated, you may wish to seek assistance in filling them out. You can check with your FBO, or call upon another party, such as the AOPA.

The AOPA, for a small fee, will provide closing services via

137

telephone, and prepare/file the necessary forms to complete the transaction. This is particularly nice if the parties involved in the transaction are spread all over the country, as would be the case if you are purchasing an airplane sight unseen.

Another source of assistance in completing the necessary paper-

---

FORM APPROVED
OMB No 2120-0029
EXP. DATE 10/31/84

UNITED STATES OF AMERICA
DEPARTMENT OF TRANSPORTATION FEDERAL AVIATION ADMINISTRATION

AIRCRAFT BILL OF SALE

FOR AND IN CONSIDERATION OF $ _____ THE UNDERSIGNED OWNER(S) OF THE FULL LEGAL AND BENEFICIAL TITLE OF THE AIRCRAFT DESCRIBED AS FOLLOWS:

UNITED STATES
REGISTRATION NUMBER **N**

AIRCRAFT MANUFACTURER & MODEL

AIRCRAFT SERIAL No.

DOES THIS _____ DAY OF _____ 19 ___
HEREBY SELL, GRANT, TRANSFER AND
DELIVER ALL RIGHTS, TITLE, AND INTERESTS
IN AND TO SUCH AIRCRAFT UNTO:

Do Not Write In This Block
FOR FAA USE ONLY

PURCHASER

NAME AND ADDRESS
(IF INDIVIDUAL(S), GIVE LAST NAME, FIRST NAME, AND MIDDLE INITIAL.)

DEALER CERTIFICATE NUMBER

AND TO _____ EXECUTORS, ADMINISTRATORS, AND ASSIGNS TO HAVE AND TO HOLD SINGULARLY THE SAID AIRCRAFT FOREVER, AND WARRANTS THE TITLE THEREOF.

IN TESTIMONY WHEREOF _____ HAVE SET _____ HAND AND SEAL THIS _____ DAY OF _____ 19 ___

SELLER	NAME (S) OF SELLER (TYPED OR PRINTED)	SIGNATURE (S) (IN INK) (IF EXECUTED FOR CO-OWNERSHIP, ALL MUST SIGN.)	TITLE (TYPED OR PRINTED)

ACKNOWLEDGMENT (NOT REQUIRED FOR PURPOSES OF FAA RECORDING: HOWEVER, MAY BE REQUIRED BY LOCAL LAW FOR VALIDITY OF THE INSTRUMENT.)

ORIGINAL: TO FAA

AC FORM 8050-2 (8-76) (0052-629-0002)

Fig. 5-2. 8050-2, Aircraft Bill of Sale.

FORM APPROVED
OMB NO. 2120-0029
EXP. DATE 10/31/84

UNITED STATES OF AMERICA DEPARTMENT OF TRANSPORTATION
FEDERAL AVIATION ADMINISTRATION-MIKE MONRONEY AERONAUTICAL CENTER
AIRCRAFT REGISTRATION APPLICATION

CERT. ISSUE DATE

UNITED STATES REGISTRATION NUMBER **N**

AIRCRAFT MANUFACTURER & MODEL

AIRCRAFT SERIAL No.

FOR FAA USE ONLY

TYPE OF REGISTRATION (Check one box)

☐ 1. Individual ☐ 2. Partnership ☐ 3. Corporation ☐ 4. Co-owner ☐ 5. Gov't. ☐ 8. Foreign-owned Corporation

NAME OF APPLICANT (Person(s) shown on evidence of ownership. If individual, give last name, first name, and middle initial.)

TELEPHONE NUMBER: (   )   –

ADDRESS (Permanent mailing address for first applicant listed.)

Number and street: ______

Rural Route: P.O. Box:

CITY	STATE	ZIP CODE

☐ **CHECK HERE IF YOU ARE ONLY REPORTING A CHANGE OF ADDRESS**

ATTENTION! Read the following statement before signing this application.

A false or dishonest answer to any question in this application may be grounds for punishment by fine and / or imprisonment (U.S. Code, Title 18, Sec. 1001).

CERTIFICATION

I/WE CERTIFY:

(1) That the above aircraft is owned by the undersigned applicant, who is a citizen (including corporations) of the United States.

(For voting trust, give name of trustee: ______), or:

CHECK ONE AS APPROPRIATE:

a. ☐ A resident alien, with alien registration (Form 1-151 or Form 1-551) No. ______

b. ☐ A foreign-owned corporation organized and doing business under the laws of (state or possession) ______, and said aircraft is based and primarily used in the United States. Records of flight hours are available for inspection at ______

(2) That the aircraft is not registered under the laws of any foreign country; and
(3) That legal evidence of ownership is attached or has been filed with the Federal Aviation Administration.

NOTE: If executed for co-ownership all applicants must sign. Use reverse side if necessary.

TYPE OR PRINT NAME BELOW SIGNATURE

EACH PART OF THIS APPLICATION MUST BE SIGNED IN INK.			
	SIGNATURE	TITLE	DATE
	SIGNATURE	TITLE	DATE
	SIGNATURE	TITLE	DATE

NOTE: Pending receipt of the Certificate of Aircraft Registration, the aircraft may be operated for a period not in excess of 90 days, during which time the PINK copy of this application must be carried in the aircraft.

AC FORM 8050-1 (1-83) (0052-00-628-9005)

Fig. 5-3. 8050-1, Aircraft Registration.

THIS FORM SERVES TWO PURPOSES
PART I acknowledges the recording of a security conveyance covering the collateral shown.
PART II is a suggested form of release which may be used to release the collateral from the terms of the conveyance.

PART I – CONVEYANCE RECORDATION NOTICE

NAME (last name first) OF DEBTOR

NAME and ADDRESS OF SECURED PARTY/ASSIGNEE

NAME OF SECURED PARTY'S ASSIGNOR (if assigned)

Do Not Write In This Block
FOR FAA USE ONLY

| FAA REGISTRA-TION NUMBER | AIRCRAFT SERIAL NUMBER | AIRCRAFT MFd. (BUILDER) and MODEL |

ENGINE MFR. and MODEL   ENGINE SERIAL NUMBER(S)

PROPELLER MFR. and MODEL   PROPELLER SERIAL NUMBER(S)

THE SECURITY CONVEYANCE DATED_____COVERING THE ABOVE COLLATERAL WAS RECORDED BY THE FAA AIRCRAFT REG-ISTRY ON_____AS CONVEYANCE NUMBER_____

_____
FAA CONVEYANCE EXAMINER

PART II – RELEASE – (This suggested release form may be executed by the secured party and returned to the FAA Aircraft Registry when terms of the conveyance have been satisfied. See below for additional information.)

THE UNDERSIGNED HEREBY CERTIFIES AND ACKNOWLEDGES THAT HE IS THE TRUE AND LAWFUL HOLDER OF THE NOTE OR OTHER EVIDENCE OF INDEBTEDNESS SECURED BY THE CONVEYANCE REFERRED TO HEREIN ON THE ABOVE-DESCRIBED COLLATERAL AND THAT THE SAME COLLATERAL IS HEREBY RELEASED FROM THE TERMS OF THE CONVEYANCE. ANY TITLE RETAINED IN THE COLLATERAL BY THE CONVEYANCE IS HEREBY SOLD, GRANTED, TRANS-FERRED, AND ASSIGNED TO THE PARTY WHO EXECUTED THE CONVEYANCE, OR TO THE ASSIGNEE OF SAID PARTY IF THE CONVEYANCE SHALL HAVE BEEN ASSIGNED: PROVIDED, THAT NO EXPRESS WARRANTY IS GIVEN NOR IMPLIED BY REASON OF EXECUTION OR DELIVERY OF THIS RELEASE.

This form is only intended to be a suggested form of release, which meets the recording requirements of the Federal Aviation Act of 1958, and the regulations issued thereunder. In addition to these requirements, the form used by the security holder should be drafted in accordance with the pertinent provisions of local statutes and other applicable federal statutes. This form may be reproduced. There is no fee for recording a release. Send to FAA Aircraft Registry, P. O. Box 25504, Oklahoma City, Oklahoma 73125.

ACKNOWLEDGEMENT (If Required By Applicable Local Law):

DATE OF RELEASE: ....

....
(Name of security holder)

SIGNATURE (in ink) ....

TITLE ....

(A person signing for a corporation must be a corporate officer or hold a managerial position and must show his title. A person signing for another should see Parts 47 and 49 of the Federal Aviation Regulations (14 CFR).

Fig. 5-4. 8050-41, Release of Lien.

work is your bank. This is particularly true if the bank has a vested interest in your airplane (i.e., they hold the note!).

INSURANCE

Insure your airplane from the moment you sign on the dotted line. No one can afford to take risks.

Basically, there are two types of insurance you will be looking at:

Liability insurance protects you, or your heirs, in instances of claims against you resulting from your operation of an airplane (i.e., bodily

140

Federal Communications Commission
Gettysburg, PA 17325

APPLICATION FOR AIRCRAFT RADIO STATION LICENSE

Approved by OMB
3060-0040
Expires 3/31/86

- Read instructions above before completing application.
- Sign and date application.
- Use typewriter or print clearly in ink.
- Place First Class Postage on the reverse side of the card and mail.

1. FAA Registration or FCC Control Number.
(If FAA Registration is not required for your aircraft, explain in item 8.)

N

2. Is application for a fleet license? ☐ No ☐ Yes
If yes, give the number of aircraft in fleet, including planned expansion............

3. Type of applicant (check one)

☐ I—Individual ☐ C—Corporation

☐ P—Partnership ☐ D—Individual with Business Name

☐ A—Association ☐ G—Governmental entity

4. Applicant/Licensee Name (See Instructions)

5. Mailing Address (Number and Street, P.O. Box or Route No., City, State, ZIP Code)

6. Frequencies Requested (check appropriate box(es) in 6.A and/or 6B.)

6A. DO NOT CHECK BOTH BOXES

☐ A—Private Aircraft ☐ C—Air Carrier

6B. ADDITIONAL INFORMATION IS REQUIRED IF YOU CHECK HERE (See Instructions))

☐ T—Flight Test HF ☐ V—Flight Test VHF ☐ O—Other (Specify)

7. Application is for:

☐ New Station ☐ Renewal

☐ Modification

8. Answer space for any required statements

9. READ CAREFULLY BEFORE SIGNING: 1. Applicant waives any claim to the use of any particular frequency regardless of prior use by license or otherwise. 2. Applicant will have unlimited access to the radio equipment and will control access to exclude unauthorized persons. 3. Neither applicant nor any member thereof is a foreign government or representative thereof. 4. Applicant certifies that all statements made in this application and attachments are true, complete, correct and made in good faith. 5. Applicant certifies that the signature is that of the individual, or partner, or officer or duly authorized employee of a corporation, or officer who is a member of an unincorporated association, or appropriate elected or appointed official on behalf of a governmental entity.

WILLFUL FALSE STATEMENTS MADE ON THIS FORM ARE PUNISHABLE BY FINE AND/OR IMPRISONMENT U.S. CODE TITLE 18, SECTION 1001.

10. Signature

Date

FCC 404
October 1984

Fig. 5-5. FCC 404, Aircraft Radio Station License.

141

Federal Communications Commission
Gettysburg, PA 17325

TEMPORARY AIRCRAFT RADIO STATION OPERATING AUTHORITY

Approved by OMB
3060-0040
Expires 3/31/86

Use this form if you want a temporary operating authority while your regular application, FCC Form 404, is being processed by the FCC. This authority authorizes the use of transmitters operating on the appropriate frequencies listed in Part 87 of the Commission's Rules.

- DO NOT use this form if you already have a valid aircraft station license.
- DO NOT use this form when renewing your aircraft license.
- DO NOT use this form if you are applying for a fleet license.
- DO NOT use this form if you do not have an FAA Registration Number.

ALL APPLICANTS MUST CERTIFY:

1. I am not a representative of a foreign government.
2. I have applied for an Aircraft Radio Station License by mailing a completed FCC Form 404 to the Federal Communications Commission, P.O. Box 1030, Gettysburg, PA 17325.
3. I have not been denied a license or had my license revoked by the FCC.

4. I am not the subject of any adverse legal action concerning the operation of a radio station.
5. I will ensure that the Aircraft Radio Station will be operated by an individual holding the proper class of license or permit required by the Commission's Rules.

WILLFUL FALSE STATEMENTS VOID THIS PERMIT AND ARE PUNISHABLE BY FINE AND/OR IMPRISONMENT.

Name of Applicant (Print or Type)	Signature of Applicant
FAA Registration Number (Use as Temporary Call Sign)	Date FCC Form 404 Mailed

Your authority to operate your Aircraft Radio Station is subject to all applicable laws, treaties and regulations and is subject to the right of control of the Government of the United States. This authority is valid for 90 days from the date the FCC Form 404 is mailed.

YOU MUST POST THIS TEMPORARY OPERATING AUTHORITY ON BOARD YOUR AIRCRAFT

NOTICE TO INDIVIDUALS REQUIRED BY PRIVACY ACT OF 1974 AND THE PAPERWORK REDUCTION ACT OF 1980

Sections 301, 303 and 308 of the Communications Act of 1934, as amended, (licensing powers) authorize the FCC to request the information on this application. The purpose of the information is to determine your eligibility for a license. The information will be used by FCC staff to evaluate the application, to determine station location, to provide information for enforcement and rulemaking proceedings and to maintain a current inventory of licensees. No license can be granted unless all information requested is provided. Your response is required to obtain this authorization.

DETACH HERE—DO NOT MAIL THIS PART

FCC 404-A
October 1984

Fig. 5-6. FCC 404, Temporary Operating Authority.

injury or property damage). If someone is injured or killed as a result of your flying you can be sure of one thing: You *will* be sued! *Hull insurance* protects your investment from loss caused by the elements of nature, by fire, by theft, by vandalism, or while being operated. There are limited coverages available that will cover losses to the airplane while on the ground, but not while in the air. You can save money here; however, discussion of coverages available is best left to you and your insurance agent. Your lending institution will require hull insurance for their protection.

A check of any of the various aviation publications will produce telephone numbers for several aviation underwriters. Many list "800" toll-free telephone numbers. Check with more than one company, as services, coverage, and rates do differ. Stay clear of policies that have exclusions, or other specific rules involving maximum preset values for replacement parts.

Something else to consider is your health and life insurance coverage. Be sure you are covered while flying a "small" airplane.

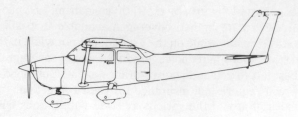

Chapter 6

Inspections

To care for your airplane and assure its continued airworthiness, it is required that certain items be inspected for proper operation and integrity.

AIRCRAFT INSPECTION

Here are the general inspection requirements, as taken from the Cessna 172 Service Manual:

To avoid repetition throughout the inspection, general points to be checked are given below. In the inspection, only the items to be checked are listed; details as to how to check, or what to check for, are excluded. The inspection covers several different models. Some items may apply only to specific models, and some items are optional equipment that may or may not be found on a particular airplane. Check the FAA Airworthiness Directives and Cessna Service Letters for compliance at the time specified by them. Federal Aviation Regulations require that all civil aircraft have a periodic (annual) inspection as prescribed by the Administrator, and performed by a person designated by the Administrator. The Cessna Aircraft Company recommends a 100-hour periodic inspection for the airplane.

Check as Applicable:

Movable Parts for: Lubrication, servicing, security of attachment, binding, excessive wear, safetying, proper operation, proper adjustment, correct travel, cracked fittings, security of hinges, defective bearings, cleanliness, corrosion, deformation, sealing, and tensions.

Fluid Lines and Hoses for: Leaks, cracks, dents, kinks, chafing, proper radius, security, corrosion, deterioration, obstructions, and foreign matter.

Metal Parts for: security of attachment, cracks, metal distortion, broken spotwelds, corrosion, condition of paint, and any other apparent damage.

Wiring for: Security, chafing, burning, defective insulation, loose or broken terminals, heat deterioration, and corroded terminals.

Bolts in Critical Areas for: Correct torque in accordance with proper torque values, when installed or when visual inspection indicates the need for a torque check.

Filters, Screens, and Fluids for: Cleanliness, contamination and/or replacement at specified intervals.

AIRPLANE FILE

Miscellaneous data, information, and licenses are a part of the airplane file. Check that the following documents are up-to-date and in accordance with current Federal Aviation Regulations. Most of the items listed are required by the United States Federal Aviation Regulations. Since the regulations of other nations may require other documents and data, owners of exported aircraft should check with their own aviation officials to determine their individual requirements.

To be displayed in the airplane at all times:

☐ Aircraft Airworthiness Certificate.
☐ Aircraft Registration Certificate.
☐ Aircraft Radio License.

To be carried in the airplane at all times:

☐ Weight and Balance and associated papers.
☐ Aircraft Equipment List.

To be made available upon request:

☐ Aircraft Logbook
☐ Engine Logbook

ENGINE RUN-UP

Before beginning the step-by-step inspection, start, run up, and shut down the engine in accordance with instructions in the Owner's Manual. During the run-up, observe the following, making note of any discrepancies or abnormalities:

- ☐ Engine temperatures or pressures.
- ☐ Static rpm.
- ☐ Magneto drop.
- ☐ Engine response to changes in power.
- ☐ Any unusual engine noises.
- ☐ Fuel selector valve; operate the engine on each position long enough to make sure the valve functions properly.
- ☐ Idling speed and mixture; proper idle cutoff.
- ☐ Alternator.
- ☐ Suction gauge.

After the inspection has been completed, an engine run-up should again be performed to ascertain that any discrepancies or abnormalities have been corrected.

PERIODIC INSPECTIONS

Continental Engine: If the engine is equipped with an external oil filter, change the engine oil and filter element at 50-hour intervals. If the engine is *not* equipped with an external oil filter, change the engine oil and clean the oil screen *every 25 hours*.

Lycoming Engine: If the engine is *not* equipped with an external oil filter, change the engine oil and clean the oil screens at 50-hour intervals. If the engine is equipped with an external oil filter, the engine oil change intervals may be extended to 100-hour intervals, providing the external filter element is changed at 50-hour intervals.

The 50-hour inspection includes a visual check of the engine, propeller, and aircraft exterior for any apparent damage or defects; an engine oil change as required above; and accomplishment of lubrication and servicing requirements. Remove the propeller spinner and engine cowling, and replace after the inspection has been completed.

The 100-hour (or annual) inspection includes everything in the 50-hour inspection, and oil change as required above. Also loosen or remove the fuselage, wing, empennage, and upholstery inspection doors, plates, and fairings only as necessary to perform a thorough, searching inspection of the aircraft. Replace after the inspection has been completed.

Note: In the following charts, numbers appearing in the time column indicate the hours between inspections/servicing.

Propeller

	Time
1. Spinner and spinner bulkhead	50
2. Blades	50
3. Hub	50
4. Bolts and/or nuts	50

Engine Compartment

Check for evidence of oil and fuel leaks, then clean the entire engine and compartment, if needed, prior to inspection.

	Time
1. Engine oil, screen, filler cap, dipstick, drain plug, and filter	50
2. Oil cooler	50
3. Induction air filter	50
4. Induction air box, air valves, doors, and controls	50
5. Cold and hot air hoses	50
6. Engine baffles	50
7. Cylinders, rocker box covers, and push rod housings	50
8. Crankcase, oil sump, accessory section, and front crankshaft seal	50
9. All Lines and hoses	50
10. Intake and exhaust systems	50
11. Ignition harness	50
12. Spark plugs and compression	100
13. Crankcase and vacuum system breather lines	50
14. Electrical wiring	50
15. Vacuum pump, oil separator, and relief valve	50
16. Vacuum relief valve filter	100
17. Engine controls and linkage	50
18. Engine shock mounts, engine	

Fuel System

Time

Landing Gear

Time

148

step and spring strut, tires,
and fairings.....................................100
3. Main and nose gear wheel bearing
lubrication 500
4. Torque link lubrication...........................50
5. Nose gear strut servicing.......................100
6. Nose gear shimmy damper service................100
7. Nose gear wheels, wheel bearings,
strut, steering system, shimmy
damper, tire, fairing, and
torque links....................................100
8. Parking brake system...........................100

Airframe

Time

1. Aircraft exterior...............................50
2. Aircraft structure..............................100
3. Windows, windshield, and doors...................50
4. Seats, stops, seat rails,
upholstery, structure, and seat
mounting 50
5. Safety belts and attaching
brackets...50
6. Control U-bearings, sprockets,
pulleys, cables, chains, and
turnbuckles 100
7. Control lock, control wheel,
and control U mechanism.........................100
8. Instruments and markings........................100
9. Gyros, central air filter.......................100
10. Magnetic compass compensation..................1000
11. Instrument wiring and plumbing..................100
12. Instrument panel, shock mounts,
ground straps, cover, and decals
and labeling....................................100
13. Defrosting, heating, and
ventilating systems, and
controls 100
14. Cabin upholstery, trim,
sun visors, and ashtrays........................100
15. Area beneath floor, lines, hoses,
wires, and control cables.......................100
16. Lights, switches, circuit breakers
fuses, and spare fuses...........................50
17. Exterior lights.................................50

18. Pitot and static system..........................100
19. Stall warning sensing unit,
    pitot warning heater............................100
20. Radio and radio controls........................100
21. Radio antennas..................................100
22. Battery, battery box, and battery
    cables 100
23. Battery electrolyte level........................50

Control Systems

In addition to the items listed below, always check for correct direction of movement, correct travel, and correct cable tension.

Time

1. Cables, terminals, pulleys, pulley
   brackets, cable guards,
   turnbuckles, and fairleads.....................100
2. Chains, terminals, sprockets, and
   chain guards...................................100
3. Trim control wheel, indicators,
   and actuator..................................100
4. Travel stops....................................100
5. All decals and labeling.........................100
6. Flap control switch (or lever),
   flap rollers and tracks,
   flap transmitter and linkage,
   and flap position indicator
   flap electric motor and
   transmission..................................100
7. Elevator trim...................................100
8. Rudder pedal assemblies and
   linkage.......................................100
9. Skin and structure of control
   surface and trim tabs.........................100
10. Balance weight attachment   100

Note: A high-time inspection is merely a 100-hour inspection with the addition of an engine overhaul. At the time of overhaul, engine accessories should be overhauled.

Summary

I am sure at this point you can understand why a proper annual takes time and costs money. Don't cut yourself short with a shoddy inspection. You may save time and money, but it could cost you your life.

PROPELLERS

The following Flying Safety Update about metal propeller care is provided courtesy of AVEMCO Insurance Company:

If you're like many pilots, you may not give much thought to your metal propeller. But you should. Even though a high margin of safety is incorporated in the design of modern metal propeller blades, failures do occur.

Reports of propeller blade failure do not show that the failures can be attributed to any particular aircraft/engine/powerplant combination. Failures can occur with any type of propeller, whether they are fixed-pitch, ground-adjustable, variable-pitch, or constant-speed.

Indeed, propellers can be quite complicated. The typical two-bladed constant-speed propeller consists of approximately 200 separate parts.

An investigation of a representative number of propeller blade failures discloses that the majority of failures occur because of fatigue cracks that started at mechanical formed dents, cuts, scars, scratches, nicks, or leading edge pits. In most cases, blade material samples did not reveal evidence of failure caused by material defects or surface discontinuities existing before the blades were placed in service.

Often, fatigue failure occurs at a place where previous damage has been repaired. This may be due to the failure actually having started prior to the repair, or improperly performed repairs. Too many blade-straightening or blade-pitching operations can overstress the metal, causing it to fail.

Metal propeller blade failure may also occur in the least suspected areas, such as under leading edge de-icer boots, under leading edge abrasion boots, and under propeller blade decals. During propeller blade overhaul, all leading-edge boots and blade decals should be removed and these areas checked for corrosion, pitting and evidence of fatigue cracks.

Another cause of metal propeller blade failure, though less frequent, is flutter. This vibration causes the ends of the blade to twist back and forth at a high frequency around an axis perpendicular to the crankshaft.

At certain engine speeds, this vibration becomes critical and, if the propeller is allowed to operate in this range, propeller blade failure may occur. For this reason, tachometer accuracy is very important. Periodic tachometer accuracy checks should be make using reliable testing instruments.

How do blades fail? The stresses that normally occur in the propeller blades may be envisioned as parallel lines of force that run within the blade approximately parallel to the surface. When a defect occurs, it tends to squeeze together the lines of force in the defect area, thereby concentrating the stress.

This increase in stress may be sufficient to cause a crack to start. Even a small defect, such as a nick or dent, may develop into a crack. The crack, in turn, results in a greater stress concentration. The resulting growth of the crack will almost inevitably result in blade failure.

There are, of course, many stresses on a propeller. The propeller is at the end of the energy chain, and is responsible for efficiently converting the brake horsepower of the engine into thrust. During normal operation, there are at least four separate stresses imposed on a propeller: thrust, torques, centrifugal force, and aerodynamic force. Additional stresses may be imposed by vibration caused by fluttering or uneven tracking of the blades.

Where do blades fail? Experience indicates that fatigue failures normally occur within a few inches of the blade tip; however, failures also occur in other portions of the blade when dents, cuts, scratches, or nicks are ignored. Since failures also occur in blades near the shank, and at the propeller hub, no damage should be overlooked or allowed to go without repair.

When performing propeller inspections and preflight inspection in particular, inspect not only the leading edge but the entire blade for erosion, scratches, nicks, and cracks. Regardless of how small any surface irregularities may appear, consider them as stress risers subject to fatigue failure.

During your preflight inspection of the propeller, be certain to consider the propeller "hot," and capable of roaring to life. More than one pilot has been surprised to find even the slightest movement results in a spinning prop.

Propeller manufacturer's manuals, service letters, and bulletins specify methods and limits for blade maintenance, inspection, service, and repair. Remove from service damaged blades that are on the manufacturer's list of blades that cannot be repaired. When repairs are possible, the manufacturer's instructions should be followed using accepted industry practices and techniques. All propeller repairs should be performed by qualified repair agencies and competent personnel.

Moreover, owners and pilots should be aware of Airworthiness Directives that apply to the propeller installed on a particular aircraft. Close attention should be paid to repetitive requirements of applicable ADs.

The following blade tips will help you care for your propeller and help it provide you with many hours of enjoyable flying:

Keep blades clean. Cracks or other defects cannot be seen if they're covered with dirt, oil, or other foreign matter.

Avoid engine run-up areas containing loose sand, stones, gravel, or broken asphalt.

Do not move the aircraft by pushing on the propeller blades; they were not designed to be used as handles. There is always the potential of injury should the engine start because someone left the ignition switch on or the engine isn't grounded.

During the normal 100-hour inspection, the engine tachometer should be checked for accuracy to preclude operation in any restricted rpm range.

Every propeller will wear and become unairworthy at some point in time. The best way to prolong its life is through regular care and maintenance.

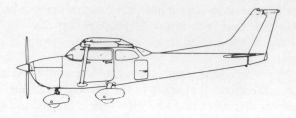

Chapter 7

Care of the 172

There are many things the owner/pilot can do to keep his airplane well maintained. Of course, this includes mechanical as well as "cosmetic" work. This is not to say there is no need for a licensed mechanic, as there are complex and sensitive workings in every aircraft that require expertise (and an FAA license). The reader is well advised that when a question comes up about maintenance, and he is unsure, *consult a competent licensed mechanic*. This could cost a few dollars, but they will be dollars well spent.

THE FAA SAYS

In case your FBO is concerned about your attempts at saving money, here is a partial reprint of Advisory Circular AC no. 150/5190-2A, dated 4 Apr 72:

d. Restrictions on Self-Service: Any unreasonable restriction imposed on the owners and operators of aircraft regarding the servicing of their own aircraft and equipment may be considered as a violation of agency policy. The owner of an aircraft should be permitted to fuel, wash, repair, paint, and otherwise take care of his own aircraft, provided there is no attempt to perform such services for others. Restrictions which have the effect of diverting activity of this type to a commercial enterprise amount to an exclusive right contrary to law.

With these words the FAA has allowed the owner of an aircraft to save his hard-earned dollars—and to become very familiar with his airplane, the latter, no doubt, contributing to safety.

The FARs (Federal Aviation Regulations) specify that preventive maintenance may be performed by pilots/owners of airplanes not utilized in commercial service.

PREVENTIVE MAINTENANCE

Preventive maintenance is defined as "simple or minor preservation operations and the replacement of small standard parts not involving complex assembly operations."

The FARs lists 28 preventive maintenance items in Appendix A of part 43.13. This means that only those operations listed are considered preventive maintenance. The items applicable to the Model 172 airplanes are included here. Procedure instructions follow.

PREVENTIVE MAINTENANCE ITEMS

1. Removal, installation and repair of landing gear tires.
2. (Does not apply to the 172.)
3. Servicing landing gear struts by adding oil, air, or both.
4. Servicing landing gear wheel bearings, such as cleaning and greasing.
5. Replacing defective safety wiring or cotter pins.
6. Lubrication not requiring disassembly other than removal of nonstructural items such as cover plates, cowlings, and fairings.
7. (Does not apply to the 172.)
8. Replenishing hydraulic fluid in the hydraulic reservoir.
9. Refinishing decorative coatings of the fuselage, wing, and tail-group surfaces (excluding balanced control surfaces), fairings, cowlings, landing gear, cabin, or cockpit interior when removal or disassembly of any primary structure or operating system is not required.
10. Applying preservative or protective material to components when no disassembly of any primary structure or operating system is involved and when such coating is not prohibited or is not contrary to good practices.
11. Repairing upholstery and decorative furnishings of the cabin or cockpit when it does not require disassembly of any primary structure or operating system or affect the primary structure of the aircraft.

12. Making small, simple repairs to fairings, nonstructural cover plates, cowlings and small patches, and reinforcements not changing the contour so as to interfere with the proper airflow.

13. Replacing side windows where that work does not interfere with the structure or any operating system, such as controls and electrical equipment.

14. Replacing safety belts.

15. Replacing seats or seat parts with replacement parts approved for the aircraft, not involving disassembly of any primary structure or operating system.

16. Troubleshooting and repairing broken landing light wiring circuits.

17. Replacing bulbs, reflectors, and lenses of position and landing lights.

18. Replacing wheels and skis where no weight and balance computation is required.

19. Replacing any cowling not requiring removal of the propeller or disconnection of flight controls.

20. Replacing or cleaning spark plugs and setting of spark plug gap clearance. (For an excellent package of information about spark plugs, write to any of the plug manufacturers. You'll be rewarded with usage charts, how-tos, and a color chart to grade your plugs. This will assist you with the identification of potential problems.)

21. Replacing any hose connection except hydraulic connections.

22. Replacing prefabricated fuel lines.

23. Cleaning fuel and oil strainers.

24. Replacing batteries and checking fluid level and specific gravity.

25. (Does not apply to the 172.)

26. (Does not apply to the 172.)

27. Replacement or adjustment of nonstructural standard fasteners incidental to operations.

28. (Does not apply to the 172.)

PROCEDURE INSTRUCTIONS
Main Wheel Removal

See Figs. 7-1 through 7-4.

Note: It is not necessary to remove the main wheel to reline brakes or remove brake parts, other than the brake disc or torque plate.

a. Jack up one main wheel of the aircraft at a time. Place the jack at the universal jack point; do not use the brake casting as a jacking point. When using the universal jack point, flexibility of the gear strut will cause the main wheel to slide inboard as the wheel is raised, tilting the jack. The jack must be lowered for a second operation. Jacking both main wheels simultaneously with universal jack points is not recommended.

b. Remove the speed fairing (if installed).

c. Remove the hub cap, cotter pin, and axle nut.

d. Remove the bolts and washers attaching back plate to brake cylinder and remove back plate.

e. Pull the wheel from the axle.

Main Wheel Disassembly

a. Remove the valve core and deflate the tire. Break the tire beads loose from the wheel rims.

WARNING

Injury can result from attempting to separate wheel halves with the tire inflated. Avoid damaging wheel flanges when breaking tire beads loose.

b. Remove the through-bolts and separate the wheel halves, removing the tire, tube, and brake disc.

c. Remove the grease seal rings, felts, and bearing cones from the wheel halves.

Wheel Inspection and Repair

a. Clean all metal parts and the grease seal felts in solvent and dry thoroughly.

b. Inspect the wheel halves for cracks. Cracked wheel halves shall be discarded and new parts used. Sand out nicks, gouges, and corroded areas. When the protective coating has been removed, the area should be cleaned thoroughly, primed with zinc chromate, and repainted with aluminum lacquer.

c. If excessively warped or scored, the brake disc should be replaced with a new part. Sand smooth small nicks and scratches.

d. Carefully inspect the bearing cones and cups for damage and discoloration. After cleaning, pack the cones with clean aircraft wheel bearing grease before installing them in the wheel half.

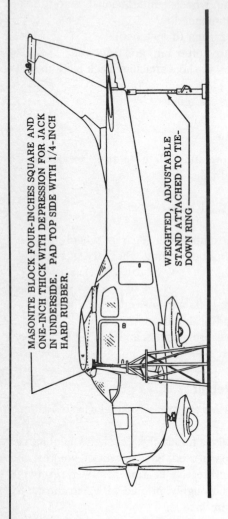

MASONITE BLOCK FOUR-INCHES SQUARE AND ONE-INCH THICK WITH DEPRESSION FOR JACK IN UNDERSIDE. PAD TOP SIDE WITH 1/4-INCH HARD RUBBER.

WEIGHTED, ADJUSTABLE STAND ATTACHED TO TIE-DOWN RING

UNIVERSAL JACK POINT (PART NO. 10004-98) AVAILABLE FROM THE CESSNA SERVICE PARTS CENTER

Wing jacks available from the Cessna Service Parts Center are REGENT Model 4939-30 for use with the SE-576 wing stands. Combination jacks are the REGENT Model 4939-70 for use without wing stands. The 4939-70 jack (70-inch) may be converted to the 4939-30 jack (30-inch) by removing the leg extensions and replacing lower braces with shorter ones. The base of the adjustable tail stand (SE-767) is to be filled with concrete for additional weight as a safety factor. The SE-576 wing stand will also accommodate the SANCOR Model 00226-150 jack. Other equivalent jacks, tail stands, and adapter stands may be used.

1. Lower aircraft tail so that wing jack can be placed under front wing spar just outboard of wing strut.

2. Raise aircraft tail and attach tail stand to tie-down ring. BE SURE the tail stand weighs enough to keep the tail down under all conditions and is strong enough to support aircraft weight.

3. Raise jacks evenly until desired height is reached.

4. The universal jack point may be used to raise only one main wheel. Do not use brake casting as a jack point.

CAUTION

When using the universal jack point, flexibility of the gear strut will cause the main wheel to slide inboard as the wheel is raised, tilting the jack. The jack must be lowered for a second operation. Jacking both main wheels simultaneously with universal jack points is not recommended.

Fig. 7-1. Proper jacking. (courtesy Cessna Aircraft Company)

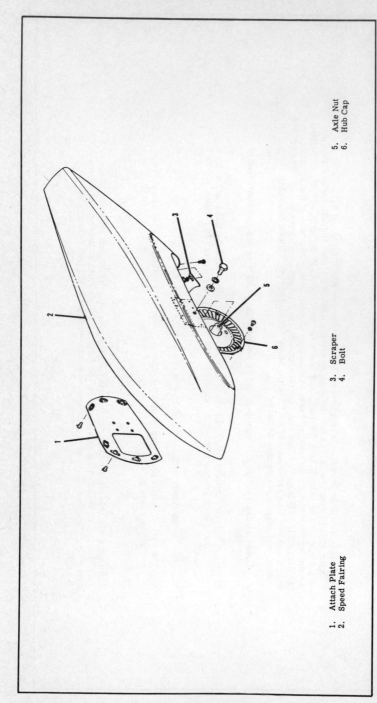

1. Attach Plate
2. Speed Fairing

3. Scraper
4. Bolt

5. Axle Nut
6. Hub Cap

Fig. 7-2. Main wheel speed fairing. (courtesy Cessna Aircraft Company)

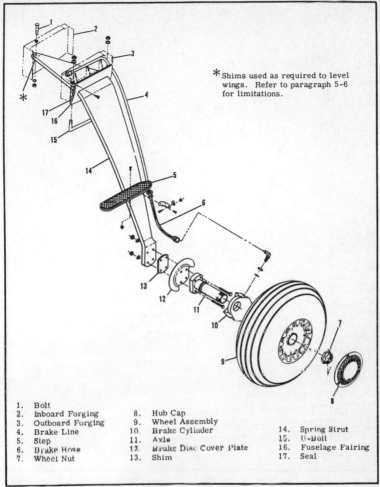

*Shims used as required to level wings. Refer to paragraph 5-6 for limitations.

1.	Bolt	8.	Hub Cap		
2.	Inboard Forging	9.	Wheel Assembly		
3.	Outboard Forging	10.	Brake Cylinder	14.	Spring Strut
4.	Brake Line	11.	Axle	15.	U-Bolt
5.	Step	12.	Brake Disc Cover Plate	16.	Fuselage Fairing
6.	Brake Hose	13.	Shim	17.	Seal
7.	Wheel Nut				

Fig. 7-3. Main gear installation. (courtesy Cessna Aircraft Company)

Main Wheel Assembly

a. Insert the through-bolts through the brake disc and position it in the inner wheel half, using the bolts to guide the disc. Ascertain that the disc is bottomed in the wheel half.

b. Position the tire and tube with the tube inflation valve through the hole in the outboard wheel half.

c. Place the inner wheel half in position on the outboard wheel half. Apply a light force to bring the wheel halves together. While maintaining the light force, assemble a washer and nut on one through-bolt and tighten snugly. Assemble the remaining washers

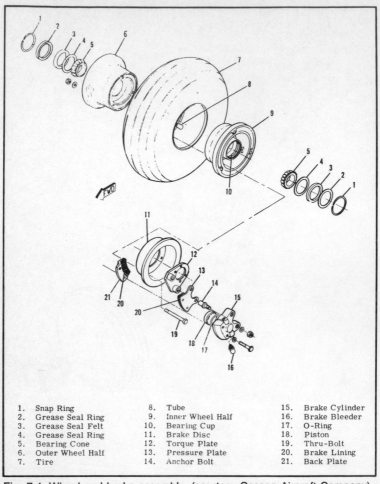

1.	Snap Ring	8.	Tube	15.	Brake Cylinder
2.	Grease Seal Ring	9.	Inner Wheel Half	16.	Brake Bleeder
3.	Grease Seal Felt	10.	Bearing Cup	17.	O-Ring
4.	Grease Seal Ring	11.	Brake Disc	18.	Piston
5.	Bearing Cone	12.	Torque Plate	19.	Thru-Bolt
6.	Outer Wheel Half	13.	Pressure Plate	20.	Brake Lining
7.	Tire	14.	Anchor Bolt	21.	Back Plate

Fig. 7-4. Wheel and brake assembly. (courtesy Cessna Aircraft Company)

and nuts on the through-bolts and torque to the value marked on the wheel.

CAUTION
Uneven or improper torque of the through-bolt nuts can cause failure of the bolts, with resultant wheel failure.

    d. Clean and pack the bearing cones with new aircraft wheel bearing grease.

    e. Assemble the bearing cones, grease seal belts, and rings into the wheel halves.

f. Inflate the tire to seat the tire beads, then adjust inflation to the correct pressure (see owner's manual).

Main Wheel Installation

a. Place the wheel assembly on the axle.

b. Install the axle nut and tighten until a slight bearing drag is obvious when the wheel is rotated. Back off the axle nut to the nearest castellation and install a cotter pin.

c. Place the brake back plate in position and secure it with bolts and washers.

d. Install the hub cap.

CAUTION

If you have speed fairings, be sure to check the scraper clearance before aircraft operation.

Nosewheel Removal and Installation

See Figs. 7-5 through 7-7.

a. Weight or tie down the tail of the aircraft to raise the nosewheel off the ground.

b. Remove the nosewheel axle bolt.

c. Pull the nosewheel assembly from the fork and remove the spacers and axle tube from the nosewheel. Loosen the scraper if necessary.

d. Reverse the preceding steps to install the nosewheel. Tighten the axle bolt until a slight bearing drag is obvious when the wheel is rotated. Back off the axle nut to the nearest castellation and install a cotter pin.

CAUTION

If you have speed fairings, be sure to check the scraper clearance before aircraft operation.

Nosewheel Disassembly

a. Remove the hub cap, completely deflate the tire, and break the tire beads loose.

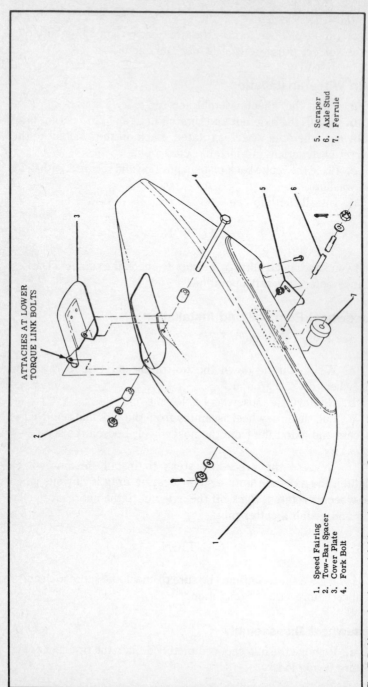

ATTACHES AT LOWER
TORQUE LINK BOLTS

1. Speed Fairing
2. Tow-Bar Spacer
3. Cover Plate
4. Fork Bolt

5. Scraper
6. Axle Stud
7. Ferrule

Fig. 7-5. Nosewheel speed fairing. (courtesy Cessna Aircraft Company)

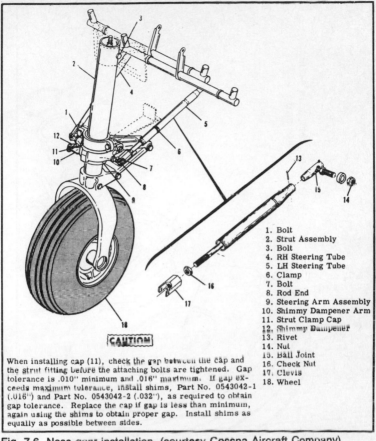

1. Bolt
2. Strut Assembly
3. Bolt
4. RH Steering Tube
5. LH Steering Tube
6. Clamp
7. Bolt
8. Rod End
9. Steering Arm Assembly
10. Shimmy Dampener Arm
11. Strut Clamp Cap
12. Shimmy Dampener
13. Rivet
14. Nut
15. Ball Joint
16. Check Nut
17. Clevis
18. Wheel

CAUTION

When installing cap (11), check the gap between the cap and the strut fitting before the attaching bolts are tightened. Gap tolerance is .010" minimum and .016" maximum. If gap exceeds maximum tolerance, install shims, Part No. 0543042-1 (.016") and Part No. 0543042-2 (.032"), as required to obtain gap tolerance. Replace the cap if gap is less than minimum, again using the shims to obtain proper gap. Install shims as equally as possible between sides.

Fig. 7-6. Nose gear installation. (courtesy Cessna Aircraft Company)

WARNING

Injury can result from attempting to separate wheel halves with the tire inflated. Avoid damaging wheel flanges when breaking tire beads loose.

b. Remove through-bolts and separate wheel halves.

c. Remove the tire and tube from the wheel halves.

d. Remove the bearing retaining rings, grease felt seals, and bearing cones.

Nosewheel Inspection and Repair

See section on Main Wheels (Wheel Inspection and Repair).

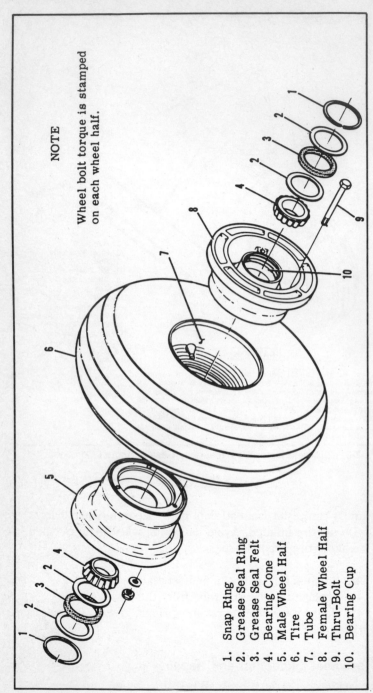

NOTE

Wheel bolt torque is stamped on each wheel half.

1. Snap Ring
2. Grease Seal Ring
3. Grease Seal Felt
4. Bearing Cone
5. Male Wheel Half
6. Tire
7. Tube
8. Female Wheel Half
9. Thru-Bolt
10. Bearing Cup

Fig. 7-7. Nosewheel. (courtesy Cessna Aircraft Company)

Nosewheel Assembly

a. Insert the tire and tube on a wheel half and position the valve stem through the hole in the wheel half.

b. Insert the through-bolts, position the other wheel half, and secure with nuts and washers. Take care to avoid pinching the tube between the wheel halves. Tighten the bolts evenly to the torque value marked on the wheel.

CAUTION

Uneven or improper torque of the through-bolt nuts can cause failure of the bolts, with the resultant wheel failure.

c. Clean and pack the bearing cones with new aircraft wheel bearing grease.

d. Assemble the bearing cones, seals, and retainers into the wheel halves.

e. Inflate the tire to seat the tire beads, then adjust to the correct pressure (see owner's manual).

f. Install the spacers, axle tube and hub caps, and install wheel assembly as described in Nosewheel Removal and Installation.

Nose Gear Shock Strut

See Figs. 7-8 through 7-11.

Fig. 7-8. Nose gear strut needing attention.

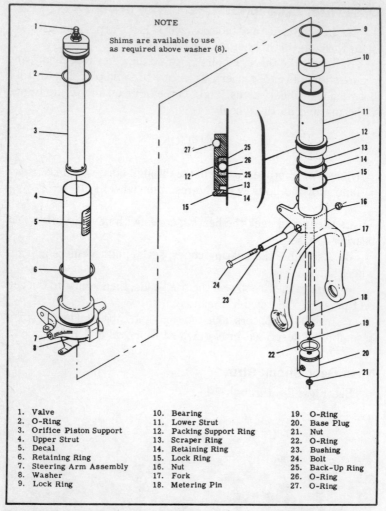

NOTE

Shims are available to use as required above washer (8).

1. Valve	10. Bearing	19. O-Ring
2. O-Ring	11. Lower Strut	20. Base Plug
3. Orifice Piston Support	12. Packing Support Ring	21. Nut
4. Upper Strut	13. Scraper Ring	22. O-Ring
5. Decal	14. Retaining Ring	23. Bushing
6. Retaining Ring	15. Lock Ring	24. Bolt
7. Steering Arm Assembly	16. Nut	25. Back-Up Ring
8. Washer	17. Fork	26. O-Ring
9. Lock Ring	18. Metering Pin	27. O-Ring

Fig. 7-9. Nosewheel gear strut. (courtesy Cessna Aircraft Company)

The nose gear shock strut requires periodic checking to ensure that the strut is filled with hydraulic fluid and is inflated to the correct air pressure. To service the nose gear strut, proceed as follows:

a. Remove the valve cap and release the air pressure.

b. Remove the valve housing.

c. Compress the nose gear to its shortest length and fill the strut with hydraulic fluid to the bottom of the filler hole.

d. Raise the nose of the aircraft, extend and compress the strut

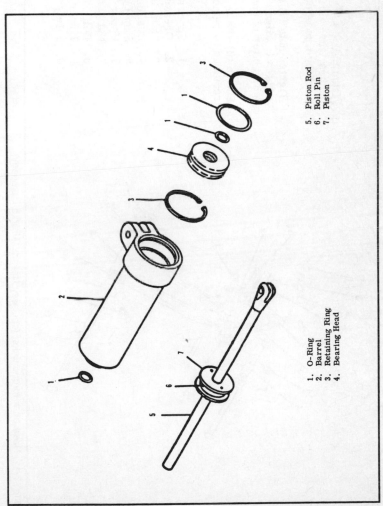

Fig. 7-10. Nose gear shimmy damper. (courtesy Cessna Aircraft Company)

1. O-Ring
2. Barrel
3. Retaining Ring
4. Bearing Head
5. Piston Rod
6. Roll Pin
7. Piston

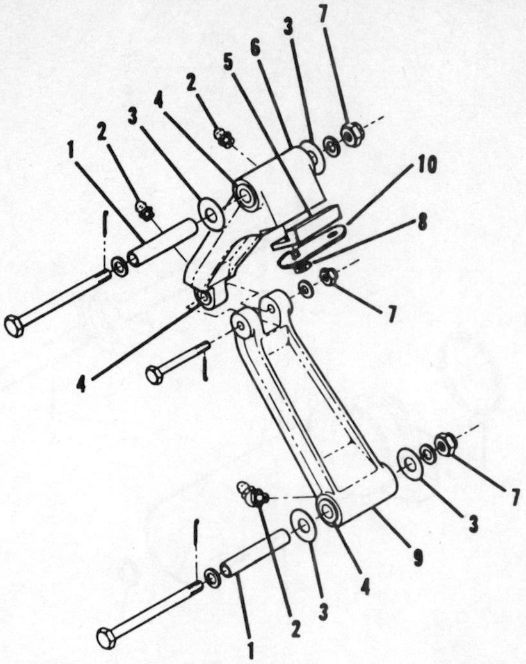

NOTE

Tighten bolts (8) to 20-25 pound-inches, then safety the bolts by bending tips of safety lug (10).

Tighten nuts (7) snugly, then tighten to align next castellation with cotter pin hole.

Shims (3) are available to use as required to remove any looseness.

1. Spacer
2. Grease Fitting
3. Shim
4. Bushing
5. Stop Lug
6. Upper Torque Link
7. Nut
8. Bolt
9. Lower Torque Link
10. Safety Lug

Fig. 7-11. Nose gear torque links. (courtesy Cessna Aircraft Company)

several times to expel any entrapped air, then lower the nose of the aircraft and repeat Step c.

e. With the strut compressed, install the valve housing assembly.

f. With the nosewheel off the ground, inflate the strut (check owner's manual for exact pressure).

NOTE

Keep the nose gear shock strut clean of dust and grit, which may harm the seals in the strut barrel.

Lubrication

See Figs. 7-12 through 7-14.

Lubrication requirements are shown in the associated figures.

Before adding grease to grease fittings, wipe dirt from the fitting. Lubricate until grease appears around the parts being lubricated, then wipe excess grease away.

Wheel bearings should be cleaned and repacked at 500-hour intervals, unless heavy use or dirt strip operations occur. If the latter is the case, then service every 100 hours.

Lubricate the nose gear torque links every 50 hours of operation (more often under dusty conditions).

Engine lubrication will be determined by your particular aircraft's owner's manual. However, as a rule of thumb, never exceed 50 hours between oil changes. Oil is cheap, and I never heard of an engine that failed due to clean oil.

Oil changing for the airplane owner is no more complicated than for the family automobile. However, there is something you should do with the oil that is not normally done with auto oil. This is to obtain an engine oil analysis at each oil change.

Engine oil analysis will give indications of what is wearing—and, over a period of time, how *quickly* it is wearing. Engine oil analysis services are available from several companies, many of which advertise in *Trade-A-Plane* and other aviation journals.

At oil change time, you may decide to put an oil additive in the crankcase, along with the regular engine oil. The object of these additives is to reduce engine wear, resulting in longer engine life. One such additive is MICROLON, a Teflon product, approved by the FAA under FAR 33.49. MICROLON is a one-time additive. That means it is added to the oil only once in the life of the engine. After initial introduction to the crankcase oil, the product bonds

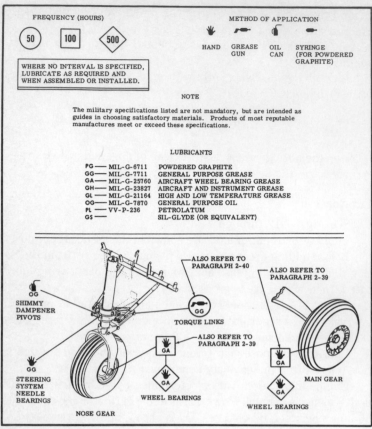

Fig. 7-12. Lubrication chart. (courtesy Cessna Aircraft Company)

itself to all surfaces within the engine, providing extremely good lubricating properties. MICROLON is available from: Econo Systems, 745 Penny Dr., Pittsburgh, PA 15235.

Hydraulic Brake Systems

Check brake master cylinders and refill with hydraulic fluid as required every 100 hours.

Fairing Repair

For fiberglass:

a. Remove the fairing and drill a hole to stop the crack from getting larger.

b. Dust the inside of the surface to be repaired with baking soda, then position a small piece of fiberglass cloth over the crack and saturate the entire area with cyanoacrylate (Super Glue). Repeat Step b.

c. From the outside, fill the crack with baking soda and harden with cyanoacrylate.

d. Sand smooth and repaint.

For metal:

a. Remove the fairing and drill a stop hole at the end of the crack to keep it from continuing further.

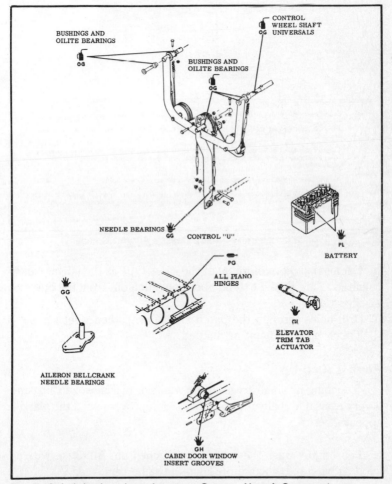

Fig. 7-13. Lubrication chart. (courtesy Cessna Aircraft Company)

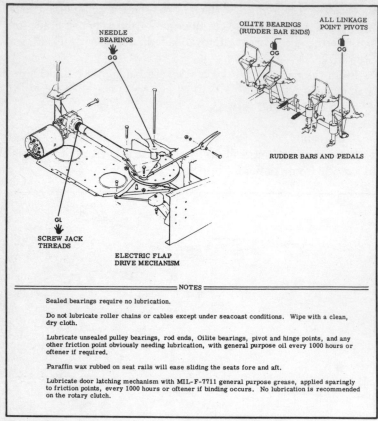

NEEDLE BEARINGS
GG

OILITE BEARINGS (RUDDER BAR ENDS)
OG

ALL LINKAGE POINT PIVOTS
OG

RUDDER BARS AND PEDALS

GL
SCREW JACK THREADS

ELECTRIC FLAP DRIVE MECHANISM

NOTES

Sealed bearings require no lubrication.

Do not lubricate roller chains or cables except under seacoast conditions. Wipe with a clean, dry cloth.

Lubricate unsealed pulley bearings, rod ends, Oilite bearings, pivot and hinge points, and any other friction point obviously needing lubrication, with general purpose oil every 1000 hours or oftener if required.

Paraffin wax rubbed on seat rails will ease sliding the seats fore and aft.

Lubricate door latching mechanism with MIL-F-7711 general purpose grease, applied sparingly to friction points, every 1000 hours or oftener if binding occurs. No lubrication is recommended on the rotary clutch.

Fig. 7-14. Lubrication chart. (courtesy Cessna Aircraft Company)

b. Cut a small piece of metal of the same type as the fairing being repaired. This should extend about one inch out from the crack in all directions.

c. Drill holes through the patch and fairing, then rivet same.

d. Touch up with paint as needed.

Paint Touch-Up

Touching-up small areas on the wings or fuselage of an airplane is very easy, and really makes a marked improvement in the plane's appearance.

a. Thoroughly wash the area to be touched up. All preservatives such as wax and silicone products must be removed.

b. If there is any loose or flaking paint, it must be removed. Carefully use very fine sandpaper for this purpose. Do not sand the bare metal.

c. If bare metal is exposed, it must be primed with an aircraft-type zinc chromate primer.

d. Using sweeping spray strokes, apply at least two coats of touch-up paint in a color matching the original surface.

For custom-packaged touch-up paints in spray cans, contact: Custom Aerosol Products, Inc., P.O. Box 1014, Allen, TX 75002, phone: (214) 727-6912.

Cabin Upholstery

See Fig. 7-15. There is probably no more hair-tearing job for the do-it-yourself airplane fixer-upper than the removal and installation of a headliner. Follow these simple instructions, and you can't miss:

Headliner Removal

a. Remove the sun visors, all inside finish strips and plates, door post upper shields, front spar trim shield, dome light panel, and any other visible retainers securing the headliner.

b. Work the edges of the headliner free from the metal tabs that hold the fabric.

c. Starting at the front of the headliner, work the headliner down, removing the screws through the metal tabs which hold the wire bows to the cabin top. Pry loose the outer ends of the bows from the retainers above the doors. Detach each wire bow in succession.

Note: Always work from front to rear when removing the headliner; it is impossible to detach the wire bows when working from rear to front.

d. Remove the headliner assembly and bows from the airplane.

Note: Due to the difference in length and contour of the wire bows, each bow should be tagged to assure proper location in the headliner.

e. Remove the spun glass soundproofing panels (these are held in place by glue).

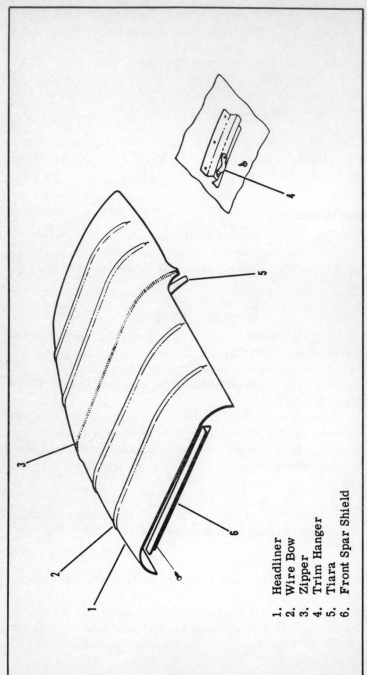

1. Headliner
2. Wire Bow
3. Zipper
4. Trim Hanger
5. Tiara
6. Front Spar Shield

Fig. 7-15. Cabin headliner. (courtesy Cessna Aircraft Company)

Headliner Installation

a. Before installing the headliner, check all items concealed by the headliner to see that they are mounted securely. Use wide cloth tape to secure loose wires to the fuselage, and to seal any openings in the wing roots. Straighten any tabs bent during the removal of the old headliner.

b. Apply cement to the skin areas where the soundproofing panels are not supported by wire bows, and press the panels into place.

c. Insert wire bows into the headliner seams, and secure the rearmost edges of the headliner after positioning the two bows at the rear of the headliner. Stretch the material along the edges to make sure it is properly centered, but do not stretch it tight enough to destroy the ceiling contours or distort the wire bows. Secure the edges of the headliner with sharp tabs, or, where necessary, rubber cement.

d. Work the headliner forward, installing each wire bow in place with the tabs. Wedge the ends of the wire bows into the retainer strips. Stretch the headliner just taut enough to avoid wrinkles and maintain a smooth contour.

e. When all bows are in place and fabric edges are secured, trim off any excess fabric and reinstall all items removed

Seat Re-Covery

Re-covering the seats is generally easier (less hair pulled out) than installing a headliner. My only advice in seat re-covery is to work in a well-ventilated area, or the glue you'll be working with will have you flying without the airplane.

Due to the wide selection of materials and styles available, I recommend you either contract the job with a professional aviation interior shop, or contact a supplier of complete interiors or slip covers. The latter method is recommended if you are the hands-on type, and also want to save a dollar. One such supplier is Cooper Aviation Supply Co., 2149 E. Pratt Blvd., Elk Grove Village, IL 60007 (Fig. 7-16). Check *Trade-A-Plane* for listings of other suppliers.

Another alternative for seats and carpets is the aircraft wrecking yards. They too advertise in *Trade-A-Plane*.

Side Window Replacement

A movable window, hinged at the top, is installed in the left

Fig. 7-16. Superflite Premium Seat Covers. (courtesy Cooper Aviation, 2149 E. Pratt Blvd., Elk Grove, IL 60007)

door (may also be installed in the right door). The window assembly may be replaced by pulling the hinge pins and disconnecting the window stop (Fig. 7-17). To remove the frame from the plastic, it is necessary to drill out the blind rivets where the frame is spliced. When replacing a window in a frame, make sure that the sealing strip and an adequate coating of a sealing compound (Presstite No. 579.6) are used all around the edges of the plastic panel.

Safety Belts

Safety belts must be replaced when they are frayed, cut, or the latches become defective. Attaching hardware should be replaced if faulty. Use only approved safety belts.

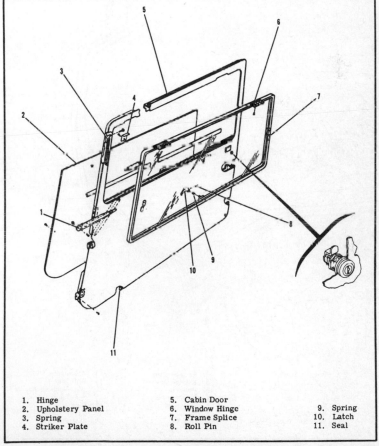

1. Hinge	5. Cabin Door		
2. Upholstery Panel	6. Window Hinge	9.	Spring
3. Spring	7. Frame Splice	10.	Latch
4. Striker Plate	8. Roll Pin	11.	Seal

Fig. 7-17. Cabin door and movable window. (courtesy Cessna Aircraft Company)

Seats

See Figs. 7-18 and 7-19. Individual seats are equipped with manually operated reclining seat backs. Rollers permit the seats to slide forward and back on seat rails. Pins, which engage various holes in the seat rails, lock the seats in selected positions. Stops limit ultimate travel.

Removal of a seat is accomplished by removing the stops and moving the seats forward and back on the rails to disengage them from the rails. Installation is in reverse order.

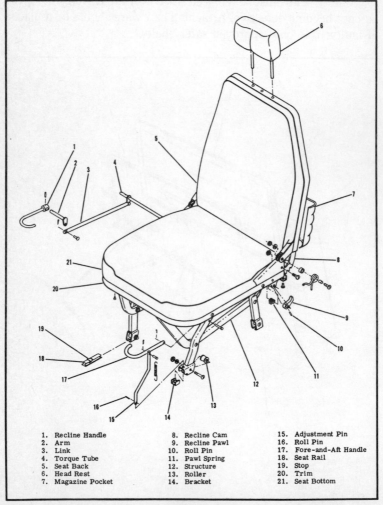

1. Recline Handle	8. Recline Cam	15. Adjustment Pin
2. Arm	9. Recline Pawl	16. Roll Pin
3. Link	10. Roll Pin	17. Fore-and-Aft Handle
4. Torque Tube	11. Pawl Spring	18. Seat Rail
5. Seat Back	12. Structure	19. Stop
6. Head Rest	13. Roller	20. Trim
7. Magazine Pocket	14. Bracket	21. Seat Bottom

Fig. 7-18. Standard single seat. (courtesy Cessna Aircraft Company)

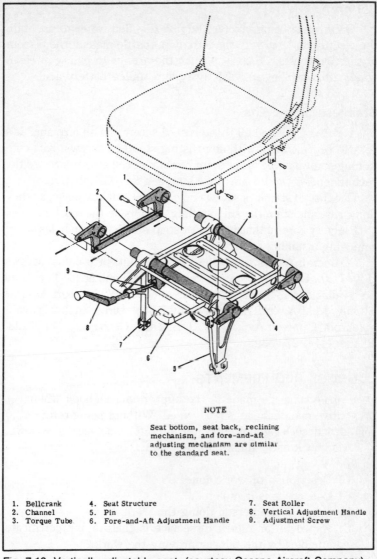

NOTE

Seat bottom, seat back, reclining
mechanism, and fore-and-aft
adjusting mechanism are similar
to the standard seat.

1. Bellcrank	4. Seat Structure	7. Seat Roller
2. Channel	5. Pin	8. Vertical Adjustment Handle
3. Torque Tube	6. Fore-and-Aft Adjustment Handle	9. Adjustment Screw

Fig. 7-19. Vertically adjustable seat. (courtesy Cessna Aircraft Company)

WARNING

It is *extremely* important that the pilot's seat stops be installed,
since acceleration and deceleration could possibly permit the
seat to become disengaged from the seat rails and create a
hazardous situation, especially during takeoff and landing.

181

Battery

Battery servicing involves adding distilled water to maintain the electrolyte level with the horizontal baffle plate at the bottom of the filler holes. Be sure to flush the area with plenty of clean water after refilling to wash away any spilled battery acid.

Stainless Screw Kits

Have you noticed all those rusted screws on an airplane? It's easy to replace them with non-rusting stainless screws. Kits containing screws in the proper number and of the proper size are the recommended way to purchase supplies for this job.

The use of stainless screws on airplanes makes sense, as they don't rust and stain the surrounding area as do the stock screws.

Be very careful that you don't strip out the screw holes when removing/installing screws.

Trimcraft Aviation supplies packaged kits of stainless screws (Fig. 7-20). Each kit contains everything you will need. Their kits are available from Sporty's, Air Components, Wil Neubert Aircraft Supply, J&M Aircraft, and from any FBOs. Direct supply is available from Trimcraft Aviation, P.O. Box 488, Genoa City, WI 53128. Phone: (414) 279-6896.

LOGBOOK REQUIREMENTS

Entries must be made in the appropriate logbook whenever preventive maintenance is performed. Without being returned to service with such logbook entry, the aircraft cannot legally be flown.

A logbook entry must include:

- ☐ Description of work done.
- ☐ Date work is completed.
- ☐ Name of the person doing the work.
- ☐ Approval for return to service (signature and certificate number) by the pilot approving the work.

The FARs require that all preventive maintenance work must be done in such a manner, and by use of materials of such quality, that the airframe, engine propeller, or assembly worked on will be at least equal to its original condition.

I strongly advise that before you undertake any of these allowable preventive maintenance procedures, you discuss your plans with a licensed mechanic. The instructions/advice you receive from

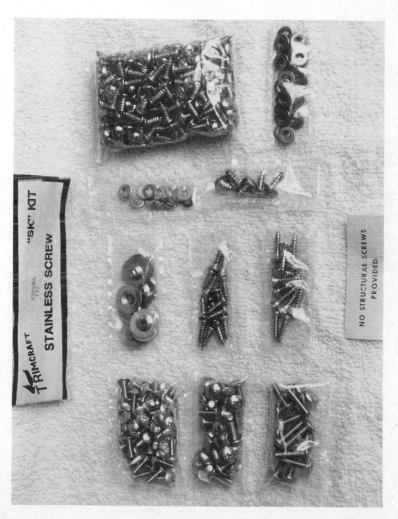

Fig. 7-20. Trimcraft stainless steel screw kit for the 172.

him may help you avoid making costly mistakes. You may have to pay the mechanic for his time, but it will be money well-spent—and, after all, his time is his money.

In addition to talking with your mechanic, get your own tools. Don't borrow from your friend the mechanic, or he won't be your friend very long.

Properly performed preventive maintenance gives the pilot/owner a better understanding of his airplane, affords substantial maintenance savings, and gives a feeling of accomplishment.

For an in-depth study of preventive maintenance, see *Lightplane Owner's Maintenance Guide*, TAB #2244, by Cliff Dossey.

STORAGE

There is much more to storing an aircraft than mere hangaring or parking. Unfortunately, a large number of owner/pilots pay little heed to the proper preserving of their airplanes during periods of non-use.

Engine Storage

The following information is taken from Teledyne Continental Motors Service Bulletin M84-10 Rev.1:

TO: Aircraft Manufacturers, Distributors, Dealers, Engine Overhaul Facilities, Owners and Operators of Teledyne Continental Motors' Aircraft Engines.
SUBJECT: ENGINE PRESERVATION FOR ACTIVE AND STORED AIRCRAFT MODELS AFFECTED:

All Models
Gentlemen:
Engines in aircraft that are flown occasionally tend to exhibit cylinder wall corrosion more than engines in aircraft that are flown frequently.

Of particular concern are new engines or engines with new or freshly honed cylinders after a top or major overhaul. In areas of high humidity, there have been instances where corrosion has been found in such cylinders after an inactive period of only a few days. When cylinders have been operated for approximately 50 hours, the varnish deposited on the cylinder walls offers some protection against corrosion. Hence a two-step program for flyable storage category is recommended.

Obviously, even then proper steps must be taken on engines used infrequently to lessen the possibility of corrosion. This is especially true if the aircraft is based near the sea coast or in areas of high humidity and flown less than once a week.

In all geographical areas, the best method of preventing corrosion of the cylinders and other internal parts of the engine is to fly the aircraft at least once a week, long enough to reach normal operating temperatures, which will vaporize moisture ad other byproducts of combustion. In consideration of the circumstances mentioned, TCM has listed three reasonable minimum preservation procedures that, if implemented, will minimize the detriments of rust and corrosion. It is the owner's responsibility to choose a program that is viable to the particular aircraft's mission.

Aircraft engine storage recommendations are broken down into the following categories:

A. Flyable Storage (Program I or II)
B. Temporary Storage (up to 90 days)
C. Indefinite Storage
A. Flyable Storage (Program I or II)
Program I—Engines or cylinders with less than 50 operating hours:
    a. Propeller pull-through every five days as per paragraph A2; and
    b. Fly every 15 days as per paragraph A3.
Program II—Engines or cylinders with more than 50 operating hours to TBO if not flown weekly:
    a. Propeller pull-through every seven days as per paragraph A2; and
    b. Fly every 30 days as per paragraph A3.

    1. Service aircraft per normal airframe manufacturer's instructions.
    2. The propeller should be rotated by hand without running the engine. For four- and six-cylinder straight-drive engines, rotate the engine six revolutions, then stop the propeller 45 to 90 degrees from the original position. For six-cylinder geared engines, rotate the propeller four revolutions and stop

the propeller 30 to 60 degrees from the original position.

CAUTION

For maximum safety, accomplish engine rotation as follows:

a. Verify that the magneto switches are OFF.
b. Throttle position to CLOSED.
c. Mixture control to IDLE CUT-OFF.
d. Set brakes and block the aircraft's wheels.
e. Leave the aircraft tiedowns installed and verify that the cabin door latch is open.
f. Do not stand within the arc of the propeller blades while turning the propeller.

3. The aircraft should be flown for thirty (30) minutes, reaching, but not exceeding, normal oil and cylinder temperatures. If the aircraft cannot be flown, it should be represerved in accordance with "B" (Temporary Storage) or "C" (Indefinite Storage). Ground running is not an acceptable substitute for flying.

Note: If "b." in each program cannot be accomplished on schedule due to weather, maintenance, etc., pull the propeller through daily and accomplish as soon as possible. It is necessary that for future reference, if required, the propeller pull-through and flight time be recorded and verified in the engine maintenance record/log with the date, time and signature.

B. Temporary Storage (up to 90 days)

1. Preparation for Storage

a. Remove the top spark plug and spray preservative oil (Lubrication Oil—Contact and Volatile Corrosion—Inhibited, MIL-L-46002, Grade 1) at room temperature through the upper spark plug hole of each cylinder with the piston approximately in bottom dead center position. Rotate the crankshaft as each pair of opposite cylinders is sprayed. Stop the crankshaft with no piston at top dead center. A pressure pot or pump-up type garden pressure sprayer may be used. The spray head should have ports around the circumference to allow complete coverage of the cylinder walls.

Note: Listed below are some approved preservative oils recommended for use in Teledyne Continental engines for temporary and indefinite storage:
MIL-L-46002, Grade 1 Oils
NOX RUST VCI-105
    Daubert Chemical Company
    4700 S. Central Avenue
    Chicago, Illinois 60600
PETROTECT VA
    Pennsylvania Refining Company
    Butler, Pennsylvania 16001
    b. Re-spray each cylinder without rotating the crank. To thoroughly cover all surfaces of the cylinder interior, move the nozzle or spray gun from the top to the bottom of the cylinder.
    c. Re-install spark plugs.
    d. Apply preservative to the engine interior by spraying the above specified oil (approximately two ounces) through the oil filler tube.
    e. Seal all engine openings exposed to the atmosphere using suitable plugs, or moisture-resistant taper and attach red streamers at each point.
    f. Engines, with propellers installed, that are preserved for storage in accordance with this section should have a tag affixed to the propeller in a conspicuous place with the following notation on the tag:
DO NOT TURN PROPELLER—ENGINE PRESERVED; PRESERVATION DATE
_____.

Note: If the engine is not returned to flyable status at the expiration of the Temporary (90-day) Storage, it must be preserved in accordance with the Indefinite Storage procedures.
    2. Preparation for Service

    a. Remove seals, tape, paper, and streamers from all openings.
    b. With bottom spark plugs removed from the

cylinders, hand turn the propeller several revolutions to clear excess preservative oil, then re-install the spark plugs.

c. Conduct normal start-up procedure.

d. Give the aircraft a thorough cleaning and visual inspection. A test flight is recommended.

C. Indefinite Storage

1. Preparation for Storage

a. Drain the engine oil and refill with MIL-C-6529 Type II. The aircraft should be flown for thirty (30) minutes, reaching, but not exceeding normal oil and cylinder temperatures. Allow the engine to cool to ambient temperature. Accomplish steps 1.a. and 1.b. of Temporary Storage.

Note: MIL-C-6529 Type II may be formulated by thoroughly mixing one part compound MIL-C-6529 Type I (Esso Rust-Ban 628, Cosmoline No. 1223 or equivalent) with three parts new lubricating oil of the grade recommended for service (all at room temperature). Single grade oil is recommended.

b. Apply preservative to the engine interior by spraying MIL-L-46002, Grade 1 oil (approximately two ounces) through the oil filler tube.

2. Install dehydrator plugs MS27215-1 or -2, in each of the top spark plug holes, making sure that each plug is blue in color when installed. Protect and support the spark plug leads with AN-4060 protectors.

3. If the engine is equipped with a pressure-type carburetor, preserve this component by the following method: Drain the carburetor by removing the drain and vapor vent plugs from the regulator and fuel control unit. With the mixture control in "Rich" position, inject lubricating oil, grade 1010, into the fuel inlet at a pressure not to exceed 10 psi until oil flows from the vapor vent opening. Allow excess oil to drain, plug the inlet, and tighten and safety the drain and vapor vent plugs. Wire the throttle in the open position, place bags of desiccant in the intake, and seal the opening with moisture-resistant paper and tape, or a cover plate.

4. If the carburetor is removed from the engine, place a bag of desiccant in the throat of the carburetor air adapter. Seal the adapter with moisture-resistant paper and tape or a cover plate.

5. The TCM fuel injection system does not require any special preservation preparation. For preservation of the Bendix RSA-7DA1 fuel injection system, refer to the Bendix Operation and Service Manual.

6. Place a bag of desiccant in the exhaust pipes and seal the openings with moisture resistant tape.

7. Seal the cold air inlet to the heater muff with moisture resistant tape to exclude moisture and foreign objects.

8. Seal the engine breather by inserting a dehydrator MS27215-2 plug in the breather hose and clamping in place.

9. Attach a red streamer to each place on the engine where bags of desiccant are placed. Either attach red streamers outside of the sealed area with tape or to the inside of the sealed area with safety wire to prevent wicking of moisture into the sealed area.

10. Engines, with propellers installed, that are preserved for storage in accordance with this section should have a tag affixed to the propeller in a conspicuous place with the following notation on the tag: DO NOT TURN PROPELLER—ENGINE PRESERVED; PRESERVATION DATE _____.

Procedures necessary for returning an aircraft to service are as follows:

1. Remove the cylinder dehydrator plugs and all paper, tape, desiccant bags, and streamers used to preserve the engine.

2. Drain the corrosion preventive mixture and reservice with recommended lubricating oil.

WARNING

When returning the aircraft to service, do not use the corrosion preventive oil referenced in paragraph C.1.a. for more than 25 hours.

3. If the carburetor has been preserved with oil, drain it by removing the drain and vapor vent plugs from the regulator and fuel control unit. With the mixture control in "Rich"

position, inject service-type gasoline into the fuel inlet at a pressure not to exceed 10 psi until all of the oil is flushed from the carburetor. Re-install the carburetor plugs and attach the fuel line.

4. With the bottom plugs removed, rotate the propeller to clear excess preservative oil from the cylinders.

5. Re-install the spark plugs and rotate the propeller by hand through compression strokes of all the cylinders to check for possible liquid lock. Start the engine in the normal manner.

6. Give the aircraft a thorough cleaning, visual inspection and test flight per airframe manufacturer's instructions.

Aircraft stored in accordance with the indefinite storage procedures should be inspected per the following instructions:

1. Aircraft prepared for indefinite storage should have the cylinder dehydrator plugs visually inspected every 15 days. The plugs should be changed as soon as their color indicates unsafe conditions of storage. If the dehydrator plugs have changed color on one-half or more of the cylinders, all desiccant material on the engine should be replaced.

2. The cylinder bores of all engines prepared for indefinite storage should be re-sprayed with corrosion preventive mixture every six months, or more frequently if a bore inspection indicates corrosion has started earlier than six months. Replace all desiccant and dehydrator plugs. Before spraying, the engine should be inspected for corrosion as follows: Inspect the interior of at least one cylinder on each engine through the spark plug hole. If the cylinder shows the start of rust, spray the cylinder with corrosion preventive oil and turn the prop over six times, then re-spray all cylinders. Remove at least one rocker box cover from each engine and inspect the valve mechanism.

The above procedures are a general recommendation for our customers. Since local conditions are different and Teledyne Continental Motors has no control over the application, more stringent procedures may be required. Rust and corrosion prevention are the owner's responsibility.

AIRFRAME STORAGE

Although Cessna aircraft are constructed of corrosion-resistant Alclad aluminum, which will last indefinitely under normal conditions, if kept clean, these alloys are subject to oxidation. The first indication of oxidation (corrosion) on unpainted surfaces is the forming of white deposits or spots. On painted surfaces, the paint is discolored or blistered. Storage in a dry hangar is essential to good preservation and should be procured if possible.

Short-Term Storage (Less Than 60 days)

a. Fill the fuel tanks with the correct grade of fuel.

b. Clean and wax the aircraft

c. Clean any grease/oil from the tires and coat them with a tire preservative. Cover the nosewheel to protect it from oil drips.

d. Block up the fuselage to remove the weight from the tires.

Note: Tires will take a set, causing them to become out-of-round, if an aircraft is left parked for more than a few days.

Long-Term Storage (Indefinite)

a. Proceed with items a through d under Short-Term Storage.

b. Lubricate all airframe items and seal or cover openings.

c. Cover all openings to the airframe. This is to keep vermin, insects, and birds out.

d. Remove the battery and store it in a cool, dry place. Service it periodically.

e. Place covers over the windshield and rear windows.

f. Inspect the airframe for signs of corrosion at least monthly. Clean and wax as necessary.

Returning to Service

a. Remove the aircraft from the blocks and check the tires for proper inflation. Check the nose strut for proper inflation.

b. Remove all covers and plugs, and inspect the interior of the airframe for debris and foreign matter.

c. Check the battery and re-install.

d. Clean and inspect the exterior of the aircraft.

EXTERIOR CARE

The care of the exterior of your airplane is not only important in the sense of appearance and value, but in safety as well. Following is a collection of some of the available products for cleaning and preserving your aircraft. These items have been selected as representative of the market. Some of the information is quoted from the manufacturers advertisements.

Windshields

Novus Polish #2 is the answer to windshield maintenance. Mildly abrasive, it will polish out those scratches and pitmarks that collect on Plexiglas. Recommended by aircraft manufacturers: Don't take chances with all-purpose plastic polishes. Novus is gentle, yet tough enough to do the job. Follow this polish with Bugaway for a windshield like new.

Bugaway is a windshield cleaning solvent developed especially for aircraft use. This remarkable formula dissolves insect splatters and bird droppings instantly. Just spray it on, wait 10 seconds, then wipe clean with a soft cloth. It's that simple. Your windshield will be sparkling clean and streak-free. Bugaway will not harm aluminum or painted surfaces.

Bugaway and Novus Polish #2 are available from Connecticut Aviation Products, Inc., P.O. Box 12, East Glastonbury, CT 06025.

Interior Heat and Sunlight Protection

The introduction of solid-state electronics in general aviation has caused great concern among owners about heat buildup within the interior of the parked aircraft.

This heat buildup will not only affect avionics, but will cause problems with instrument panels, upholstery, and a variety of other "plastic things."

Research shows us that the interior temperature of a parked aircraft can reach as much as 185 degrees. This is the reason that many aircraft you see tied down outside have some type of cover over the windshields, either inside or outside (Fig. 7-21).

Inside covers protect the interior and keep heat down by reflecting the sun's rays away with their metalic-type reflective surfaces. The heat shields, as they are called, attach to the interior of the aircraft by means of Velcro fasteners.

Interior reflective heat shields are available from many sources including Connecticut Aviation Products, Inc., P.O. Box 12, East Glastonbury, CT 06025.

Exterior covers will provide similar protection for the interior of the aircraft, yet give additional exterior protection or refueling caps and to fresh air vents.

Exterior reflective heat shields are available from Aero Draft,

Fig. 7-21. Interior reflective heat shield.

430 Budding Ridge, Cheshire, CT 06410.

Interior Surface Protection

The interior of the airplane is seen by all, including the pilot and his passengers. It is also used by all, and is a problem to keep clean. My recommendation is a very thorough cleaning by use of standard automobile cleaning methods, with similar materials, then coating fabric surfaces (seats and carpets) with Scotch Guard, which is available in most grocery stores. Follow the directions on the can for best results.

Exterior Surface Protection

Complete washing with automotive-type cleaners will produce acceptable results, and the materials used will be cheaper than "air-craft cleaners." Automotive wax will also provide adequate protection for painted or unpainted surfaces. When I say wax, that includes the new "space-age" silicone preparations called sealers. Just remember, there are a lot of surfaces on an airplane . . . many square feet.

A new product on the market for sealing aviation paints is TST 5000 by Total Systems Technology, Inc. It is a Teflon-based system that "locks" into the paint for up to five years. The name, by the way is based upon the 500 Teflon particles per inch that are applied to painted surfaces. For further information, contact Total Systems Technology, 65 Terence Dr., Pittsburgh, PA 15236 or call (800) 472-2775.

For those of you interested in polishing a bare metal airplane, there is the Cyclo Wonder Tool, a dual orbital polishing machine. I can say from personal experience that this machine is well worth the investment if you wish to keep a shiny unpainted bird in tip-top condition. It is also useful in stripping before painting, and will polish hard waxes (Fig. 7-22). For further information, contact Cyclo Manufacturing Co., 3841 Eudora Way, P.O. Box 2038, Denver, CO 80201.

Other Cleaning Aids

The following items are available at most grocery stores or automotive supply houses.

Pledge: Use on most hard surfaces including the windshield, vinyl surfaces (seats, dash panel, and doors).

409: Heavy-duty cleaner for the hard-to-remove stuff. Keep it away from the windshield, instruments, and painted surfaces.

Windex: An excellent product for small cleanup jobs. However, keep it away from Plexiglas. *Never use it on the windshield or other*

Fig. 7-22. Cyclo Wonder Tool for polishing. (courtesy Cyclo Manufacturing)

windows! Its use on such surfaces will cause a characteristic clouding, and spoil the clear qualities. In time, you will have to replace the window.

Armor-All: Good for a final coat on the dash panel, kick panels, seats, etc. It makes vinyl look and smell new.

Gunk: Used for degreasing the engine area and front strut. It dissolves grease and can be washed off with water. When using it in the engine compartment, cover the mags and alternator with plastic bags to keep the Gunk and the rinse water out. This product is also good for cleaning the belly. It is reasonably safe on painted surfaces if rinsed per instructions.

WD-40: General lubricant used to stop squeaks and ease movement. It's good on cables, controls, seat runners, and doors. Keep it off the windows.

LPS: A line of several lubricants available in various viscosities. It's similar in use to WD-40, but with more "staying power."

Rubbing compound: Used to clean away stains from exhaust. Use this product carefully, as you could remove the stains *and* the paint by overdoing it.

Touch-up paint: Many colors on airplanes are unavailable to the owner in small quantities for touch-up use. However, don't despair, as a good automotive supply house (and some department stores) have inexpensive cans of spray paint to match almost any automotive color. Try to find one that closely matches your airplane's paint. Remember that a touch-up is just that, not a complete repaint, and don't expect it to be more. Touching-up of small blemishes, chips, etc., is done to protect the airframe—and perhaps make the appearance slightly better.

Tools You Should Carry with You

A small quantity of quality tools should allow the owner to perform maintenance on his airplane. These include:

- ☐ Multipurpose knife (Swiss Army knife).
- ☐ 3/8″ ratchet drive with a flex head as an option.
- ☐ 2, 4, 6-inch 3/8″ extensions.
- ☐ Sockets from 3/8″ to 3/4″ in 1/16″ increments.
- ☐ 6″ crescent wrench.
- ☐ 10″ monkey wrench.
- ☐ 6 or 12-point closed (box) wrenches from 3/8″ to 3/4″. In addition, I recommend a set of open-end wrenches of the same dimensions.

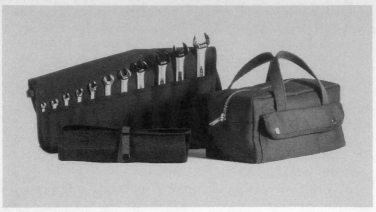

Fig. 7-23. Handy foldable cloth tool bags and pouches are available from Helsper Sewing Co., 80 Highbury Dr., Elgin, IL 60120.

☐ Pair of channel lock pliers (medium size).
☐ Phillips screwdriver set in the three common sizes.
☐ Blade screwdriver set to include short (2″) to long (8″) sizes.
☐ Plastic electrical tape.
☐ Container of assorted nuts and bolts.
☐ Spare set of spark plugs.

A carrying bag or box will be very handy to keep your tools in order and protected (Fig. 7-23).

A PARTING WORD

Again, before you attempt any task, *be sure you know what you are doing*. If unsure, ask someone . . . such as your mechanic. He might charge you for his time in showing you how to perform a step in maintenance, but it is well worth the cost to learn the proper methods. So far as his charging, just remember that he has a large amount of experience in aircraft servicing, you possibly have none, and he will have to take his time to show you what he has learned. This time he takes is his money—after all, he is paid by the hour.

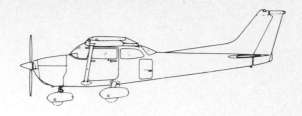

Chapter 8
Updating the Avionics

The Cessna 172 series airplanes are very versatile transporters of people. However, to get all from them that they can provide, you may have to upgrade the avionics—particularly on the older birds, or those minimally equipped (Figs. 8-1 through 8-3).

There are more-or-less set standards in the industry as to how an airplane should be equipped, avionics-wise. There are also FARs setting forth minimum standards for all airplanes, and more demanding standards for those utilized in IFR operations.

Equipment	VFR	IFR
COMM	x	x
NAV	x	x
DME		x
MBR		x
LOC/GS		x
XPNDR	x	x
Audio Panel		x
ELT	x	x
Clock	x	x
Encoding Altimeter		x

Other items that would be nice to have include RNAV, ADF, and LORAN C.

Anything extra added to the recommended minimums is all the better. One place for additions would be in duplicating some equipment: NAV/COMM, LOC/GS, etc.

Fig. 8-1. Example of a very early
Cessna 172 panel.

TYPES OF AVIONICS

COMM:	VHF transceiver for voice radio communications (Figs. 8-4, 8-5).
NAV:	VHF navigation receiver for utilizing VORs (Fig. 8-6).
NAV/COMM:	Combination of COMM and NAV in one unit (Figs. 8-7 through 8-10).
LOC/GS:	Localizer/Glideslope. Visual output is via CDI, with the addition of a horizontal indicator to show glide path.
CDI:	Course Deviation Indicator is panel-mounted and gives a visual output of the NAV radio's data (Figs. 8-11 through 8-16).
PNDR:	Transponder; may or may not have altitude encoding (Figs. 8-17 through 8-20).
ADF:	Automatic Direction Finder (Fig. 8-21).
DME:	Distance Measuring Equipment (Fig. 8-22).
NAV:	Random Area Navigation, microprocessor-based system that allows considerable flexibility in course planning and flying (Fig. 8-23).
LORAN C:	A system of very accurate radio/computer-based navigation completely separate from the VOR based systems (Figs. 8-24, 8-25).
A-Panel:	Audio panel; allows centralized control of all radio equipment (Fig. 8-26).
ELT:	Emergency Locator Transmitter (required by FARs for all but local flying).
MBR:	Marker Beacon Receiver (Fig. 8-27).

FLYING NEEDS

If you are a casual flier, and do little cross-country flying, then

Fig. 8-4. Terra TX720 COMM radio. This particular model is one-half the size of the standard centerline-mounted COMM radio. (courtesy Terra)

Fig. 8-5. Narco HT800 makes a fine back-up COMM radio. (courtesy Narco)

you can get by with a minimum of equipment:

- ☐ NAV/COMM
- ☐ XPNDR
- ☐ ELT

Although it wasn't too many years ago that most cross-country flying was done by pilotage (reading charts and looking out the windows for checkpoints), today's aviator has become accustomed to

Fig. 8-6. Terra TN200 NAV receiver, matching the TX720 in size. (courtesy Terra)

Fig. 8-7. Terra TXN920, a single panel combination of the TX720 COMM and TN200 NAV radios into what is referred to as a NAV/COMM. (courtesy Terra)

Fig. 8-8. Narco MK12D state-of-the-art digital, with memory, NAV/COMM. (courtesy Narco)

Fig. 8-9. King KX175B NAV/COMM (same in appearance as the KX170 series). These are among the most popular NAV/COMMs found in general aviation. (courtesy King)

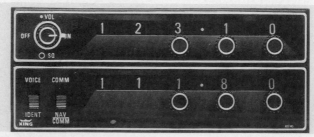

Fig. 8-10. King KX145 NAV/COMM. (courtesy King)

Fig. 8-11. King KI 205 VOR/LOC indicator. (courtesy King)

Fig. 8-12. King KI 204—206 VOR/LOC/GS indicator. Notice the horizontal indicator for glideslope. (courtesy King)

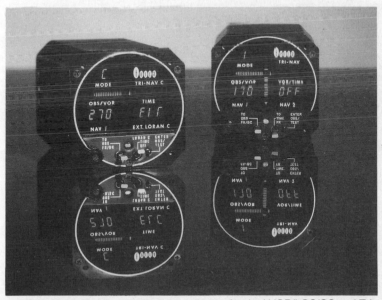

Fig. 8-13. Terra Tri-Nav gas discharge display for dual VOR/LOC/GS and Tri-Nav C for a single VOR/LOC/GS and LORAN. (courtesy Terra)

Fig. 8-14. Davtron digital VOR readout. (courtesy Davtron)

the advantages of modern navigation systems. Therefore, I feel that an airplane equipped in such a minimal fashion would be inappropriate for the typical pilot of today.

If you do a lot of VFR cross-country flying, as most family pilots do, you will need a little more equipment to ease your work-

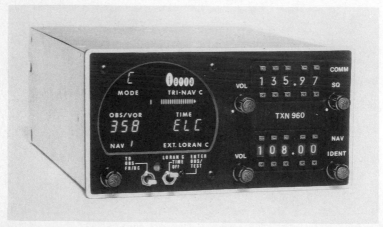

Fig. 8-15. Terra TXN960 NAV/COMM with built-in display. (courtesy Terra)

Fig. 8-16. Narco Escort II NAV/COMM with display all in a unit small enough to fit a standard 3-inch panel hole. (courtesy Narco)

load, and to give you backup in case of failure:

- ☐ Dual NAV/COMM
- ☐ DME
- ☐ XPNDR
- ☐ ELT
- ☐ LORAN C

Fig. 8-17. Terra TRT250 XPNDR. (courtesy Terra)

Fig. 8-18. Narco AT150 XPNDR. (courtesy Narco)

Fig. 8-19. Collins TDR950 XPNDR. (courtesy Collins)

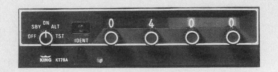

Fig. 8-20. King KT76A XPNDR. (courtesy King)

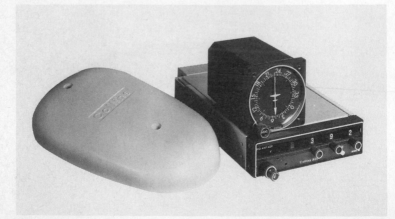

Fig. 8-21. Collins ADF650 shown with antenna and display. (courtesy Collins)

KING   KN 64   DME

```
9 2 . 4      1 8 0      3 1
  NM           KT         MIN
```

RMT   FREQ.   GS/T   DME

KN 64   OFF

1. SOLID STATE TRANSMITTER
2. SIMULTANEOUS READOUT OF DIST., GS, & TTS
3. INTERNAL OR REMOTE CHANNELING
4. COMLETELY PANEL MOUNTED
5. OPERATES 11-33 VDC

Fig. 8-22. King KN64 DME (distance measuring equipment). (courtesy King)

The additional NAV/COMM can be used in easing your workload, as well as providing backup in case of partial equipment failure. If you want to add one more thing that will really ease your workload on long cross-country trips, get an autopilot. It doesn't have to be a complex model; even a wing-leveler would be a great assist.

If you fly IFR—and the Cessna 172s are certainly capable of it—you will need still more equipment, in addition to the above:

☐ LOC/GS

Fig. 8-23. Narco RNAV860 (random area navigation). (courtesy Narco)

Fig. 8-24. II Morrow Apollo II LORAN C "Flybaby" has all federally listed airports and VORs preprogrammed into memory, and allows the entry of 100 more locations. (courtesy II Morrow)

Fig. 8-25. ARNAV 60 LORAN. (courtesy ARNAV)

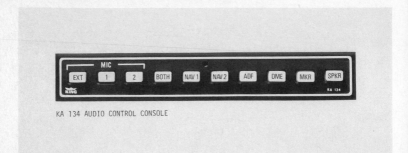

Fig. 8-26. King KA134 audio control panel for selecting of which NAC/COMM/etc. will be used. (courtesy King)

Fig. 8-27. Collins ARMR350 audio control panel with MB (marker beacon). (courtesy Collins)

☐ MBR
☐ ADF
☐ XPNDR (altitude reporting)
☐ RNAV
☐ LORAN C

The entire IFR installation must be certified, so be prepared to spend some money if you are planning to completely re-outfit a plane for IFR. It might be worthwhile entertaining thoughts about changing airplanes, rather than just avionics. Often you can purchase a newer airplane, equipped as you want, for less than it would cost you to update your present airplane.

UPDATING YOUR AIRPLANE

There are several ways of going about filling those vacant spots on your instrument panel. Some are more expensive than others.

New Equipment

New equipment is state-of-the-art, offering the newest innovations, best reliability, and—best of all—a warranty. An additional benefit is the fact that the new solid-state electronics units draw considerably less electric power than did their tube-type predecessors. This is extremely important for the person wanting a "full panel."

New avionics can be purchased from your local avionics dealer, or from a discount house.

You can visit your local dealer and purchase all the equipment you want, and have it installed. Of course, this will be the most expensive route you can take when upgrading your avionics. However, in the long run, it can be the most cost-effective. You'll have new equipment, expert installation, and service backup. You will also have a nearby dealer you can "discuss" problems with, should they arise.

The discount house will be considerably cheaper for the initial purchase; however, you may be left out when the need for warranty service raises its ugly head. Some manufacturers will not honor warranty service requests unless the equipment was purchased from, *and installed by,* an authorized dealer. Perhaps this sounds unfair to you; however, it will keep the authorized dealers in business. And if they stay in business, you can find them to repair your equipment.

Used Equipment

Used avionics can be purchased from dealers or individuals. The aviation magazines and *Trade-A-Plane* are good sources of used equipment. However, a few words of caution about used avionics: *Purchasing nothing:*

- [ ] with tubes in it.
- [ ] more than six years old.
- [ ] made by a defunct manufacturer (parts could be difficult to obtain).
- [ ] "as is."
- [ ] "working when removed."

Used equipment can be a wise investment, but it is very risky unless you happen to be an avionics technician, or have access to one. I recommend against the purchase of used avionics unless you are *very* familiar with the source. Even then, I would not recommend their purchase for use as primary IFR equipment.

Reconditioned Equipment

Currently there are several companies that advertise reconditioned avionics at bargain—or at least low—prices.

The equipment has been removed from service and completely checked out by an avionics shop. Parts that have failed, are near failure, or are likely to fail will have been replaced.

These radios offer a fair buy for the airplane owner, and are usually warrantied by the seller.

However, be advised that reconditioned is not "new." Everything in the unit has been used, but not everything will be replaced during reconditioning. You will have some new parts and some old parts. Being aware of this drawback, I feel that reconditioned equipment purchases make sense for the budget-minded owner. Also, few pieces of reconditioned equipment will exceed six or seven years of age.

LORAN

Long range navigation, called LORAN, is based on low-frequency radio signals, rather than the VHF FAA navaids normally associated with flying. Actually, LORAN was not really intended for general aviation usage, but it has become very popular. The latest type of LORAN is "C," which indicates computer.

The newest versions of LORAN offer distinct advantages over normal VHF navaids such as VORs. Due to the propagation properties of radio waves at the frequencies utilized by LORAN, there is no VHF line-of-sight usable range limit. This means that unlike most VORs, usable only within a short range of less than 50 to 100 miles, LORAN is usable many hundreds of miles from the actual station. This opens up some very interesting possibilities for use.

In small plane flying, much activity is conducted at low (under 2000 feet) altitude, and in very isolated areas . . . i.e., the boondocks! This can be a limiting factor when navigating by use of standard VORs. The use of low altitude means that the VOR may be of little or no use, as the signals are line-of-sight. Here is where LORAN shines; it is usable right on down to the ground.

Many LORAN units you will see on the aviation market are reworked marine versions. They are not certified for IFR work; however, this does not mean they are incapable or inaccurate. This only means the manufacturer was unwilling to spend the many dollars necessary for certification. It is also an indicator of price. The simpler uncertified versions are generally available for under $1000, while the certified units will run better than $4000.

Without going into extensive theory about operation, the LORAN C unit can, by receiving several LORAN signals at one time and comparing them, determine its exact location within a few feet! This will be displayed on the readout as latitude and longitude. Then, by use of "waypoints," the pilot can navigate. The waypoints are geographical locations entered into the LORAN by the operator via the keyboard. The unit will then compare the known signals to the geographical inputs and give constant information concerning course direction, time elapsed, estimated time enroute, distance traveled, distance to destination, etc.—all this in one box!

There are many makes of LORAN C units on the market. They vary primarily in the number and type of features found on the individual unit. Prices vary accordingly.

By the way, LORAN is operated by the United States Coast Guard, not the FAA.

PURCHASING SUMMARY

My strongest recommendation when contemplating the purchase of additional avionics is to save your money until you can purchase new equipment. The new boxes offer more features each model year, the size goes down, the electrical appetite is reduced, and the reliability factor goes up. Additionally, due to inflation, current avionics are more of a bargain than were those of 20 years ago.

Don't even think about trading in equipment that is currently working properly. You cannot replace it for what a dealer will give you. Keep it as your second system.

Recommended reading: *Upgrading Your Airplane's Avionics,* TAB #2301 by Timothy R. V. Foster.

INTERCOMS AND HEADSETS

After sitting for many hours in an airplane, whether it is a Cessna or any other make, your ears will be ringing from all the constant noise. In fact, it is possible to damage your hearing with constant assaults of loud noise.

The FAA recently issued Advisory Circular AC 91-35, partially reprinted here for your information.

AC: 91-35

Subject: Noise, Hearing Damage, and Fatigue in General Aviation Pilots

1. Purpose. This circular will acquaint pilots with the hazards of regular exposure to cockpit noise. Especially pertinent are piston-engine, fixed-wing, and rotary-wing aircraft.

2. Background.

a. Modern general aviation aircraft provide comfort, convenience, and excellent performance. At the same time that the manufacturers have developed more powerful engines, they have given the occupants better noise protection and control, so that today's aircraft are more powerful, yet quieter than ever. Still, the levels of sound associated with powered flight are high enough for general aviation pilots to be concerned about participating in continuous operations without some sort of personal hearing protection.

b. Most long-time pilots have a mild loss of hearing. Many pilots report unusual amounts of fatigue after flights in particularly noisy aircraft. Many pilots have temporary losses of hearing sensitivity after flights, and many pilots have difficulty understanding transmissions from the ground, especially during critical periods under full power, such as takeoff.

3. Discussion

Like carbon monoxide, noise exposure has harmful effects that are cumulative—they add together to produce a greater effect on the listener both as sound intensity is increased, and as the length of time he listens is increased. A noise that could cause a mild hearing loss to a man who heard it once a week for a few minutes might make him quite deaf if he worked in it for eight hours.

However, as with everything, there is a "fix." For the airplane driver and his passengers there is the headphone intercom system (Figs. 8-28, 8-29).

Intercom systems come in all types and with varied capabilities. Some are an extension of the audio panel, primarily for the use of the pilot in his duties; others stand alone. "Stand alone" means they are not hooked to anything in the airplane, but rather are completely portable.

No matter what type you select, the ear protection will be con-

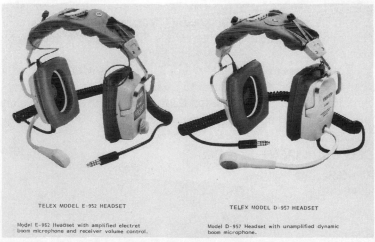

TELEX MODEL E-952 HEADSET

TELEX MODEL D-957 HEADSET

Model E-952 Headset with amplified electret boom microphone and receiver volume control.

Model D-957 Headset with unamplified dynamic boom microphone.

Fig. 8-28. Telex sound reducing headsets. (courtesy Telex)

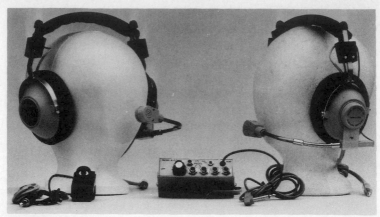

Fig. 8-29. Hush-A-Com headsets and intercom control box. (courtesy Revere Electronics)

trolled by the quality of the headphones used. For proper ear protection, you must use full ear cover headsets, not the lightweight stereo types so popular with the high-school set. There are several manufacturers of adequate headsets, and you will see their ads in the magazines and *Trade-A-Plane*. Don't make a selection based solely on an advertisement. Talk to other pilots, then go to an aviation supply store and try a few. Pay particular attention to the weight, as the weight will become a fatigue factor over long periods of flying. After you find a system you like, purchase it and *use* it.

If you wish to roam through the skies and listen to the stereo, this is your chance; just plug your headsets into a stereo and listen to your heart's content while you go zooming through the mountains and valleys of the mighty clouds that create the geography of the skies.

Just in passing, I have heard of some pilots who supply only headsets without microphones to their passengers. I don't advocate this, as I feel flying is a fun thing, and no one should be shut out, but it is an interesting observation.

OLD EQUIPMENT MODELS

Aire-Sciences

Model	NAV/COMM Channels	
RT-551A	200	720
RT-553	200	360
RT-553A	200	720

Model	NAV/COMM Channels	
RT-557	XPNDR	
RT-667	XPNDR	
RT-777	XPNDR	
RT-787	XPNDR	
RT-887	XPNDR	
RT-563	200	360
RT-563A	200	720
RT-661A	200	720
RT-773	200	360

Cessna (ARC)

Model	NAV/COMM Channels
400	300

The Cessna 300 and 400 series of NAV/COMMs have come in 90, 100, 360, and 720-channel versions. These units were first placed into production about 1960, and have been improved on a yearly basis. The 300/400 series also includes ADF and XPNDR equipment. The individual model numbers changed each year.

Genave

Model	NAV/COMM Channels	
Alpha 100	100	
Alpha 190	100	90
Alpha 200	200	100
Alpha 200A	200	100
Alpha 200B	200	100
Alpha 300	100	360
Alpha 360	100	360
Alpha 500	200	360
Alpha 600	200	360
Alpha 720	720	
Beta 500	XPNDR	
Beta 5000	XPNDR	
GA-1000	200	720
Sigma 1500	ADF	

King

Model	NAV/COMM Channels
KR-80	ADF

Model	NAV/COMM Channels	
KR-85	ADF	
KR-86	ADF	
KR-87	ADF	
KT-75	XPNDR	
KT-76	XPNDR	
KT-78	XPNDR	
KX-100A	90	190
KX-120	tune	360
KX-130	100	360
KX-145	200	720
KX-150A,B	100	100
KX-155	200	720
KX-160	100	360
KX-165	200	720
KX-170	200	360
KX-170A	200	360
KX-170B	200	720
KX-175B	200	720
KY-90A	90	
KY-95	360	
KY-195B	720	

Narco

Model	NAV/COMM Channels	
10A	200	360
11A	360	
100	360	
110	200	360
ADF-140	ADF	
ADF-29	ADF	
ADF30A	ADF	
ADF-31(all)	ADF	
AT-6	XPNDR	
AT-50	XPNDR	
AT-150	XPNDR	
Escort 110	100	110
VHT-3	tune	19
MK-2	tune	27
MK-3	190	90
MK-4	tune	27
MK-5	190	
MK-7	360	
MK-8	100	

218

Model	NAV/COMM Channels	
MK-10	190	360
MK-12(90)	100	90
MK-12(360)	100	360
MK-12A(90)	100	90
MK-12A(360)	100	360
MK-12B	100	360
MK-12D	200	720
MK-16	200	360
MK-24	100	360
Nav-11	200	
Nav-12	200	

Terra

Model	NAV/COMM Channels	
ML-200	200	100
R250	XPNDR	
R360-200-1	200	360
TX-720	720	

OTHER DEVICES

In this, the day of modern technology and digital readouts, some owners have been fit to add numerous bells and whistles to the

Fig. 8-30. Davtron digital OAT (outside air temperature). (courtesy Davtron)

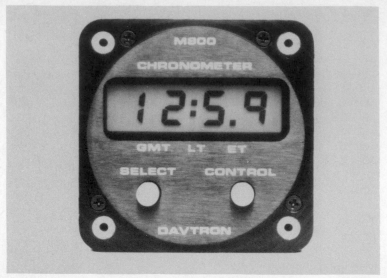

Fig. 8-31. Davtron chronometer. (courtesy Davtron)

panels of their airplanes. Among the more common are the digital outside air temperature gauge and the digital chronometer (Figs. 8-30, 8-31).

To some, the instrument panel is a functional device; to others it's a statement made by the owner. In either case, much care must be taken when filling up the panel—not just to provide instrumentation, but to functionally plan it well and accomplish it economically.

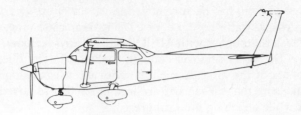

Chapter 9

Painting an Airplane

Although most owners would never attempt to paint their airplane, they should know just what a good painting job involves. For those of you thinking of painting your airplane, these are your instructions.

The following information is provided by Randolph Products Co., Carlstadt, NJ 07072. Phone: (201) 438-3700

PAINT STRIPPING OF ALUMINUM AIRCRAFT
List of Required Materials

B-5000 Rand O Strip Remover: Rand O Strip is a fast-acting water wash paint remover designed for use on aircraft aluminum surfaces. It conforms to Military specification MIL-R-25134.

Application

Stir contents before proceeding. Apply liberally by brush or non-atomizing spray to metal surface. When brushing, be sure to brush only in one direction. Keep surface wet with remover. If an area dries before the paint film softens or wrinkles, apply more remover. It is sometimes advisable to lay an inexpensive polyethylene drop cloth over the applied remover in order to hold the solvents longer, giving more time for penetration of the film. After the paint softens and wrinkles, use a pressure water hose to thoroughly flush off all residue.

In the case of an acrylic lacquer finish, the remover will only soften and will not wrinkle the film. A rubber squeegee or stiff bristle brush can be used to help remove more of this type of finish.

After all paint has been removed, flush the entire aircraft off with a pressure water hose. Let dry. Using clean cotton rags, wipe all surfaces thoroughly with MEK (Methly Ethyl Ketone).

Note: Do not let remover come in contact with any fiberglass components of the aircraft such as radomes, wingtips, fairings, etc. Make sure that these parts are well masked or removed from aircraft while stripping is in progress.

Caution

While using remover, always wear rubber gloves and protect your eyes from splashes. If remover gets on skin, flush with plenty of water; if any comes in contact with your eyes, flood repeatedly with water and call a physician. Have adequate ventilation.

CORROSION REMOVAL

After paint stripping, any traces of corrosion on the aluminum surface must be removed.

Aircraft Corrosion Control, a manual published by Aviation Maintenance Publishers, deals with this problem in details and is available from your local Randolph Products distributor.

If corrosion is found, every trace must be removed with fine sandpaper (no emery), aluminum wool, or a Scotch Brite pad. Never use steel wool or a steel brush, as bits of steel will imbed in the aluminum, causing much worse corrosion.]

FINISHING PROCEDURE
List of Required Materials (Metal Pretreatment and Painting):

- ☐ G-6304 Rand O Prep (Metal Pretreatment).
- ☐ 1100 MEK (Methyl Ethyl Ketone).
- ☐ G-2404 Randthane Epoxy Primer (Component A).
- ☐ G-2405 Randthane Epoxy Primer (Component B).
- ☐ G-4201 Randthane Primer Reducer.

Conditions for Painting

For optimum results, temperature and humidity should be

within the following limits:

Relative Humidity: 20% to 60%
Temperature: Not less than 70 degrees F.

Departure from these limits could result in various application or finish problems.

Drying time of the various coatings will vary with temperature, humidity, amount of thinner used, and thickness of paint film.

Painting Safety Tips

1. Ground the surface you are painting or sanding.
2. Do not use an electric drill to mix dope or paint.
3. Wear leather-soled shoes in the painting area.
4. Wear cotton clothes while painting.
5. Keep solvent-soaked rags in fireproof safety container.
6. Keep the spray area and floor clean and free of dust buildup.
7. Have adequate ventilation. Do not allow mist or fumes to build up in a confined area.
8. Do not smoke or have any type of open flame in the area.

Metal Pretreatment (Aluminum)

In the case of an aircraft that has been stripped of its previous coating, make sure that all traces of paint or paint remover residue have been removed. Give special attention to areas such as seams and around rivet heads.

Aircraft should be flushed with plenty of clean water to ensure removal of all contaminants. Let dry. Using clean cotton rags, wipe all surfaces thoroughly with MEK.

Apply G-6304 Rand O Prep metal pretreatment liberally to all the aluminum surfaces of the aircraft. While keeping these surfaces thoroughly wet with Rand O Prep, scrub briskly with a Scotch Brite pad. It is advisable to wear rubber gloves and to protect your eyes from splashes during this procedure.

Rand O Prep may be applied with clean rags or a brush.

After the entire aircraft has been treated with this procedure, flush very thoroughly with plenty of clean water. Let dry.

The next step is to thoroughly wipe down the entire aluminum surface with MEK using clean cotton rags. This will ensure all contaminants are removed prior to application of primer.

Ranthane Epoxy Primer: Specifically designed for aircraft, this primer affords the utmost in corrosion protection. It gives the best adhesion possible both to the substrate aluminum surface and to the finish top coat. "Hold out" is excellent, with little or no primer absorption of finish coat.

Primer Application

Ranthane Epoxy Primer is mixed as follows:

☐ One part by volume of G-2404 Ranthane Primer (Component A).

☐ One part by volume of G-2405 Ranthane Primer (Component B).

☐ 1 1/2 parts by volume of G-4201 Ranthane Primer Reducer.

After the three components are thoroughly mixed, let stand for 15 to 20 minutes prior to starting application.

Pot life after mixture is six hours.

Ranthane Primer can be applied using any conventional, electrostatic, or airless type of spray equipment.

Care must be taken that only enough primer be used to prime the surface evenly to about 0.0005 in., or one-half a mil film thickness. This means that the aluminum substrate should show through with a light yellow coating of the primer coloring the metal.

Drying time of the primer will vary slightly due to differences in temperature and relative humidity at the time of application; but as a general rule, primer should be ready for application of the finish coat within four to six hours.

After the primer is thoroughly dry, wipe entire surface with clean, soft, cotton rags using a little pressure, as in polishing. Next, tack-rag the entire surface.

You are now ready for application of the top coat finishing system you have selected.

If more than 24 hours after priming have elapsed prior to applying the top coat finish, it is advisable to very lightly scuff the primer with 600 sandpaper and tack-rag before proceeding.

List of Required Materials
(Selected Top Coat Finishing System)

A. Ranthane Polyurethane Enamel
☐ Selected Ranthane Color

☐ G-2403 Catalyst
☐ G-4200 Reducer
B. Randacryl Acrylic Lacquer
☐ Selected Randacrylic Color
☐ B-0161 Thinner for Randacrylic
☐ Y-9910 Universal Retarder
C. Randolph Aircraft Enamel
☐ Selected Enamel Color
☐ #257 Enamel Reducer

Topcoat Finishing System

Ranthane Polyurethane Enamel: Ranthane is a "state of the art" modern-day aircraft finished developed after years of research and testing at the Randolph laboratories. It encompasses "flight proven" characteristics such as superior gloss and color retention, abrasion, chemical, fuel, hydraulic fluid, and thermal shock resistance.

Ranthane will maintain these film characteristics with little or no maintenance over many years of active flying.

Ranthane Topcoat Application: Thoroughly mix one (1) part by volume of Ranthane Color to one (1) part by volume G-2403 Catalyst. Adding G-4200 Ranthane Reducer, thin mixture to 18 to 20 seconds using the #2 Zahn viscosity cup. Let stand for 15 to 20 minutes.

Pot life after mixing is approximately six hours, but will vary with color, temperature, and humidity.

Spray a relatively light tack coat on first application. Let dry for at least 15 minutes.

Second coat is applied as a full wet cross-coat.

Care should be taken that too much paint is not being applied, resulting in runs or sags.

Ranthane is a high-solid material giving excellent hiding characteristics without excessive paint buildup.

An overnight dry is preferable before taping for trim color application unless forced drying is used. In such a case, one to two hours at 140 degrees F. is sufficient.

After masking and before applying the trim color, lightly scuff the trim color surface using the #400 wet-or-dry sandpaper.

Tack-rag and apply trim color. Remove masking tapes as soon as paint has started to "set."

Randacrylic Acrylic Lacquer: Randalcrylic is a "flight proven" finish used for many years by some of the largest prime aircraft manufacturers. It has outstanding durability with good color and gloss retention characteristics.

Randacrylic Topcoat Application: Thoroughly mix Randacryl Color with B-0161 Randacrylic Thinner as follows:

☐ Four (4) parts by volume Randacryl Color
☐ Five (5) parts by volume B-0161 Randacryl Thinner

Adjustments to this mixture might be necessary due to spray equipment used or operator technique.

Spray relatively light tack coat on first application. Let dry for approximately 30 minutes. Follow this first coat with at least three full wet cross coats, letting each dry for approximately 30 minutes between coats.

If the material is too heavy, orange peel or pinholes are likely to appear.

The gloss in the final coat can be enhanced by adding about a fourth as much Y-9910 Universal Retarder as you have thinner in the material.

An overnight dry is preferable before taping for trim color application.

Remove masking tape as soon as paint has started to set.

Randolph Aircraft Enamel: Randolph Aircraft Enamels have been "flight proven" over many years of service and will give good durability and a full, rich luster.

Randolph Aircraft Enamel Topcoat Application: Thoroughly mix Enamel with only enough #257 Enamel Reducer to arrive at a viscosity of 25 to 28 seconds using a #2 Zahn viscosity cup.

Spray on a light tack coat. Allow to dry for 15 to 20 minutes, then apply a full, wet cross coat.

Allow dry at least 48 hours before taping for trim colors.

After masking and before applying trim color, lightly scuff the trim color surface using #400 wet-or-dry sandpaper. Tack-rag and apply trim color.

Remove masking tapes as soon as paint has started to set.

REFINISHING FIBERGLASS COMPONENTS

When refinishing any fiberglass component of the aircraft such as randomes, wingtips, antenna, fairings, etc., it is extremely important that they are protected from paint remover or solvents. The only safe method of removing paint from these components is to sand it off.

After paint is removed by sanding, tack-rag the surface and apply a light coat of Ranthane Primer.

When Ranthane Primer is dry (four to six hours), briskly wipe the entire surface clean with soft cotton rags (as in polishing). Next, tack-rag the surface and finish in selected finishing system.

Note: After repainting any aircraft, it is advisable to check your Owner's Manual or check with your inspection facility as to whether the control surfaces of the aircraft require rebalancing.

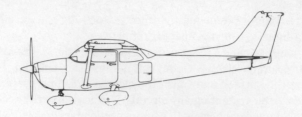

Chapter 10

Modifications and STCs for the 172

The following is a list of STCs (supplementary type certificate) for Cessna 172 airplanes. When reading the list, the STC number appears first, followed by the item/part modified by the STC, the airplane models the STC applies to, and the name and address of the holder of the STC.

AVIONICS AND AUTOPILOTS

SA1-9: 69A115 gyro-stabilizer; Globe Industries, Inc., 125 Sunrise Pl., Dayton, OH 45401.

SA1-116: Federal F-300 Autopilot; Aircraft Components, Inc., 755 Woodward Ave., Benton Harbor, MI 49023.

SA3-90: Lear ADF Loop and housing; Capitol Aviation, Inc., Capitol Airport, Springfield, IL 62705.

SA3-108: Single-axis automatic pilot A-2 or A-3; Javelin Aircraft Co., Inc., 9175 East Douglas, Wichita, KS 67207.

SA4-40: Automatic rudder control; Motorola Aviation Electronics, Inc., 3302 Airport Ave., Santa Monica, CA 90406.

SA4-531: Federal F-200 autopilot; Aircraft Components, Inc., 755 Woodward Ave., Benton Harbor, MI 49023.

SA4-602: Autopilot; Brittain Industries, Inc., 12027 South Prairie Ave., Hawthorne, CA 90250.

SA313DO: Federal FS103 autopilot; A and E Service, McCollum Airport, Marietta, GA 30060.

SA1308WE: Installation of Brittain model CSA-1 Stability Augmentation System; Brittain Industries, P.O. Box 51370 Tulsa, OK 74151.

SA1468WE: Installation of Brittain model B2C Autopilot system; Brittain Industries. P.O. Box 51370, Tulsa, OK 74151.

SA1806WE: Installation of Brittain Industries B2C Flight Control system; Brittain Industries, P.O. Box 51370, Tulsa, OK 74151.

SA1221SW: Mitchell automatic flight system AK312 consisting of Century I with optional omni tracker (172, 172A,B,C,D,E,F,G,H,I,K,L); Century Flight Systems, Inc., F.M. 1195, P.O. Box 610. Mineral Wells, TX 76067.

SA1406SO: Installation of Model CC-1 checkpoint computer (172,172A,B,C,D,E,F,G,H,I,K,L,M,N,P); Perception Systems, 4500 N Dixie Highway, #C-24, West Palm Beach, FL 33407.

SA4717SW: Installation of Texas Instruments Model 9100 LORAN C navigator (172, 172A,B,C,D,E,F,G,H,I,L,M,N,P); Texas Instruments, P.O. Box 405 M/S 3439, Lewisville, TX 75067.

SA5124SWD: S-TEC System 60 single-axis autopilot (14 volt) (172, 172A,B,C,D,E,F,G,H,I,K,L); S-Tec Corporation, Route 4, Building 946, Wolters Industrial Complex, Mineral Wells, TX 76067

SA5200SWD: S-TEC System 40 single-axis automatic flight guidance system ST-182-40 (172,172A,B,C,D,E,F,G,H,I,K,L); S-Tec Corporation, Route 4, Building 946, Wolters Industrial Complex, Mineral Wells, TX 76067.

SA232EA: Installation of Tactair omni-lock model OL-1 and optional installation of Tactair localizer adapter Model LA-1 (for use with Tactair model omni-lock model OH-4) (172B,C); Avionics, Inc., Terminal Building, Lunken Airport, Cincinnati, OH 45226.

SA17EA: Installation of Tactair T-101 autopilot and optional installation of Tactair T-201 autopilot accessory kit (for use with Tactair T-101 autopilot) (172D,P172D); Avionics, Inc., Terminal Building, Lunken Airport, Cincinnati, OH 45226.

SA603SW: Installation of Mitchell automatic flight system model AK-191 consisting of Century II and radio coupler and model AK192 automatic aileron stabilizer (172D,E,F,G,H,I,K,L); Century Flight System, Inc., F.M. 1195, P.O. Box 610, Mineral Wells, TX 76067.

SA1645SW: Mitchell automatic flight system AK403, consisting of Century IIB autopilot with optional radio coupler (172D through 172I,K,L); Century Flight Systems, Inc., F.M. 1195,

P.O. Box 610, Minral Wells, TX 76067.

SA2268WE: Installation of Brittain Industries B2C flight control systems (172D,E); Brittain Industries, P.O. Box 51370, Tulsa, OK 74151.

SA2619WE: Installation of Pathfinder model P1 autopilot (172D through M); Astronautics Corporation of America, 2416 Amsler Street, Torrance, CA 90505.

SA2620WE: Installation of Pathfinder Model P2 autopilot system (172C through L); Astronautics Corp. of America, 2416 Amsler Street, Torrance, CA 90505.

SA2654WE: Installation of Pathfinder model P2A autopilot (172D,E,F,G,H,I,K,L,M); Astronautics Corp. of America, 2416 Amsler Street, Torrance, CA 90505.

SA3046SWD: Mitchell automatic flight system AK524 consisting of Century IIB autopilot with optional radio coupler (172D,E,F,G,H,I,K,L); Century Flight Systems, Inc., FM 1195, P.O. Box 610, Mineral Wells, TX 76067.

SA5111SWD: S-TEC System 60 two-axis automatic flight guidance system ST-095 (172D,E,F,G,H,I,K,L); S-TEC Corporation, Route 4, Building 946, Wolters Industrial Complex, Mineral Wells, TX 76067.

SA5113SWD: S-TEC system 60-pitch stabilization system ST-096 (172D.E,F,G,H,I,K,L); S-TEC Corporation, Route 4, Building 946, Wolters Industrial Complex, Mineral Wells, TX 76067.

SA5201SWD: S-TEC system 50 two-axis automatic flight guidance system, ST-182-50 (172D,E,F,G,H,I,K,L); S-TEC Corporation, Route 4, Building 946, Wolters Industrial Complex, Mineral Wells, TX 76067.

SA299GL: Installation of Cessna Nav-O-Matic 200A autopilot (172G); Galesburg AP and L,R.R. 2, Airport, Galesburg, IL 61401.

SA3824SWD: Mitchell automatic flight system AK730 consisting of Century I autopilot with optional omni tracking system (172K); Mitchell Industries, Inc., P.O. Box 610, Mineral Wells, TX 76067.

SA494SO: Installation of radio equipment in instrument panel (172L); Burnside-Ott Aviation Training Center, 12800 S.W. 137th Avenue, Miami, FL 33156.

SA1798SW: Mitchell Automatic Flight System AK467 consisting of Century IIB Autopilot with optional Radio Coupler (172M);

Century Flight Systems, Inc., F.M. 1195, P.O. Box 610, Mineral Wells, TX 76067.

SA1799SW: Mitchell Automatic Flight System AK472 consisting of Century I Autopilot with optional omni tracker (172M); Century Flight Systems, Inc., F.M. 1195, P.O. Box 610, Mineral Wells, TX 76067.

SA380GL: Installation of Tull microwave landing system airborne equipment (172M,N); Burlington Northern Automotive, 3600 East 70th Street, Minneapolis, MN 55450.

SA3200SWD: Automatic flight system AK467 consisting of Century II autopilot with optional radio coupler (172M,N); Century Flight Systems, Inc., F.M. 1195, P.O. Box 610, Mineral Wells, TX 76067

SA3201SWD: Automatic flight system AK472 consisting of Century I autopilot with optional omni tracker (172M,N); Century Flight Systems, Inc., F.M. 1195, P.O. Box 610, Mineral Wells, TX 76067.

SA4221SW: S-TEC system 60 (two-axis) flight guidance system, Model ST-019, with optional flight director steering horizon and vertical speed selector (14 volt system) (172M,N); S-TEC Corporation, Route 3, Building 946, Wolters Industrial Complex, Mineral Wells, TX 76067.

SA4230SW: S-TEC 60-roll flight guidance kit, Model ST-008 (172M,N); S-TEC Corporation, Route 3, Building 946, Wolters Industrial Complex, Mineral Wells, TX 76067.

SA4338SW: S-TEC pitch stabilization system, Model ST-042 (14 volt system) (172M,N); S-TEC Corporation, Route 3, Building 946, Wolters Industrial Complex, Mineral Wells, TX 76067.

SW5133SWD: S-TEC system 60 two-axis automatic flight guidance system ST-019 with optional flight director steering horizon (172M,N); S-TEC Corporation, Route 3, Building 946, Wolters Industrial Complex, Mineral Wells, TX 76067.

SA5150SWD: S-TEC System 60-pitch stabilization ST-042 (172M,N); S-TEC Corporation, Route 3, Building 946, Wolters Industrial Complex, Mineral Wells, TX 76067.

SA5195SWD: S-TEC System 40/50 single and two-axis automatic flight guidance systems, ST-183-40/50 (172M,N); S-TEC Corporation, Route 3, Building 946, Wolters Industrial Complex, Mineral Wells, TX 76067.

SA5309SWD: Installation of S-TEC System 60 single-axis automatic flight guidance system Model ST-008 (172M,N); S-TEC

Corporation, Route 3, Building 946, Wolters Industrial Complex, Mineral Wells, TX 76067.

SA5192SWD: S-TEC 40/50 single and two-axis automatic flight guidance systems ST-184-40/50 (172M,N,P); S-TEC Corporation, Route 3, Building 946, Wolters Industrial Complex, Mineral Wells, TX 76067.

SA5291SWD: Installation of S-TEC System 60 single-axis automatic flight guidance system ST-012 (172M,N,P,Q); S-TEC Corporation, Route 3, Building 946, Wolters Industrial Complex, Mineral Wells, TX 76067.

SA168GL Install Heath Kit Model 01-1154 aircraft digital clock/timer (172N); The Heath Company, Hilltop Road, Benton Harbor, MI 49022.

SA3301SWD: Mitchell automatic flight system AK730, consisting of Century I autopilot with optional omni tracking system (172N); Century Flight Systems, Inc., F.M. 1195, P.O. Box 610, Mineral Wells, TX 76067.

SA3302SWD: Mitchell automatic flight system AK731 consisting of Century IIB autopilot with optional radio coupler (172N); Century Flight Systems, Inc., F.M. 1195, P.O. Box 610, Mineral Wells, TX 76067.

SA3303SWD: Mitchell automatic flight system AK732 consisting of Century III autopilot with optional radio and glide slope couplers (172N); Century Flight Systems, Inc., F.M. 1195, P.O. Box 610, Mineral Wells, TX 76067.

SA3417SWD: EDO Avionics automatic flight system AK904 consisting of Century 31 autopilot (172P); Century Flight Systems, Inc., F.M. 1195, P.O. Box 610, Mineral Wells, TX 76067.

SA3418SWD: EDO Avionics automatic flight system AK920 consisting of Century 21 autopilot (172P); Century Flight Systems, Inc., F.M. 1195, P.O. Box 610, Mineral Wells, TX 76067.

SA4243SW: S-TEC system 60 (two-axis) flight guidance system Model ST-025 with optional flight director/steering horizon and optional vertical speed/indicator selector (28 volt system) (172N); S-TEC Corporation, Route 3, Building 946, Wolters Industrial Complex, Mineral Wells, TX 76067.

SA4244SW: S-TEC system 60 single-axis flight guidance system, Model ST-012 (28 volt system) (172N); S-TEC Corporation, Route 3, Building 946, Wolters Industrial Complex, Mineral Wells, TX 76067.

SA4417SW: Installation of S-TEC System 60 stabilization system ST-060 (28 volt) (172N): S-TEC Corporation, Route 3, Building 946, Wolters Industrial Complex, Mineral Wells, TX 76067.

SA5139SWD: S-TEC System 60 two-axis automatic flight guidance system ST-025 with optional flight director steering horizon (172N,P); S-TEC Corporation, Route 3, Building 946, Wolters Industrial Complex, Mineral Wells, TX 76067.

SA5151SWD: S-TEC System 60 pitch-stabilization system ST-060 (172N,P); S-TEC Corporation, Route 3, Building 946, Wolters Industrial Complex, Mineral Wells, TX 76067.

SA4197SW: S-TEC System 60 (two-axis) flight guidance system, Model ST-011, with optional flight director/steering horizon and vertical speed indicator/selector (14 volt system) (172P,Q); S-TEC Corporation, Route 3, Building 946, Wolters Industrial Complex, Mineral Wells, TX 76067.

SA3417SWD: EDO Avionics automatic flight system AK904 consisting of Century 31 autopilot (172P); Century Flight Systems, Inc., F.M. 1195, P.O. Box 610, Mineral Wells, TX 76067.

SA3418SWD: EDO Avionics automatic flight system AK920 consisting of Century autopilot (172P); Century Flight Systems, Inc., F.M. 1195, P.O. Box 610, Mineral Wells, TX 76067.

SA1570CED: Installation of KAP 100 single-axis, KAP 150 two-axis, or KFC 150 two-axis flight control system (172P); King Radio Corporation, 400 North Rogers Rd., Olathe, KS 66062.

SA1-219: Gyro stabilizer 69A133 (172), Glode Industries, Inc., 125 Sunrise Place, Dayton, OH 45401.

AS1098W: Automatic pilot AK106 (172); Mitchell Industries, Inc., P.O. Box 610, Municipal Airport, Mineral Wells, TX 76067.

SA393WE: Pneumatic pitch assist PC-1 and optional altitude hold AH-1 (172); Brittain Industries, Inc., P.O. Box 51370, Tulsa, OK 74151.

SA411SW: Automatic pitch trim AK138 (172); Mitchell Industries, Inc., P.O. 610, Municipal Airport, Mineral Wells, TX 76067.

SA895WE: Kienzla 65 flight time recorder (172); Burrows and Sons, 1829 Bridgeport Avenue, Claremont, CA 91711.

ENGINES AND PROPELLERS

SA1-438: Lycoming O-360-A1A engine and McCauley 2D36C14/78 KM-4 propeller with Woodward 2101055 AA governor; Albert E. Zotack, 295 First Ave., Stratford, CT 06497.

SA3-11: Propeller installations—two-position controllable, hub 2B-36C7, blades 78K-2 or 78K-4; McCauley Industrial Corp., 1840 Howell Ave., Dayton, OH 45401.

SA3-126: Lycoming C-340-A1A engine and Hartzell HC-82XG-1DB/8433-12 propeller; KWAD Co., 4530 Jettridge Dr., NW., Atlanta, GA 30327.

SA792WE: Lycoming O-360 series engines and Sensenich M67EMM propellers; McKinzie Aircraft Repair, Inc., 1300 North 26th St., Springfield, OR 97477.

SA1078WE: Franklin 6A-335-B engine with McCauley 2A31C/84S-6 propeller using EDO 89-2000 floats; Columbia Marine, Inc., P.O. Box 179, Vancouver, WA 98663.

SA3-571: Lycoming O-360-A1D engine, McCauley 2D36C14-78KM-4 or Hartzell HC-C2YK-1A/7666-2 propellers (172,172A,B,C,D,E,F,G,H); KWAD Co., 4530 Jettridge Dr., NW, Atlanta, GA 30327.

SA420CE: Lycoming O-360-A1A or A1D engine, McCauley 2D36C14/78KM-4 or Hartzell KC-C2YK-1B/7666-2 propeller (172, 172A,B,C,D,E,F,G,H landplanes; 172D,E,F,G,H floatplanes; EDO 89-2000 floats only); Robert L. or Barbara V. Williams, Box 431, 213 North Clark, Udall, KS 67146.

SA807CE: Installation of Lycoming 180-hp engine and constant-speed propeller (172,172A through I,K,L,M,N; landplane, normal category only); Robert L. or Barbara V. Williams, 117 East First, Udall, KS 67146

SA181GL: Installation of McCauley 1A200/DFA propeller (172A seaplane); Les G. Taylor, 1115 19th Street South, St. Cloud, MN 56301.

SA1334WE: Installation of Franklin 6A-350-C2 engine and McCauley 2A31C/84S-6 propeller (172B through G); Columbia Marine, Inc., P.O. Box 179, Vancouver, WA 98663.

SA1774WE: Installation of Lycoming O-320-E2D engine and McCauley 1C172.MTM7653 propeller (172B through H); Columbia Marine, Inc., P.O. Box 179, Vancouver, WA 98663.

SA2375SW: Install Lycoming O-320-D2G engine rated for 160 hp takeoff and 150 METO (172D,E,F,G,H); RAM Aircraft Modifications, Inc., P.O. Box 5219, Madison Cooper Airport, Waco, TX 76708.

SA204GL: Installation of AVCO Lycoming O-320-E2D engine (172H); Professional Aviation, Inc., Porter County Airport, 3801 Murvihill Rd., Valparaiso, IN 46383.

SA414NW: Installation of Lycoming O-360-A1F6D engine and McCauley Propeller (172H); Salem Aviation, 2680 Aerial Way, S.E., Salem, OR 97302.

SA87NW: Installation of Lycoming O-360-A1A 180-hp engine and

Hartzell HC-C2YK-1A/7666A-O propeller (172I,K,L); Kenmore Air Harbor, Inc., P.O. Box 64, Kenmore, WA 98028.

SA332GL: Installation of Lycoming O-360 Series engine and McCauley 1A200/DFA propeller (172I,K,L,M,N,P seaplane); Penn Yan Aero Product Development Division, R.R. 1, Box 165, Mahomet, IL 61853.

SA647CE: Install Lycoming O-360-A1A 180-hp engine and constant-speed propeller (172I,K,L,M,N land and floatplanes using EDO 89-2000 floats only); Barbara or Bob Williams, Box 431, 213 North Clark, Udall, KS 67146.

SA703GL: Installation of Lycoming O-360-A4A, A4M, or A4N series engines and Sensenich propeller models 76EM8S5 or 76EM8SPY (172I,K,L,M,N,P); Penn Yan Aero Product Development Division, R.R. 1, Box 165, Mahomet, IL 61853.

SA1225CE: Installation of Lycoming O-320-E2D/STC SE1226CE or O-320-D2G engine and McCauley 1C160/CTM 7557 or 1C160/DTM 7557 propeller (172I,K,L,M landplane); Schneck Aviation, Inc., Greater Rockford Airport, P.O. Box 6417, Rockford, IL 61125.

SA4428SW: Lycoming O-360-A2F engine and McCauley 1A170/CFA-76-60 propeller (172I,K,L,M,N); Mike Kelley Aircraft, Inc., Box 541, Wellington, KS 67152.

SA1324CE: Installation of Lycoming O-360-A1A engine and Hartzell HC-C2YK-1B/7666A-2 propeller (172N); Avcon Industries, Inc., 1006 West 53rd Street North, P.O. Box 4248, North Wichita Station, Wichita, KS 67204.

SA610SW: Lycoming O-320 and O-360 series engines with Hartzell HC-82XL-7636D-4; HC-C2YK-2R/7666 or HC-92OZ-2B/8447-128 propeller (172); R.F.B. Company, Chandler Field, Purcell, OK 73080.

FLOATS AND SKIS

SA3-179: A3500A or A2500A main skis and NA1200A nose skis; FluiDyne Engineering Corp., 5900 Olson Memorial HWY, Minneapolis, MN 55422.

SA3-256: Main ski AWB2500A and nosewheel ski AWN1200; FluiDyne Engineering Corp., 5900 Olson Memorial HWY, Minneapolis, MN 55422.

SA3-355: C3000 main ski and AWN1200 nose wheel ski; FluiDyne Engineering Corp., 5900 Olson Memorial HWY, Minneapolis, MN 55422.

SA3-614: Model 3000 main skis and model 2000 nose ski; Flui-Dyne Engineering Corp., 5900 Olson Memorial HWY, Minneapolis, MN 55422.

SA88CE: C-3000 main skis and AWN-1200A nose ski; FluiDyne Engineering Corp., 5900 Olson Memorial HWY, Minneapolis, MN 55422.

SA315GL: Installation of Fluidyne skis (172, 172A,B,C,D,E,F,G,H,I,K,L,M,N); Robert L. or Barbara V. Williams, Box 608, Udall, KS 67146.

SA340NW: Installation of Pee Kay Model 2300 floats (172, 172D,K); Seaplane Flying, Inc., P.O. Box 2164, Vancouver, WA 98661.

SA650CE: Installation of Fleet Model 2500 floats (172A through 172K); Trifield Associates, 560 Daytona Drive, Fort Erie, Ontario, Canada.

SA358NW: Installation of Pee Kay Model 2300 seaplane floats (172A through 172N); Devore Aviation Corporation, 6104-B Kircher Blvd., N.E., Albuquerque, NM 87109.

SA365NW: Installation of Pee Kay model 2300 seaplane floats. Approval is intended for installation in listed models with Franklin 6A-0360-C2 engine installation IAW Seaplane Flying, Inc., STC SA340NW (172D through 172K); Devore Aviation Corp., 6104-B Kircher Blvd., N.E., Albuquerque, NM 87109.

SA665CE: Installation of model 2400 Acqua floats (172D,E,F,G,H,I,K,M,N,R172K): Claggett Aircraft Products Research and Engineering, Inc., 805 Geiger Rd., Zephyrhills, FL 33599.

SA1000EA: Installation of Pee Kay Model 2300 or B2300 (TSO-C27-2) seaplane floats (172I,K,L,M,N seaplane); Pee Kay Floats Devore Aviation Corporation, 6104-B Kircher Boulevard, N.E., Albuquerque, MN 87109.

SA584NW: Installation of EDO model 689-2130 seaplane floats (172L,M,N,P); EDO Corporation Government Systems Division, Farmingdale OPS, Republic Airport, East Farmingdale, NY 11735.

SA1168SO: Installation of Aqua Model 2200 floats (172N); Claggett Aircraft Products Research and Engineering, Inc., 805 Geiger Rd., Zephyrhills, FL 33599.

SA584NW: Installation of EDO 689-2130 seaplane floats (172N,P); EDO-Aire Seaplane Division of EDO Corporation, Republic Airport, East Farmingdale, NY 11735.

STOL AND SPEED

SA3-655: Wheel fairings; Marsh Flying Club, Inc., 812 East 34th St., Sioux Falls, SD 57101.

SA3-690: Installation of DOYN swept-tail assembly kit 1400; KWAD Co., 4530 Jettridge Dr., NW, Atlanta, GA 30327.

SA44SO: Cessna L-19 wing conversion; Marrs Aircraft, Avion Park, FL 33825.

SA1677SW: Wing leading edge cuff; Southern Aircraft Corp., P.O. Box 78, Page, OK 74939.

SA3-576: Installation of speed kit (172, 172A,B): Aircraft Development Co., 1326 North Westlink Blvd., Wichita, KS 67212.

SA296GL: Convert to conventional landing gear (172, 172A,B,C,D,E,F,G,H,I,K,L,M,N); Robert L. or Barbara V. Williams, Box 608, Udall, KS 67146.

SA902CE: Installation of STOL kit (172, 172A through 172I, 172K, 172L, 172M, 172N, 172P); Robert L. or Barbara V. Williams, Box 608, Udall, KS 67146.

SA910CE: Installation wing leading edge cuffs, drooped tips, stall fences and aileron gap seals (172 landplane, 172A through 172P landplane and floatplane); Horton STOL-Craft, Inc., Wellington Municipal Airport, Wellington, KS 67152.

SA1484CE: Installation of flap and aileron seals (172, 172A,B,C,D,E,F,G,H,I,K,L,M,N,P); Aircraft Development Company, 1326 North Westlink Boulevard, Wichita, KS 67212.

SA1665CE: Installation strut/wing and strut fuselage fairings, lightening hole covers, and aerodynamic putty (172, 172A through 172G landplanes and floatplanes, 172, 172H through 172I landplanes only); Aircraft Development Company, 1326 North Westlink Boulevard, Wichita, KS 67212.

SA2002WE: Installation of recontoured wing leading edge, stall fences, wingtips and positive aileron seals (172 through 172I); Robertson Aircraft Cooperation, 839 W. Perimeter Road, Renton, WA 98055.

SA2075: Installation of Madras Air Service Inc. "Super Tips" (172, 172A through 172L normal category); Madras Air Service, Inc., Route 2, Box 1225, Madras, OR 97741.

SA2852: Installation of leading edge cuffs, stall fences, aileron seals, wingtips (172,172A,B,C,D,E,F,G,H,I,K,L,M); Bob Williams DBA Bush Conversions, P.O. Box 431, Udall, KS 67146.

SA3105WE: Installation of flapgap fairing (172, 172A,B,C,D,E,F,G,H,I,K,L,M,N normal and utility categories);

Thermal Aircraft Company, 56-850 Tyler Street, Thermal, CA 92274.

SA3788WE: Installation of the "liftrol" wing spoiler system (172, 172A,B,C,D,E,F,G,H,I,K,L); Esther E. Cleaves, 4542 Norma Drive, San Diego, CA 92115.

SA5433SW: Conversion from tricycle to conventional landing gear (172, 172A,B,C,D,E,F,G,H,I,K,L,M,N,P); Custom Aircraft Conversions, 234 West Turbo Drive, San Antonio, TX 78216.

SA319GL: Installation of Bolen wheel extenders on Cessna models modified per STC SA296GL (172D,E,F,G,H,I,K); Robert L. or Barbara V. Williams, Box 608, Udall, KS 67146.

SA596WE: Installation of Doyn Aircraft co. kit per STC SA3-571 (172D,E (seaplane); Barbara or Bob Williams Box 431, 213 North Clark, Udall, KS 67146.

SA2671WE: Installation of upper wing surface stall fences and aileron gap sealing strips (172M); Group One, 2915 Earhat Apron, Torrance, CA 90505.

SA1402CE: Install wing stall fences and aileron gap seals (172M,N); Barbara or Bob Williams, Box 431, 213 North Clark, Udall, KS 67146.

SA4080SW: Installation of leading edge cuffs, stall fences, aileron seals, wing tips (172M,N); Bob Williams, DBA Bush Conversions, P.O. Box 431, Udall, KS 67146.

SA974EA: Installation of L/R wing tip transparent fairing and sensor mounting bracket (172M); Rock Avionics Systems, Inc., 412 Avenue of the Americas, New York, NY 10011.

SA4-893: Installation of wheel fenders on nose gear and main gear (172); Aurora Air, Inc., DBA Madras Air Service, Madris, OR 97741.

SA480CE: Nose and main gear wheel fairing (Jetstreams) using standing unaltered Cessna landing gear and nose gear for model and year using 500 × 5 nose and 600 × 6 main gear tires (172); Creative Designs, 1338 Orkla Dr., Minneapolis, MN 55427.

OTHERS

SA3-82: Retractable lifting handles model H,P/N 50-9; Woychik Aircraft Equipment, Middleton, WI 53562.

SA3-89: Equipment shelves and Grimes D-7080 rotating beacon; Capitol Aviation, Inc., Capitol Airport, Springfield, IL 62705.

SA3-107: Rudder trim system; Javelin Aircraft Co., Inc., 9175 East Douglas, Wichita, KS 67207.

SA4-198: 13-gallon auxiliary fuel system; Met-Co-Aire, P.O. Box

2216, Fullerton, CA 92633.

SA4-686: Full flow lube oil filter 30409A with element 1A0235; Winslow Aerofilter Corp., 4069 Hollis St., Oaklard, CA 94608.

SA64CE: Sky-Lite B-100 beacon light; Gas Equipment and Engine Co., 1015 Diamond Ave., Evansville, IN 47708.

SA94CE: Removal of right cabin door; Skylane Flying Service, Inc., 2029 Allens La., Evansville, IN 47708.

SA117EA: Flow lube oil filter PB 55-1; Fram Aerospace, Division of Fram Corp., 750 School St., Pawtuckett, RI 02860.

SA242EA: 40-0040 and 40-0043 supplemental light system; Grimes Manufacturing Co., 515 North Russell St., Urbana, OH 43078.

SA414SW: Jump step or mud guard on right landing gear; Curtis J. Smith Jr., Route 2, Box 314, Breaux Bridge, LA 70517.

SA531NW: Installation of windshield; Jack Shannon, 216 Terminal Building, Boeing Field, Seattle, WA 98101.

SA533CE: Installation of Canairco 1214WS supplementary light; Canairco Ltd., 400 First Avenue North, Minneapolis, MN 55401.

SA548GL: Installation of Flitefile console (172 1965 through 1981); David L. Benson, 7474 Carmel La., Grand Ledge, MI 48837.

SA861WE: Pilot and passenger restraint harness; Pacific Scientific Co., 1346 South State College Blvd., Anaheim, CA 92803.

SA1513SO: Installation of front seat modification; Civil Air Patrol, Maxwell AFB, AL 36112.

SA1584SO: Installation of Appalachian Accessories brake rotor P/N 75-27; Appalachian Accessories, P.O. Box 1077, TCAS, Blountville, TN 37617.

SA3072WE: Installation of emergency warning system; Systems Management Associates, Inc., P.O. Box 957, Palo Alto, CA 94302.

SA3-664: Install model 113A6, 200CW-6 or 212CW-6 dry vacuum pump and instrument vacuum system (172, 172A,B,C,D,E,F); Airborne Manufacturing Co., 711 Taylor St., Elyria, OH 44035.

SA21GL: Installation of Grimes multi-plexed anti-collision light system (172, 172A through 172I,K,L,M,N,P); Grimes Manufacturing Co., 515 North Russell St., Urbana, OH 43078.

SA43EA: Installation of Re-Vue Agency "nite-lite" and electronic aerial advertising sign (172, 172A,B,C); Re-Vue Agency, Inc., 616 East 4th. St., Pueblo, CO 80204.

SA211GL: Installation of windshield P/N W-2055, W/T-2055, W/G-2055 on Cessna 172 and 172A, and P/N W-2056, W/T-2056

✓ or W/G-2056 on Cessna 172B and 172C; Great Lakes Aero Products, 1021 North Chevrolet Ave., Flint, MI 48504.

SA326GL: Installation of fuel tank caps (172, 172A,B,C,D,E,F,G,H,I,K,L,M); John J. Francissen, 426 Pleasant Dr., Roselle, IL 60172.

SA729EA: Replacement of existing wheel/brake assemblies with Goodyear wheel/brake assemblies 9543679/95444295 (172, A through I); Aviation Products Division, The Goodyear Tire and Rubber Company, 1144 East Market St., Akron, OH 44315.

SA761GL: Modify airplane to fly on unleaded automotive gasoline, 87 minimum antiknock index (172, 172A,B,C,D,E,F [T-41A], G,H [T-41A]); EAA Aviation Foundation, P.O. Box 2592, Oshkosh, WI 54903.

SA864CE: Installation of electro pneumatic stall warning system (172, S/N 17254893 and on); Keaton Engineering Company, 1000 West 55th Street South, Wichita, KS 67217.

SA135EA: Installation of engine exhaust combustion monitor (172, 172A,B,C,D); Rosemount Engineering Co., 12001 West 78th St., Eden Prairie, MN 55343.

SA1947CE: Replace existing engine driven vacuum pump with engine driven piston-type vacuum pump (172 through 172Q); Sigma-Tek, Inc., 1326 South Walnut Street, Wichita, KS 67213.

SA3338WE: Recognition light installation on horizontal stabilizer (172, 172A,B,C,D,E,F [T-41], H [T-41], I,K,L,M,N); Devore Aviation Corporation, Suite B, 6104 Kicher Street, N.E., Albuquerque, NM 87109.

SA3796WE: Installation of Elano P/N 099001-063 F, or later FAA-approved revision muffler in lieu of original Avcon muffler (172, 172A through 172H (landplane only, normal category); Del-Air, P.O. Box 746, Strathmore, CA 93267.

SA4242WE: Installation of SDI CFS-1000, -1001, of FT-100 fuel flow indication system and facet P/N 480543 auxiliary fuel pump (172, 172A through 172H (landplane only, normal category); Del-Air, P.O. Box 746, Strathmore, CA 93267.

SA4283WE: Installation of electric inflatable door seal (172, 172A,B,C,D,E,F,G,H,K,L,M,N); Bob Fields Accessories, 5673 Stanford Street, Ventura, CA 93003.

SA3418WE: Installation of SDI Novastar II combined position/anticollision lighting system; Symbolic Displays, Inc., 1762 McGaw Avenue, Irvine, CA 92714.

SA18EA: Wet-to-dry vacuum pump conversion kit 300-1 (172A,B,C,D,E,F,G,H); Airborne Manufacturing Company, 711

Taylor Street, Elyria, OH 44035.

SA1813NM: Installation of Lompoc Aero inner plexiglasspane in swing-out window frames presently employing a single window (172A,B,C,D,E,F,G,H,I,K,L,M,N,P,T-41A); Lompoc Aero Specialties, Lompoc Airport, P.O. Box 998, Lompoc, CA 93436.

SA751EA: Installation of winterization kit (172B,G); Franklin Engine Company, Inc., Old Liverpool Road, Syracuse, NY 13206.

SA1311CE: Chrome-plated brake disc installation (172F,G,H,I,K,L); Engineering Plating and Processing, Inc., 641 Southwest Boulevard, Kansas City, KS 66103.

SA992CE: Installation of 10-inch diameter camera hole (172I,K,L,M,N,P); Ryan International Airways Corporation, 1640 Airport Rd., Mid-Continental Airport, Wichita, KS 67209.

SA1395SO: Remove pipe plug, Cessna P/N MS20913-1 or MS20913-1D from bottom of fuel selector valve body and replace with drain valve, MT-1072-77 (172I,K,L,M); Middle Tennessee Aircraft, P.O. Box 472, Smithville, TN 37166.

SA1531NM: Modification of the Union Aviation Supplemental Type Certification No. SA860SO for portable rudder/brake hand-control by adapting the control to "Nylafil" rudder pedals (172I,K,L,M,N,P); Dave Flock, 1009 West 31st Street, Loveland, CO 80537.

SA1826CE: Installation of photo bubble in baggage door opening (172I,K,L,M,N,P); Hue Aire, Inc., 930 North Main, Hutchinson, KS 67501.

SA1948CE: Operation on unleaded and/or leaded automotive gasoline (172I,K,L,M); Petersen Aviation, Inc., Route 1, Box 19, Minden, NE 68959.

SA3777WE: Installation of flexible stainless steel oil cooler hoses (172I,K through N); Aircraft Metal Products Corporation, 4206 Glencoe Avenue, Venice, CA 90291.

SA3858WE: Installation of an air/oil separator (172I,K,L,M,N); Walker Engineering Company, 5760 West 3rd Street, Los Angeles, CA 90036.

SA702GL: Installation of a cooling shroud on engine-driven dry air pumps (172K,L,M,N,P,Q); S & M Products, 2515 East Bonnie Brook Lane, Waukegan, IL 60087.

SA2575WE: Installation of observer station in rear seat-baggage compartment area, searchlight and dual speakers in bottom of aft fuselage, windows in baggage compartment area (baggage was removed), and a muffler (172K,M, normal category landplane only); World Associates, Inc., 430 Wilshire Boulevard,

Suite 204, Santa Monica, CA 90401.

SA965CE: Installation of Model IU328-001 vacuum pump and IU292-003 suction relief valve (172L ser 17259224 through 17260758); Edo-Aire Wichita Division, 1326 South Walnut, Wichita, KS 67213.

SA6NE: Installation of Whelan anti-collision strobe light power supplies, Models HS-41 and HD-42 as direct replacements for Models HS and HD installed in accordance with STC SA615EA or STC SA800EA (172M); Whelan Engineering Company, Inc., Winter Avenue, Deep River, CT 06417.

SA1258EA: Installation of Cosco Model 78 child restraint system (172M); Stuart R. Miller, P.O. Box 926, Grand Central Station, New York, NY 10163.

SA146GL: Installation of EPA portable enviro pod (172M,N); Air Force Wright Aero Lab, AFWAL/AARF.

SA1211EA: Installation of EPA portable enviro-pod with Tensor-Hasselbad camera configuration (172M,N); Tensor Industries, Inc., 117 Schley Avenue, Lewes, DE 19958.

SA5621SW: Installation of electrically driven vacuum pump (172M,N,P,Q); Aero Safe Corporation, P.O. Box 10206, Fort Worth, TX 76114.

SA1396SO: Remove drain plug, Cessna P/N AN814-3DL from bottom of fuel selector valve body and replace with drain valve MT-1072-77 (172N); Middle Tennessee Aircraft, P.O. Box 472, Smithville, TN 37166.

SA4-1601: Conversion of aircraft for parachute jumping and aerial photography operations (172); Air Oasis Company, Municipal Airport, Long Beach, CA 90801.

SA4-306: Roto-Nav bracket and Grimes D 7080 anti-collision light on vertical fin (172); Air Oasis Company, Municipal Airport, Long Beach, CA 90801.

SA10WE: Arens Vernier type throttle control (172); Van Nuys Skyways, Inc., 16700 Roscoe Blvd, Van Nuys, CA 91408.

SA462WE: Jump door 62-500 (172); Sky Motive, Inc., Route 1, Box 32, Snohomish, WA 98290.

SA2362WE: Installation of lure toxicant dispenser AEY 70, Model # 1 (172); USDA, 3701 West Nob Hill Blvd, Yakima, WA 98902.

SA105NW: Mounting and wiring for occasional installation and use of Barnes Engineering Company airborne fire spotter system (172); State of Washington, Dept. of Natural Resources, Route 13, Box 62, Olympia, WA 98501.

SA271NW: Removal of paper air induction filter (172); Kenmore Air Harbor, P.O. Box 64, Kenmore, WA 98028.

SA1-193: Conversion of aircraft for parachute jumping operations (172); Parachute Club of America, P.O. Box 409, Monterey, CA 93940.

SA116EA: Installation of Fram Part Flow Lube Oil Filter Model PB 55-1 (172); Fram Aerospace Division of Fram Corporation, 750 School Street, Pawtucket, RI 02860.

POPULAR MODIFICATIONS

The following are some of the more popular modifications owners can make to their 172s:

STOL

STOL conversions are perhaps king of all the modifications available to the 172 owner. STOL is the military designation for Short Take-off and Landing aircraft. STOL has been extended into general aviation markets, resulting in some rather spectacular—performance-wise—conversion aircraft. The typical STOL modification involves changes to the overall shape of the wing (usually in the form of a leading edge cuff), the addition of stall fences (to stop the stall from proceeding along the wing spanwise (Fig 10-1), gap seals, wingtips, and perhaps an increase in power.

Fig. 10-1. Most STOL conversions make use of stall fences.

These are the specifications Horton STOLcraft lists for a converted Cessna 172:

Gross weight:	2200 lbs
Takeoff Speed:	38 mph
Takeoff over 50' obst:	840 ft
Cruise Speed:	133 mph
Approach Speed:	38 mph
Landing over 50' obst:	625 ft

(These figures represent maximum performance)

Note: Sometimes an owner will make STOL modifications one part at a time, and often with STCs from several sources. Before proceeding with this method, check with your local GADO about the various STCs you are considering, as some are not compatible with others.

STOL modifications/kits are available from:

Bush Conversions, Inc.
P.O. Box 431
Udall, KS 67146

Horton STOLcraft
Wellington Municipal Airport
Wellington, KS 67152
Phone: (800) 835-2051
KS: (316) 326-2241

R/STOL, Inc.
Snohomish County Airport
Building C-72
Everett, WA 98204
Phone: (206) 355-2736

Turbotech, Inc.
1115 E. 5th Street
P.O. Box 61586
Vancouver, WA 98666
Phone: (206) 694-6287

Power

Power modifications are the second most popular type of work done to 172s, and are often done in conjunction with STOL modifications. These mods consist of engine replacement to increase the useful load and flight performance figures of the aircraft. The modifications can be extensive and costly, although most are not much above the level of a good engine rebuild charge (Figs. 10-2, 10-3). The following firms provide power modifications for Cessna 172 airplanes:

Avcon Industries, Inc., installs the Lycoming O-360-A1A engine with a constant-speed propeller on the 172. For further information, contact:

Avcon Industries, Inc.
P.O. Box 654
Udall, KS 67146

Penn Yan Aero installs the 180-hp O-360 engine in the 172 and claims that it increases the cruise speed from 139 to 160 mph. The rate of climb is brought from 730 fpm to 1100 fpm, and the takeoff distance reduced from 730 to 400 feet, yet still retaining the simplicity of a fixed-pitch propeller. For further information, contact:

Penn Yan Aero
Penn Yan Airport
2499 Bath Rd.
Penn Yan, NY 14527
Phone: (315) 536-2333

RAM Aircraft Corp. installs the AVCO Lycoming O-320-D2G 160-hp engine in all model 172s. This is done as a replacement of the older Continental O-300 series 145-hp engines, and to replace the O-320-H2AD engine, which has had so many ADs issued against it. For more information, contact:

RAM Aircraft Corp.
Waco-Madison Cooper Airport
P.O. Box 5219
Waco, TX 76708
Phone: (817) 752-8381

Turbotech, Inc., installs the Franklin 220-hp engine or a turbocharged Franklin of 250 hp on 172 and 175 models. These modifi-

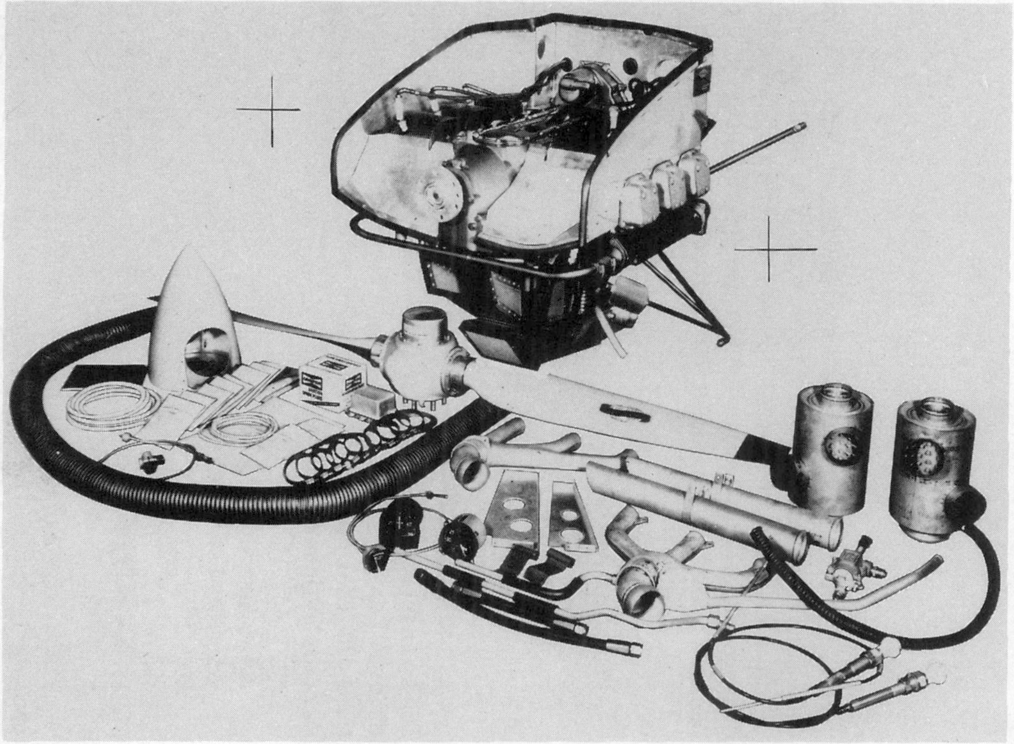

Fig. 10-2. Franklin 220-hp engine and conversion for a Cessna 172. (courtesy Turbotech, Inc.)

Fig. 10-3. Lineup of Franklin engines for power-up conversions on the Cessna 172. (courtesy Turbotech, Inc.)

cations give a maximum speed of 170 mph and a rate of climb of 1800 fpm. This conversion is particularly popular among the float-plane fliers, giving a cruise of 155 mph. This is the most powerful conversion for the 172/175 airplanes available. Flying a 220 or 250-hp 172 is a real thrill, and will give you a look at the hidden capabilities of this fine airplane. For further information, contact:

Turbotech, Inc.
1115 E. 5th Street
P.O. Box 61586
Vancouver, WA 98666
Phone: (206) 694-6287

Wingtips

Wingtips are often changed to increase performance. Dr. Sighard Hoerner, Ph.D, designed a high-performance wingtip for the U.S. Navy, which provided information that led to the development of improved wingtips for lightplanes. A properly designed wingtip can provide an increase of three to five mph in cruise speed and a small increase in climb performance, but most important are the improved low-speed handling characteristics: 10 to 20 percent reduction in takeoff roll, four to five mph lower stall speed, and improved slow-flight handling. Installation time can be as low as two to three hours. This is one of the most popular modifications for 172 owners (Figs. 10-4, 10-5). For more information, contact:

Ace Deemers
Madras Air Service
1914 NW Deemers Dr.
Madras, OR 97741

Met-Co-Aire
P.O. Box 2216
Fullerton, CA 92633
Phone: (714) 870-4610

Landing Gear

Taildragger conversions have become popular among owners of 172s. Basically, the nosewheel is removed, the main gear moved forward, and a tailwheel installed (Fig. 10-6). Performance benefits

Fig. 10-4. The Met-Co-Aire (Hoerner-style) wingtip. (courtesy Met-Co-Aire)

of eight to ten mph increase in cruise, shorter takeoff distances and better rough-field handling are claimed. My own opinion is that if the need for a rough-field machine is real, then a proper STOL and power-up modification should also be made. This will cost a large amount of money, and the 172 owner would be well advised to consider the possibility of purchasing a more appropriate aircraft for the job, such as a Cessna 180 or 185, or a Maule.

Fig. 10-5. This downturned style wingtip is often seen on Cessna airplanes.

Fig. 10-6. Taildragger conversion. (courtesy Custom Aircraft Conversions, Inc.)

Typical taildragger modifications and kits are available from:

ACT
P.O.Box 119
Georgetown, CA 95634
Phone: (916) 333-2466

Bush Conversions, Inc.
P.O. Box 431
Udall, KS 67146

Gap Seals

Gap seals are extensions of the lower wing surface from the rear spar to the leading edge of the flap and/or aileron. They cover approximately six square feet of open space, allowing a smoother flow of air around the wing. In addition to the reduction of parasitic drag, the aircraft will cruise from one to three mph faster, and stall from five to eight mph slower. Gap seals are often part of a STOL installation.

B&M Aviation produces all aluminum gap seals. The units are riveted into place and require two to three hours of installation time. For further information, contact:

B&M Aviation
2048 Airport Way
Bellingham, WA 98226
Phone: (206) 676-1750

Flight Bonus manufacturers gap seals made of a thin, flexible strip of neoprene-impregnated nylon fabric that is bonded to the aileron and the wing during installation. Installation time is five to six hours. For further information, contact:

Flight Bonus, Inc.
P.O. Box 120773
Arlington, TX 76012
Phone: (817) 265-1650

Other sources of gap seal kits are:

Aircraft Development
1326 N. Westlink Blvd.
Witchita, KS 67212
Phone: (316) 722-7736

Davids Aviation
Superplane
22962 Clawiter Rd. #24
Hayward, CA 94545
Phone: (415) 782-5425

Weight

Weight increases are available that increase the gross weight of the 172 to 2550 pounds. These STCs are available for the 172N and P Models only. For further information, contact:

Penn Yan Aero
Penn Yan Airport
2499 Bath Rd.
Penn Yan, NY 14527
Phone: (315) 536-2333

Fuel

Fuel tanks are sometimes added to increase operational range. Such modifications are available from:

Flint Aero
8665 Mission Gorge Rd.
Building D1
Santee, CA 92071
Phone: (619) 448-1551

Noise

Noise reduction has been a problem for all small airplane owners; however, one manufacturer produces an inner window. To reduce cabin noise, the inner windows are installed in the doors, and amount to "storm" windows (Fig. 10-7). By increasing the window thickness and including a dead air space, interior noise is reduced. For further information, contact:

Lompoc Aero Specialties
Lompoc Airport
P.O. Box 998
Lompoc, CA 93438
Phone: (805) 736-1273

Fig. 10-7. Noise-reducing interior windows. (courtesy Lompoc Aero Specialties)

Other noise reduction installations are available from:

Aircraft Development
1326 N. Westlink Blvd.
Wltchita, KS 67212
Phone: (316) 722-7736

Doors

Door catches on older 172s are usually rusted and no longer function to hold the doors open. The installation of a Sky Catch will eliminate this problem. For further information, contact:

Sky Craft Quality Aviation Products
8933 Pawnee Rd.
Homerville, OH 44235
Phone: (216) 948-2778

Drain Valve

Fuel Safety—or, more exactly, the inability to completely clear the fuel system of water—is easily corrected by the addition of a belly drain valve. The item costs only a few dollars, and takes about 10 minutes to install. It could save your life, as the location of installation is the lowest point in the fuel system, where water will gather. For further information contact:

C-Mods
P.O. Box 506
Morrisville, NC 27560
Phone: (919) 544-5137

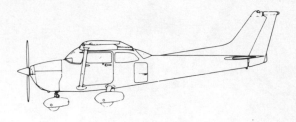

Chapter 11
Fun Flying on Floats

Ever wish you could go someplace and *really* get away from it all? Well, perhaps the answer to your dreams is a floatplane. A floatplane is a land-based aircraft that has had the landing gear removed and floats installed in their place (Figs. 11-1 and 11-2).

The fun of float flying attracts many people, and such planes offer a means of transportation to otherwise inaccessible locations. However, even with their capabilities, there are a few things you should know before you consider this type of aircraft or flying:

1. You will need a seaplane rating on your license. This is relatively easy to obtain, as there are many flying schools around the country that offer seaplane training. The training is completely practical, and involves flying skills only, nothing written. Often the price is fixed, and the rating guaranteed. Check *Trade-A-Plane* and other publications for appropriate advertising.

2. Your insurance rates will go up considerably, unless you have extensive floatplane experience with no accident history. Even then, rates will be higher for a float-equipped airplane than for a land-only plane. The reasoning behind the higher rates is the higher loss ratio with floatplanes as compared to land planes. For example, a typical ground loop in a land-based aircraft can result in several hundred dollars of damage. The damaged aircraft can often be taxied to a repair facility. The same type of mishap on the water could mean a sunken aircraft, resulting in difficult or impos-

Fig. 11-1. Cessna Skyhawk on floats. (courtesy EDO)

Fig. 11-2. Cessna Hawk XP on floats. (courtesy EDO)

sible recovery, and thousands of dollars in damages.

3. You are forever limited to water flying. The Cessna 172 cannot be equipped with amphibious floats, due to weight limitations.

4. Aircraft performance is reduced, as the aircraft performance figures show on the following pages.

5. There is considerably more maintenance on aircraft used for water operations. Much of this in the form of corrosion control.

PERFORMANCE FIGURES

The following are the official specifications for the various models of 172s listed by horsepower of the engine. If you compare these to the land performance figures (specifications) found in Chapter 2, you will see quite a large difference in performance between land and floatplanes.

This large performance difference is quite normal; after all, the floats and rigging are heavy and extremely bulky.

Specifications

145-hp Version:

Speed
    Max Speed at Sea Level: 108 mph
    Cruise, 75 percent power at 6500 ft: 106 mph
Range
    Cruise, 75 percent at 6500 ft: 500 mi
    38 Gallons, no reserve: 4.7 hrs
                                      106 mph

    Cruise, 75 percent at 6500 ft: 625 mi
    48 Gallons, no reserve: 5.9 hrs
                                      106 mph

    Optimum Range at 10,000 ft: 530 mi
    38 Gallons, no reserve: 5.5 hrs
                                      97 mph

    Optimum Range at 10,000 ft: 670 mi
    48 Gallons, no reserve: 7.0 hrs
                                      97 mph

Rate of Climb at Sea Level: 580 fpm
Service Ceiling: 12,000 ft
Takeoff
    Water Run: 1620 ft
    Over 50-ft Obstacle: 2390 ft
Landing
    Water Roll: 590 ft

Over 50-ft Obstacle:	1345	ft
Stall Speed		
Flaps Up, Power Off:	59	mph
Flaps Down, Power Off:	52	mph
Baggage:	120	lbs
Wing Loading: (lbs/sq ft)	12.7	
Power Loading: (lbs/hp)	14.8	
Fuel Capacity		
Standard:	42	gal
Long-range Tanks:	52	gal
Oil Capacity:	8	qts
Engine:	Continental O-300	
TBO:	1800	hrs
Power:	145	hp
Propeller: (diameter)	80	in
Wingspan:	35 ft 10	in
Wing Area: (sq ft)	174	
Length:	27 ft 00	in
Height:	9 ft 11	in
Gross Weight:	2220	lbs
Empty Weight:	1415	lbs
Useful Load:	805	lbs

150-hp Version:

Speed		
Max Speed at Sea Level:	98	kts
Cruise, 75 percent power at 7500 ft:	97	kts
Range		
Cruise, 75 percent at 7500 ft.	365	nm
38 Gallons usable fuel:	3.8	hrs
Cruise, 75 percent at 7500 ft:	480	nm
48 Gallons usable fuel:	5.0	hrs
Maximum Range at 10,000 ft:	385	nm
38 Gallons usable fuel:	4.4	hrs
Maximum Range at 10,000 ft:	510	nm
48 Gallons usable fuel:	5.9	hrs
Rate of Climb at Sea Level:	715	fpm
Service Ceiling:	12,000	ft
Takeoff		
Water Run:	1620	ft
Over 50-ft Obstacle:	2390	ft
Landing		
Water Roll:	590	ft
Over 50-ft Obstacle:	1345	ft
Stall Speed		

Flaps Up, Power Off:	46	kts
Flaps Down, Power Off:	44	kts
Baggage:	120	lbs
Wing Loading: (lbs/sq ft)	12.7	
Power Loading: (lbs/hp)	14.8	
Fuel Capacity		
Standard:	42	gal
Long-range Tanks:	52	gal
Oil Capacity:	8	qts
Engine:	Lycoming O-320-E2D	
TBO:	2000	hrs
Power:	150	hp
Propeller: (diameter)	80	in
Wingspan:	35 ft 10	in
Wing Area: (sq ft)	174	
Length:	27 ft 00	in
Height:	9 ft 11	in
Gross Weight:	2220	lbs
Empty Weight:	1574	lbs
Useful Load:	646	lbs

160-hp Version:

Speed		
Max Speed at Sea Level:	96	kts
Cruise, 75 percent power at 4000 ft:	95	kts
Range		
Cruise, 75 percent power at 4000 ft:	360	nm
40 Gallons usable fuel:	3.8	hrs
Cruise, 75 percent power at 4000 ft:	475	nm
50 Gallons usable fuel:	5.0	hrs
Maximum Range at 10,000 ft:	435	nm
40 Gallons usable fuel:	5.6	hrs
Maximum Range at 10,000 ft:	565	nm
50 Gallons usable fuel:	7.3	hrs
Rate of Climb at Sea Level:	740	fpm
Service Ceiling:	15,000	ft
Takeoff		
Water Run:	1400	ft
Over 50-ft Obstacle:	2160	ft
Landing		
Water Roll:	590	ft
Over 50-ft Obstacle:	1345	ft
Stall Speed		
Flaps Up, Power Off:	48	kts
Flaps Down, Power Off:	44	kts

Baggage:	120	lbs
Wing Loading: (lbs/sq ft)	12.7	
Power Loading: (lbs/hp)	13.9	
Fuel Capacity		
Standard:	43	gal
Long-range Tanks:	54	gal
Oil Capacity:	8	qts
Engine:	Lycoming O-320-D2J	
TBO:	2000	hrs
Power:	160	hp
Propeller: (diameter)	80	in
Wingspan:	35 ft 10	in
Wing Area: (sq ft)	174	
Length:	26 ft 08	in
Height:	11 ft 11	in
Gross Weight:	2220	lbs
Empty Weight:	1621	lbs
Useful Load:	606	lbs

195-hp Version:

Speed		
Max Speed at Sea Level:	118	kts
Cruise, 75 percent power at 6000 ft:	116	kts
Range		
Cruise, 80 percent power at 6000 ft:	395	nm
49 Gallons usable fuel:	3.4	hrs
Cruise, 80 percent power at 6000 ft:	570	nm
66 Gallons usable fuel:	4.9	hrs
Maximum Range at 10,000 ft:	495	nm
49 Gallons usable fuel:	5.5	hrs
Maximum Range at 10,000 ft:	705	nm
66 Gallons usable fuel:	7.9	hrs
Rate of Climb at Sea Level:	870	fpm
Service Ceiling:	15,500	ft
Takeoff		
Water Run:	1135	ft
Over 50-ft Obstacle:	1850	ft
Landing		
Water Roll:	675	ft
Over 50-ft Obstacle:	1390	ft
Stall Speed		
Flaps Up, Power Off:	50	kts
Flaps Down, Power Off:	44	kts
Baggage:	200	lbs
Wing Loading: (lbs/sq ft)	14.7	

Power Loading: (lbs/hp)	13.1	
Fuel Capacity		
Standard:	52	gal
Long-range Tanks:	68	gal
Oil Capacity:	9	qts
Engine: Teledyne-Cont.	IO-360-KB	
TBO:	2000	hrs
Power:	195	hp
Propeller: (diameter) C/S	80	in
Wingspan:	35 ft 10	in
Wing Area: (sq ft)	174	
Length:	26 ft 08	in
Height:	12 ft 05	in
Gross Weight:	2550	lbs
Empty Weight:	1808	lbs
Useful Load:	750	lbs

FLOATS FOR THE 172

The following floats are available for the Cessna 172 airplanes:

For the 172: Canadian model 2000, available from:

Canadian Aircraft Products, Ltd.
2611 Viscount Way
Richmond, BC V6V1M9
Canada
Phone: (604) 278-9821

For the 172: Capre 2200 and 2400
For the 172XP: Capre 2400, available from:

Capre Inc.
805 Geiger Rd.
Zephyrhills, FL 33599
Phone: (813) 782-9541

For the 172: Edo 2000, 2130 and 244OB
For the 172XP: Edo 244OB, available from:

Edo Corp.
Float Operations
14-04 111 Street
College Point, NY 11356
Phone: (212) 445-6000

For the 172: Fiberfloat 2400

For the 172XP: Fiberfloat 2400, available from:

Fiberfloat Corp.
895 Gay St.
Bartow, FL 33830
Phone: (813) 533-8001

For the 172: PK B2300
For the 172XP: PK B2300, available from:

DeVore Aviation Corp.
6104B Kircher Blvd., NE
Albuquerque, NM 87109
Phone: (505) 345-8713

FLOAT PRICES

Floats themselves are expensive. The following list reflects
1987 suggested retail prices.

Canadian 2000		$11,400
Capre	2200	13,490
	2400	14,450
EDO	2000	13,850
	2440B	15,540
Fiberfloat 2400		14,400
PK B2300		14,750

MODIFICATIONS

There are precious few 172s on floats available in the used market. It is, however, possible to covert an existing 172 for use on floats. This conversion can be done in the field, meaning no extensive disassembly is necessary.

The conversion kits, available from Cessna, consist of the necessary materials to strengthen the airframe and make attachment points for the floats. Stainless steel control cables are a part of the kit. At the time of modification, it is required that zinc chromate be applied inside, outside, and between all panels of the airframe.

The 172XP with the 195-hp engine makes a fine floatplane, but it is now out of production. This is unfortunate, as the 172XP is a true four-place floatplane. The basic 172 is really considered to be two " + " place, due to the weight and horsepower limitations. The latter can often be helped with the installation of a larger engine.

For engine and performance modification information, see Chapter 10.

AREAS OF FLOATPLANE ACTIVITY

There is a floatplane flying in every state of the union; however, some states have more than others.

The following states have considerable float flying:

☐ Alaska
☐ California
☐ Florida
☐ Louisiana
☐ Maine
☐ Massachusetts
☐ Minnesota
☐ Washington
☐ Wisconsin

Canada offers some of the best floatplane flying in the world, as there are many locations that are accessible *only* by floatplane.

ASSOCIATIONS

The AOPA sponsors the Seaplane Pilots Association. The group was formed in 1972, and now claims several thousand members. The objective is to assist seaplane pilots with technical problems, provide a national lobbying effort, and explore possible economy measures.

Membership in the Seaplane Pilots Association will bring you a quarterly magazine called *Water Flying.* Additionally, you will receive the *Water Flying Annual,* and other written communications that include timely tips and safety measures. The SPA sponsors numerous fly-ins annually. For further information, contact:

Seaplane Pilot's Association
421 Aviation Way
Frederick, MD 21701
Phone: (301) 695-2000

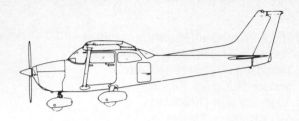

Chapter 12
Hangar Flying

The following pages are devoted to comments, statements, rumors, and facts that are often heard about the Cessna 172 airplanes.

CLUBS

For the most information about your airplane, join a club that supports your airplane. In the field of the Cessna 172 there are two such clubs.

The Cessna Pilots Association

The Cessna Pilot Association's sole purpose is to support owners/pilots of Cessna single-engine airplanes.

The association publishes a fine monthly newsletter, with color photos, and a large amount of well-documented information pertinent to the safe and cost-effective ownership of an airplane.

The newsletter is not a promoter of advertised products; however, it does recommend products the association feels are worthwhile.

For further information about this fine organization, contact:

Cessna Pilots Association
P.O. Box 12948
Witchita, KS 67277
Phone: (316) 946-4777

The Cessna Skyhawk Association

The Cessna Skyhawk Association, part of the Cessna Owners Organizations, offers a monthly newsletter which includes:

- ☐ Maintenance and Modification Ideas
- ☐ Exchange of Technical Information
- ☐ Manufacturers' Service Letters
- ☐ Service Difficulty Reports
- ☐ Airworthiness Directives
- ☐ Airworthiness Alerts
- ☐ Safety Corner
- ☐ The Av-Mart

. . . and much more! Additionally, the association provides a group insurance program for your aircraft, a family-oriented annual fly-in, and help as close as a telephone. For more information, contact:

Cessna Skyhawk Association
P.O. Box 75068
Birmingham, AL 35253
Phone: (800) 247-8360

WHO SAYS WHAT

The Cessna 172 is a very talked-about airplane. After all, there are a lot of them around. Here is a synopsis of many comments I have heard regarding the 172:

Insurance Carriers Say:

"Insuring the Cessna 172 is easy, as there are no real secrets to them. They are reliable, easy to fly, and replacement parts are available everywhere."

"We feel very comfortable about insuring low-time pilots in the 172."

"The 172 makes flying a family affair, and that generally makes for safer flying."

"The 172 airplanes are quite forgiving of pilot inattention, therefore provide a low risk for insurance coverage."

Lineboys Say:

"I see all kinds of planes, and some are real expensive, but I really like to see an old 172 that has been all fixed up. The pilot is usually the guy who fixed it, and he's real proud of it."

"High wings are harder to fuel than low wings."

"Wish all Cessnas had steps on them."

"All the old Cessna drivers were sure happy to see 'red' [80/87 octane] fuel again."

"Some of the 172 drivers are refueling out of their cars. Guess it saves money, but it doesn't guarantee I'll be employed much longer."

Mechanics Say:

"There's not much that can go wrong with a Cessna high wing that creates any mystery. They were built tough."

"The four-cylinder Lycoming 150-hp engines seem to be very solid. The Continental O-300 engines develop cracks in the jugs, and the H2AD has been real headaches for all concerned."

"The O-300 engine is more expensive to overhaul then the O-320."

"Get the 100LL valve kit for the O-300; it really helps."

"The 'H' engines from S/N 7970 and up are modified, and the factory considers them to be the 'answer' ".

"These planes are simple enough for the typical owner to care for with little supervision."

"Poor fuel sump draining is a real problem, but it can be fixed for less than $50 by installing a belly drain."

"The seat attach points on the seat rails are a weak point."

NTSB Says:

The following tables of comparative accident data are a compilation of a study made by the NTSB (National Transportation Safety Board). All figures are based on the adjusted rate of 100,000 hours of flying time.

It's interesting to note where the various makes/models are placed on these charts. Placement is determined by: *worst* at the top; *best* at the bottom.

If you are unsure of what some of the mentioned makes/models are, I suggest you consult *The Illustrated Buyer's Guide to Used Airplanes* (TAB #2372).

Fatal Accident Rate Comparison by Manufacturer

Make	Mean Fatal Accident Rate
Bellanca	4.84
Grumman	4.13
Beech	2.54
Mooney	2.50
Piper	2.48
Cessna	1.65*

Engine Failure

Aircraft	Rate
Globe GC-1	12.36
Stinson 108	10.65
Ercoupe	9.50
Grumman AA-1	8.71
Navion	7.84
Piper J-3	7.61
Luscombe 8	7.58
Cessna 120/140	6.73
Piper PA-12	6.54
Bellanca 14-19	5.98
Piper PA-22	5.67
Cessna 195	4.69
Piper PA-32	4.39
Cessna 210/205	4.25
Aeronca 7	4.23
Aeronca 11	4.10
Taylorcraft BC	3.81
Piper PA-24	3.61
Beech 23	3.58
Cessna 175	3.48
Mooney M-20	3.42
Piper PA-18	3.37
Cessna 177	3.33
Cessna 206	3.30
Cessna 180	3.24
Cessna 170	2.88
Cessna 185	2.73

Aircraft	Rate
Cessna 150	2.48
Piper PA-28	2.37
Beech 33, 35, 36	2.22
Grumman AA-5	2.20
Cessna 182	2.08
Cessna 172	1.41*

In-Flight Airframe Failure

Aircraft	Rate
Bellanca 14-19	1.49
Globe GC-1	1.03
Ercoupe	0.97
Cessna 195	0.94
Navion	0.90
Aeronca 11	0.59
Beech 33, 35, 36	0.58
Luscombe 8	0.54
Piper PA-24	0.42
Cessna 170	0.36
Cessna 210/205	0.34
Cessna 180	0.31
Piper PA-22	0.30
Aeronca 7	0.27
Beech 23	0.27
Cessna 120/140	0.27
Piper PA-32	0.24
Taylorcraft BC	0.24
Piper J-3	0.23
Mooney M-20	0.18
Piper PA-28	0.16
Cessna 177	0.16
Cessna 182	0.12
Cessna 206	0.11
Grumman AA-1	0.09
Cessna 172	0.03*
Cessna 150	0.02

Stall

Aircraft	Rate
Aeronca 7	22.47

269

Aircraft	Rate
Aeronca 11	8.21
Taylorcraft BC	6.44
Piper J-3	5.88
Luscombe 8	5.78
Piper PA-18	5.49
Globe GC-1	5.15
Cessna 170	4.38
Grumman AA-1	4.23
Piper PA-12	3.27
Cessna 120/140	2.51
Stinson 108	2.09
Navion	1.81
Piper PA-22	1.78
Cessna 177	1.77
Grumman AA-5	1.76
Cessna 185	1.47
Cessna 150	1.42
Beech 23	1.41
Ercoupe	1.29
Cessna 180	1.08
Piper PA-24	0.98
Beech 33, 35, 36	0.94
Cessna 175	0.83
Piper PA-28	0.80
Mooney M-20	0.80
Cessna 172	0.77*
Cessna 210/205	0.71
Bellanca 14-19	0.60
Piper PA-32	0.57
Cessna 206	0.54
Cessna 195	0.47
Cessna 182	0.36

Hard Landing

Aircraft	Rate
Beech 23	3.50
Grumman AA-1	3.02
Ercoupe	2.90
Cessna 177	2.60
Globe GC-1	2.58
Luscombe 8	2.35
Cessna 182	2.17
Cessna 170	1.89

Aircraft	Rate
Beech 33, 35, 36	1.45
Cessna 150	1.37
Cessna 120/140	1.35
Cessna 206	1.30
Piper PA-24	1.29
Aeronca 7	1.20
Piper J-3	1.04
Grumman AA-5	1.03
Cessna 175	1.00
Cessna 180	0.93
Cessna 210/205	0.82
Piper PA-28	0.81
Cessna 172	0.71*
Piper PA-22	0.69
Taylorcraft BC	0.48
Cessna 195	0.47
Piper PA-18	0.43
Piper PA-32	0.42
Cessna 185	0.42
Navion	0.36
Mooney M-20	0.31
Piper PA-12	0.23
Stinson 108	0.19

Ground Loop

Aircraft	Rate
Cessna 195	22.06
Stinson 108	13.50
Luscombe 8	13.00
Cessna 170	9.91
Cessna 120/140	8.99
Aeronca 11	7.86
Aeronca 7	7.48
Cessna 180	6.49
Cessna 185	4.72
Piper PA-12	4.67
Piper PA-18	3.90
Taylorcraft BC	3.58
Globe GC-1	3.09
Grumman AA-1	2.85
Piper PA-22	2.76
Ercoupe	2.74

Aircraft	Rate
Beech 23	2.33
Bellanca 14-19	2.10
Piper J-3	2.07
Cessna 206	1.73
Cessna 177	1.61
Grumman AA-5	1.47
Piper PA-32	1.42
Cessna 150	1.37
Piper PA-28	1.36
Piper PA-24	1.29
Cessna 210/205	1.08
Cessna 182	1.06
Cessna 172	1.00*
Mooney M-20	0.65
Beech 33, 35, 36	0.55
Navion	0.36
Cessna 175	0.17

Undershoot

Aircraft	Rate
Ercoupe	2.41
Luscombe 8	1.62
Piper PA-12	1.40
Globe GC-1	1.03
Cessna 175	0.99
Grumman AA-1	0.95
Taylorcraft BC	0.95
Piper PA-22	0.83
Piper PA-32	0.70
Bellanca 14-19	0.60
Aeronca 11	0.59
Piper PA-28	0.59
Aeronca 7	0.59
Piper PA-24	0.57
Piper J-3	0.57
Stinson 108	0.57
Cessna 120/140	0.53
Cessna 195	0.47
Grumman AA-5	0.44
Piper PA-18	0.43
Beech 23	0.43
Cessna 185	0.41
Mooney M-20	0.37

Aircraft	Rate
Cessna 170	0.36
Navion	0.36
Cessna 150	0.35
Cessna 210/205	0.33
Cessna 206	0.32
Cessna 172	0.26*
Cessna 182	0.24
Beech 33, 35, 36	0.21
Cessna 180	0.15
Cessna 177	0.10

Overshoot

Aircraft	Rate
Grumman AA-5	2.35
Cessna 195	2.34
Beech 23	1.95
Piper PA-24	1.61
Piper PA-22	1.33
Cessna 175	1.33
Stinson 108	1.33
Cessna 182	1.21
Aeronca 11	1.17
Luscombe 8	1.08
Piper PA-32	1.03
Globe GC-1	1.03
Mooney M-20	1.01
Cessna 172	1.00*
Cessna 170	0.99
Grumman AA-1	0.95
Piper PA-12	0.93
Cessna 210/205	0.89
Cessna 177	0.88
Piper PA-18	0.81
Cessna 206	0.81
Piper PA-28	0.80
Cessna 120/140	0.71
Piper PA-28	0.80
Cessna 120/140	0.71
Ercoupe	0.64
Bellanca 14-19	0.60
Cessna 180	0.56
Navion	0.54

Aircraft	Rate
Aeronca 7	0.48
Cessna 150	0.35
Piper J-3	0.34
Cessna 185	0.31
Beech 33, 35, 36	0.23

Owners Say:

"Maintenance is what I like about my Hawk. It requires very little."

"We recently traded down to a 172 from a '65 Beech 35. The service it required was breaking me. Now we can afford to fly again—slower, but we get there."

"I just replaced the last of six cylinders on my Continental O-300. That's at 150 SMOH. Not all overhauls are created equal."

"My last annual cost $325, and that's in the high-cost Washington, D.C. area. I'm real happy with that."

"My bird has King avionics and I love them. I've never had a lick of trouble with them. My brother has ARC and is jealous. His is in the shop all the time."

"Had to replace several landing lights before I heard about the vibration kit available from Cessna. Why don't people (FBOs and dealers) tell you about these things?"

"I could afford to buy a retractable if I wanted it, but why pay for all the extra maintenance for a little extra speed? Slow down and enjoy life."

Pilots Say:

"The 172 flies just like a 150, just bigger."

"It's no tiger on takeoff in the summer, but it gets there, even when we (four) are all aboard."

"I've never attained the published cruise speed in my '65, but it still gets me there."

"The nosewheel shimmies, just like the one on my old 150."

"We bought the 172 instead of a PA-28/140 to have the capability to really carry four people."

"I fly from a mountain airport at the 7,000-foot line. Don't think I would ever try to get out with four on board in the summer."

"My wife gave me a set of sheepskin seat covers for Christmas last year—real class, in a class bird."

"I just had a 180-hp engine installed, wow! What get-up-and-go! This really helps, as the ranch strip is kinda bad in the spring."

"Most of the time I fly by myself, but I prefer the extra 'weight' of the 172 over the lighter 150. This is very true when I am flying IFR."

"The visibility in a busy traffic pattern is poor, but that's the same for all high-wingers."

"Love the barn door flaps; can really save a high approach."

"I have a '63 model with manual flaps, and plan to keep it. I don't like the electric flaps; there's too much that can break on them."

"A faster airplane would be nice, but most of my trips are less than 300 miles, and the actual time saved would be small, but the increased maintenance would be large."

"My wife is learning to fly, and when my son gets old enough, he will, too. Flying our Hawk has become a family affair."

"I have the Deemers tips on the plane, and they allow me to make it into my farm strip easier. The strip is only 990 feet long, but clear on both ends."

"It's too noisy, but most small planes are."

"There's only the two of us, so we can take all the baggage and other stuff we want to. Loads of room."

"After ground-looping my 180 a couple of times, I sold it and got this 172 with the 180-hp STC. It is really super here on the ranch; I use it like a station wagon."

"I use mogas in my '64 Hawk. Seems okay, and it saves me money. Just wish the FBO would pump it; the gas in the trunk of the car scares me."

Sales People Say:

"I like to sell 172s to first-time buyers because they make people happy, not broke."

"172s sell themselves. They are roomy, look good, and are reasonable in price. They're just real good value . . . something you don't often see these days."

"I have rarely seen a bargain 172; generally, you get what you pay for."

"There is such a 172 market that the prices are almost fixed."

"I wouldn't recommend the 172 models with the Lycoming 'H' engine—too many expensive problems."

"A 172 makes a good investment. If you keep it in good shape, you'll always get your money out of it."

"As a purchasing broker, I look at a lot of 172s for my customers. I am always able to find a plane to fill the bill. There are just so many around.''

TIPS

Never leave your airplane unattended not tied down. It could not only move in the wind and get damaged, it could damage someone else's airplane.

Put plugs in the air intakes of the cowling to keep birds out.

Use pitot tube covers to keep bugs from blocking the little holes.

Mount a fire extinguisher in the cabin where you can quickly get at it.

Keep a working flashlight on board.

Always carry a complete first-aid kit in your plane.

If you are flying over sparsley populated areas it would be a good idea to have survival water, food, and cover (blankets or sleeping bags) on board.

Having flares on board can be handy if you are down and trying to attract the attention of a rescue team.

Appendix A

Advertising Abbreviations

AD	Airworthiness Directive
ADF	Automatic Direction Finder
AF	airframe
AF&E	airframe and engine
AI	aircraft inspector
ALT	altimeter
ANN	annual inspection
ANNUAL	annual inspection
AP	autopilot
ASI	airspeed indicator
A&E	airframe and engine
A/P	autopilot
BAT	battery
B&W	black and white
CAT	carburetor air temperature
CHT	cylinder head temperature
COMM	communications radio
CS	constant-speed propeller
C/S	constant-speed propeller
C/W	complied with
DBL	double
DG	directional gyro

DME	Distance Measuring Equipment
FAC	factory
FBO	fixed based operator
FGP	full gyro panel
FWF	firewall forward
GAL	gallons
GPH	gallons per hour
GS	glideslope
HD	heavy-duty
HP	horsepower
HSI	horizontal situation indicator
HVY	heavy
IFR	Instrument Flight Rules
ILS	Instrument Landing System
INS	Instrument Navigation System
INSP	inspection
INST	instrument
KTS	knots
L	left
LDG	landing
LE	left engine
LED	light emiting diode
LH	left hand
LIC	license
LOC	localizer
LTS	lights
L&R	left and right
MB	marker beacon
MBR	marker beacon

MP	manifold pressure
MPH	miles per hour
MOD	modification
NAV	navigation
NAV/COM	navigation/communication radio
NDH	no damage history
OAT	outside air temperature
OX	oxygen
02	oxygen
PMA	parts manufacture approval
PROP	propeller
PSI	pounds per square inch
R	right
RC	rate of climb
REMAN	remanufactured
REPALT	reporting altimeter
RH	right hand
RMFD	remanufactured
RMFG	remanufactured
RNAV	Random Area Navigation
ROC	rate of climb
SAFOH	since airframe overhaul
SCMOH	since (chrome/complete) major overhaul
SEL	single engine land
SFACNEW	since factory new
SFN	since factory new
SFNE	since factory new engine
SFREM	since factory remanufacture
SFREMAN	since factory remanufacture
SFRMFG	since factory remanufacture
SMOH	since major overhaul
SNEW	since new

SPOH	since propeller overhaul
STC	supplemental type certificate
STOH	since top overhaul
STOL	short takeoff and landing
TAS	true airspeed
TBO	time between overhaul
TLX	telex
TNSP	transponder
TNSPNDR	transponder
TSN	time since new
TSO	Technical Service Order
TT	total time
TTAF	total time airframe
TTA&E	total time airframe and engine
TTE	total time engine
TTSN	total time since new
TXP	transponder
T&B	turn and bank
VAC	vacuum
VFR	Visual Flight Rules
VHF	very high frequency
VOR	Visual Omni Range
XC	cross-country
XMTR	transmitter
XPDR	transponder
XPNDR	transponder
3LMB	three light marker beacon

Appendix B

Telephone Area Codes

201	NJ north
202	Washington, DC
203	CT
205	AL
206	WA west
207	ME
208	ID
209	CA Fresno
212	NY City
213	CA Los Angeles
214	TX Dallas
215	PA east
216	OH northeast
217	IL central
218	MN north
219	IN north
301	MD
302	DE
303	CO
304	WV
305	FL southeast
307	WY
308	NE west
309	IL Peoria area

312	IL northeast
313	MI east
314	MO east
315	NY north central
316	KS south
317	IN central
318	LA west
319	IA east
401	RI
402	NE east
404	GA north
405	OK west
406	MT
408	CA San Jose area
409	TX southeast
412	PA southwest
413	MA west
414	WI east
415	CA San Francisco
417	MO southwest
419	OH northwest
501	AR
502	KY west
503	OR
504	LA east
505	NM
507	MN south
509	WA east
512	TX south central
513	OH southwest
515	IA central
516	NY Long Island
517	MI central
518	NY northeast
601	MS
602	AZ
603	NH
605	SD
606	KY east
607	NY south central
608	WI southwest

609	NJ south
612	MN central
614	OH southeast
615	TN east
616	MI west
617	MA east
618	IL south
619	CA southeast
701	ND
702	NV
703	VA north & west
704	NC west
707	CA Santa Rosa area
712	IA west
713	TX Houston
714	CA southwest
715	WI north
716	NY west
717	PA central
718	NY southeast & NYC
801	UT
802	VT
803	SC
804	VA southeast
805	CA west central
806	TX northwest
808	HA
812	IN south
813	FL southwest
814	PA northwest & central
815	IL north central
816	MO northwest
817	TX north central
818	CA southwest
901	TN west
904	FL north
906	MI northwest
907	AK
912	GA south
913	KS north
914	NY southeast

Appendix C

Cessna 172
Current Price Guide

The following is a guide to prices for the many models of Cessna 172 airplanes. The prices are based on average asking/selling prices for 1987. As with most aircraft, there are no real set prices. This is meant as a guide only.

Price is controlled by several factors:

☐ The age and general condition of the airplane.
☐ How well equipped the plane is, and the age/condition of that equipment.
☐ The remaining time left on limited-life components.
☐ The history of the aircraft, its past usage and damage record.

These factors all are based on the physical characteristics of the airplane. There are, however, two other points to consider, and they are perhaps the most important in setting the asking/selling price of an aircraft:

1. How badly does the present owner want to sell his airplane?
2. How badly does the purchaser desire to buy the aircraft?

The meeting of these two points is called bargaining. Plan to do lots of it in purchasing an airplane. No price is ever set in concrete!

The following prices are based on a plane with average equipment (avionics) and with middle time on the engine. Middle time on the engine is defined as the middle one-third of the TBO (i.e., on an 1800-hr engine, this would be 600 to 1200 hrs SMOH).

Year	Model	Asking
1956	172	$ 8300
1957	172	8400
1958	172	8450
1958	175	8500
1959	172	8500
1959	175	8700
1960	172A	8900
1960	175A	9000
1961	172B	9300
1961	175B	9400
1962	172C	9500
1962	175C	9600
1963	172D	9800
1964	172E	10,000
1965	172F	10,500
1966	172G	10,700
1967	172H	11,400
1968	172I	11,600
1969	172K	12,200
1970	172K	13,000
1971	172L	13,400
1972	172L	14,500
1973	172M	15,200
1974	172M	16,900
1975	172M	15,000
1976	172M	23,500
1977	172N	16,000
1977	R172K-XP	25,000
1978	172N	17,000
1978	R172K-XP	26,500
1979	172N	20,000
1979	R172K-XP	30,000
1980	172N	32,000
1980	R172K-XP	28,000
1980	172 -Cut RG	34,900
1981	172P	44,500
1981	R172K-XP	39,000
1981	172 -Cut RG	60,000
1982	172P	46,000
1982	172 -Cut RG	
1983	172P	

286

Year	Model	Asking
1983	172Q-Cut	55,000
1983	172 -Cut RG	70,000
1984	172P	n/a
1984	172Q-Cut	n/a
1984	172 -Cut RG	n/a

SH—Skyhawk
SL—Skylark
Cut—Cutlass
RG—retractable gear

The prices for SH and SHII are slightly higher than for the Standard Model 172. This is because the Skyhawk and Skyhawk II have more factory-installed options than the Standard. The same applies to the Skylark, Hawk, and Cutlass Series. Additionally, there may be slight differences between the plain upgraded version and the II version, depending on inclusion of the NAV PAC.

Index

Supplemental Type Certificate
(STC), 111
swept-tail fastback design, 48

T

T-37 jet trainer, 14, 15
T-41 military primary trainer, 17, 20
Taylorcraft Ranchwagon, 22
TBO, 103
telephone area codes, 281-284
temporary operating authority, 142
test flight, 132
throttle control, 242
title search, 135
tools, 195
top overhaul, 104
toxicant dispenser, 242
Travel Air Manufacturing Company,
2
Tri-Pacer, 22
tricresyl phosphate (TCP), 110
tricycle landing gear, 14, 22

U

undershoot rates, 272
used equipment, 212

V

vacuum pumps, 240, 242
VFR operation, 197
VOR, 206
VOR/LOC, 204
VOR/LOC/GS, 205

W

Waco CG-4A Glider, 4
walk-around inspection, 128
weight, modifications for increased,
252
weight and balance papers, 145
wheels, 162
  inspection and repair of, 157
  modifications for, 240
windows, modifications for, 241
windshields, 239
  care of, 192
wings, modifications for, 237, 248
winterization kit, 241
wiring, 145

X

XPNDR, 40, 197, 207, 208
XT-37A jet airplane, 14

Other Bestsellers From TAB

☐ **PILOT'S SKETCHBOOK—Lt. Col. Joseph P. Tracy, USAF (Ret.)**

Joe Tracy describes—through poetry, prose, and sketches—the various airplanes he has flown over the last 50 years. He takes you on 90-horsepower biplanes and the multi-multi thousand pound thrust giants that can seat 500 passengers. Tracy has compiled over a half a century's worth of his sketches, poetry, and prose into a unique piece of aviation literature that you'll enjoy for many years to come. 176 pp., Hardcover.

**Paper $14.95   Hard $21.95
Book No. 27408**

☐ **ARV FLIER'S HANDBOOK—Joe Christy**

Here's a practical, in-depth look at this increasingly popular new aviation category with a realistic assessment of the ARVs advantages and problems. It includes an overview of the ARV's available today—machines on both sides of the 254 lb./55kt. dividing line. Covered are costs, materials, construction standards, obtaining a license, insurance facts, even cost comparisons with traditional lightplanes. (A "fun" plane that will do 80 mph costs about $12,000.) 192 pp., 96 illus.

Paper $12.95   Book No. 2407

☐ **AIM/FAR 1987 Airman's Information Manual/Federal Aviation Regulations—Aero Staff Editors**

This single essential source book contains the latest Federal Aviation Regulations for pilots plus reprints of the latest FAA Airman's Information Manual! Thoroughly revised and updated, this handy 1987 edition of essential AIMs and FARs makes it easy to quickly locate exactly the information you need when you need it. Illustrated with invaluable charts, diagrams, and tables. 400 pp., illustrated.

**Paper $11.95   Hard $16.95
Book No. 24387**

☐ **THE ILLUSTRATED HANDBOOK OF AVIATION AND AEROSPACE FACTS—Joe Christy**

A complete look at American aviation—civil and military. All the political, social, economic, and personality factors that have influenced the state of U.S. military airpower, the boom-and-bust cycles in Civil aviation, America's manned and unmanned space flights, and little-known facts on the birth of modern rocketry, it's all here in this complete sourcebook! 480 pp., 486 illus.

Paper $29.50   Book No. 2397